MW00567174

Centre for Research
on Canadian-Russian Relations
at Carleton University

Slavic Research Group
at the University of Ottawa

CANADA/RUSSIA SERIES

Volume 4

General Editors
J.L. Black
Andrew Donskov

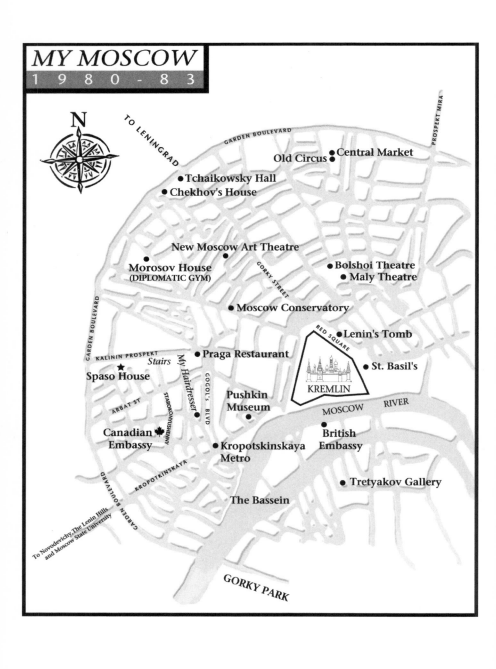

MY MOSCOW
1 9 8 0 - 8 3

N

TO LENINGRAD

GARDEN BOULEVARD

PROSPEKT MIRA

Old Circus • • Central Market

• Tchaikowsky Hall
• Chekhov's House

New Moscow Art Theatre
•

• Morosov House
(DIPLOMATIC GYM)

GORKY STREET

• Bolshoi Theatre
• Maly Theatre

• Moscow Conservatory

GARDEN BOULEVARD

RED SQUARE

•Lenin's Tomb

KALININ PROSPEKT
Stairs • Praga Restaurant
★
Spaso House

My Hairdresser

GOGOL'S BLVD

• St. Basil's

KREMLIN

ARBAT ST

STAROKONYUSHENNY

Pushkin
Museum
•

MOSCOW   RIVER

Canadian ❦
Embassy

• Kropotskinskaya
Metro

British
Embassy

KROPOTKINSKAYA

GARDEN BOULEVARD

To Novodevichy,The Lenin Hills
and Moscow State University

• Tretyakov Gallery

The Bassein

GORKY PARK

Letters from Moscow

Landon Pearson

PENUMBRA PRESS

Copyright © Landon Pearson and Penumbra Press, 2003
Published by PENUMBRA PRESS
Printed and bound in Canada.
Cover and book design by Tammy d'Entremont.
No part of this publication may be reproduced, stored in a retrieval system
or transmitted, in any form or by any means, without the prior written con-
sent of the publisher or a licence from The Canadian Copyright Licensing
Agency (Access Copyright). For an Access Copyright licence, call toll free to
1-800-893-5777 or visit www.accesscopyright.ca

NATIONAL LIBRARY OF CANADA CATALOGUING IN PUBLICATION

Pearson, Landon
    Letters from Moscow / Landon Pearson.

(Canada/Russia series ; 4)
ISBN 1-894131-44-4
    1. Pearson, Landon--Correspondence.   2. Diplomats' spouses--
Canada--Correspondence.   3. Soviet Union--Social conditions--1970-1991.
4. Diplomatic and consular service, Canadian--Soviet Union.
I. Title. II. Series.
DK276.P42 2003   947.085'4   C2003-905525-6

Canada    Canada Council
for the Arts

Penumbra Press gratefully acknowledges the Canada Council for the Arts
and the Ontario Arts Council for supporting its publishing programme. The
publisher further acknowledges the financial support of the Government of
Canada through the Book Publishing Industry Development Program
(BPIDP) for our publishing activities. We also acknowledge the Government
of Ontario through the Ontario Media Development Corporation's Ontario
Book Initiative.

To my correspondents, one and all,
whose affection and interest kept me writing

INTRODUCTION

We never meant to go to Moscow. When Geoffrey was approached in the spring of 1980 to succeed Robert Ford as Ambassador to the Soviet Union (USSR) we were both surprised. Not that Geoffrey wasn't up for an ambassadorial appointment; he already had a solid diplomatic career behind him. But we had never served in the Soviet Union or in Eastern Europe and we knew no Russian. However, Robert Ford, highly respected as a poet and a Russian scholar, had been Ambassador in Moscow for sixteen years, the last ten as dean of the diplomatic corps, and had outlasted his logical successors, officers who had served under him. They had gone on to other things. Since the Cold War was still on, Geoffrey's experience in arms control and disarmament argued in his favour. So we talked it over, and he accepted.

Both of us were ready for a new challenge. We had been back in Ottawa for seven years. Geoffrey had had a number of absorbing tasks in what was then known as the Department of External Affairs and I had completed a Master's degree in education, co-founded a prevention programme in children's mental health based in local elementary schools, and acted as vice-chairperson of the Canadian Commission for the International Year of the Child (1979). Except for the youngest, our children were either at university or working. It was a good time to set out for what proved to be our final foreign posting.

Mr. Ford had asked that his posting be extended for a year beyond retirement age so that he could preside over Canadian participation in the 1980 Moscow Olympics. But the Soviet invasion of Afghanistan in December 1979 threw these plans into disarray. The period of détente that promised to bring the countries of the world together in an Olympic stadium came to an abrupt end. Canada joined the United States and most other western countries in boycotting the games. Relations between Canada and the USSR soured. In the end the Fords were glad to leave. They never returned.

When we arrived in October 1980 we thought it would be difficult to replace such a well-known couple, but it seems that not only the Fords but everyone else were ready for change. We were warmly welcomed by all. What did prove to be difficult, however, was the polit-

ical climate. Fallout from the invasion of Afghanistan had been inten-
sified by fears raised by the simmering discontent in Poland that had
led to the emergence of the trade union Solidarity during the summer
of 1980. Would the Soviets invade Poland as they had once invaded
Hungary and Czechoslovakia? During our first weeks in Moscow no
one talked of anything else. And then, in November, Ronald Reagan
became president of the United States and characterized the Soviet
Union as the "Evil Empire." The Cold War became colder as the rhetoric, on both sides, polarized. This was the atmosphere in which we
took up our diplomatic duties and tried to find our way, an atmosphere that continued to surround us throughout our entire posting. It
culminated in September 1983, just before our scheduled departure,
with the shooting down of KAL flight 007, off course on its way to
Japan and carrying nine Canadians among its 269 passengers. It was
not an easy time to be in the Soviet Union and yet it was fascinating.
I found that I liked the people I met, especially the women, and yet I
hated the system. How come? I wrote my letters often struggling
with this dilemma. Later, to resolve it, I wrote a whole book about
childhood in the Soviet Union, because I was convinced that it was in
the richness of the Soviet response to children that my answers lay.
Children of Glasnost was published in 1990.

I had no thoughts, however, of publishing my letters. At the time,
I wrote them to help me sort out my own impressions and to communicate with my family and friends. But when Geoffrey suggested
to the Centre for Research on Canadian-Russian Relations that perhaps the letters merited publication in the Centre's series I took a second look.

I had never read the letters straight through before and so had
never reflected on them as a whole. But once I did, I could see two
distinct story-lines and a surprising consistency of tone. The first
"story-line" is the account of diplomatic life at the ambassadorial
level experienced by a Canadian living in Moscow in the declining
days of the Soviet Empire. The second "story-line" is my slow discovery through day-to-day living, encounters with people, travelling,
and reading, of the nature and complexity of the Soviet overlay on
Russian history and character and the variety of human reactions
that evolved in response to an oppressive regime.

The tone of the letters is the product of two distinct interacting factors. The first factor is the nature and composition of my correspondents. Each letter was replicated twenty-five times; twelve copies went to family—our five children living in different parts of Canada, my mother, my brothers, Geoffrey's sister, a couple of nieces, an elderly aunt. I was and am deeply attached to all of these people. Family and friendship mean a great deal to me and my separation from those close to me certainly coloured my life in Russia. This was before e-mail and the direct phone line embassies now enjoy. Letters took three to four weeks to turn around and phone calls cost $11.50 a minute (provided you could get through!). The fact that most of my correspondents actually came to visit during our time there greatly enriched our experience.

The second factor contributing to the tone of the letters was that although they were normally sent by the diplomatic bag, I was always conscious that once words are consigned to paper and sent to so many people they become, to some extent, public, and as a representative of my country abroad I had to be discreet. On the other hand, these were personal letters, so I wanted my correspondents to have as clear an understanding of my perceptions of life around me as possible. Russian friends now living in Canada immediately recognize the allusive style I employed; it was so common at the time.

The letters are arranged chronologically and have been edited only to exclude unnecessary information, description of trips outside the Soviet Union, or references that would make no sense to anyone except those to whom they were directed. Gaps in time can be explained by the fact that when we were in Canada on business or on home leave there was no need for me to write. I have included maps at the request of several of my correspondents, who wanted to be able to track our trips and get a sense of where the Embassy was situated with respect to the parts of Moscow I wrote about. And I hope the photos, which have been arranged in narrative form, will bring life to my text. They were all taken by me or with my camera except for a few official ones, which I am unable to credit because they are not marked.

Finally, I would like to thank all who supported me in preparing these letters for publication. First of all, Geoffrey for suggesting the

idea and Larry Black and the advisory group at the Centre for
Research on Canadian-Russian Relations for accepting it, Robin
Hannah for transferring my error-strewn typewritten originals onto
diskette, Yolande Arsenault for adjusting the text as I cut it (as well as
many other invaluable acts of assistance), Ambrose Pottie for the
maps, Tammy d'Entremont for the cover design, Douglas Campbell
for editing, and John Flood for shepherding it through Penumbra
Press.

Any royalties earned will go to Street Kids International in
Toronto so that support can be sent to their partner organizations
working with the hundreds of thousands of street kids in Russia mar-
ginalized by an economy and a culture in transition.

PART I

LETTER NUMBER 1

**Moscow
October 20, 1980**

Dear one and all,

Two weeks ago I left Canada. It does not seem possible that I should already feel so comfortable here at Starokonyushenny Per. 23 (Old Horsestable Lane). I am sitting at my desk overlooking the trees in the back garden of the Embassy, which is suffused with yellow autumn light. Beyond the Embassy wall I can see a couple of large functional apartment buildings, a pale, blue sky, and a huge construction crane which I haven't seen move in the ten days that we have been here. Behind me, in the bedroom, the photographs are already hanging and the bed is very comfortable. Through the door from the family sitting room I can hear Keith Jarrett playing the Köln concert and admire my new jade plant that I just acquired at the plant *commissione*, one of the many stores where people take things to be sold on consignment. The sitting room is bright, with a yellow carpet and yellow and green curtains and a huge Russian television set on which we will watch *Spartacus* tonight danced by the Bolshoi, and on which we watched the arrival of President Babrak Kamal from Afghanistan the other day, heard all the speeches, and looked to see which Russian leaders were present and which weren't. Of course I don't know the difference yet but Geoffrey is beginning to.

The rest of the official residence is not nearly so comfortable but it is very elegant. The residence is on the second floor of the building that also serves as the chancery. It was built in the 1890s by a rich sugar merchant for his mistress and has great, high ceilings, beautiful plasterwork and mouldings, and a very handsome parquet floor in the dining room, which is the only room not fully carpeted and

also one of the most beautiful rooms I have ever seen anywhere. It is
a grand European apartment and Mrs. Ford expended, I understand,
a great deal of time and energy assuring that it be furnished in a style
appropriate to its dimensions. So she brought chandeliers from Brazil
and mirrors from Italy and rugs from France. The furniture is generally mahogany; Chippendale in the dining room, Regency or Louis
XVI in the reception rooms. The colours are lovely; old rose, dove
grey, smoky blue. It does not look Canadian but we will do what we
can with the paintings. The David Milne looks marvellous in the
drawing room.

We are moving everything else around to see what fits best where
and I find that a difficult process. Our air shipment was here when
we arrived but there is no sign yet of our sea shipment. There was
some damage en route but none of it too serious. It's hard to convey
in words what it all looks like except to say that I consider it a great
privilege to be able to live in something that is both beautiful and
comfortable and which should be manageable. There is a garden but
it is not easily accessible and while that does not matter at the
moment, it may in warmer weather. We will see.

To go on for a bit about domestic matters. Living above the
chancery has certain distinct advantages. The most important, from
my point of view at the moment, is the easy access to the Embassy
translators. The servants who at present staff the residence speak
very little English, and two of them are completely new, one of them
having started work only this morning. Servants come from UPDK,
the diplomatic service agency, and you take what you are sent. I
think we are the beneficiaries, for the moment, of a "honeymoon"
period. The Soviets are anxious, one is guessing, to improve relations between Russia and Canada and Geoffrey's appointment
appears to be a popular one. (He is slated to see the foreign minister,
Andrei Gromyko, on Thursday, which is considered something of a
coup.) So they are prepared to make things as easy as possible. The
result is that we have been sent an excellent cook, who also happens
to be a delightful person, with whom I can hardly wait to converse
when I have enough Russian. We all know these people have to play
a political role of sorts and the professional quality of the staff they
send is much determined by the political climate, but I fully expect

from what I have seen so far of Tamara and Nikolai that we will be able to establish quite warm human relationships and we won't worry too much about what they say in their monthly meetings with UPDK! Besides, they work an eight-hour, five-day-a-week contract and are gone, on normal evenings, by 5:30. I find that suits us very well indeed.

Last week was very busy, as you can imagine. Not only am I trying to get us properly established in our daily routines but we are also trying to get to know all the members of the mission, find out what they do and what they are interested in, and get a feel for the problems and issues of life in Moscow for the Canadian community. So we are trying to meet people in many different ways and contexts: here at lunch as individuals; in their offices as I find out who is responsible for what as it affects the residence; at a tea where I met many of the wives, a large proportion of whom seem to have jobs and to be quite happy but some of whom are confined to apartments with one or two small children and are not; and, finally, at the Canadian Club, which meets in the basement of the Embassy every Friday night for pizza and a movie. It is too early to tell what they are really like but it does seem to be a real community and there is a certain reassurance in that. It is a surprisingly large one, well over a hundred altogether, and of course it changes frequently so by the time I have gotten to know everyone, some of them will already be gone.

Just one more comment about Canadians—we had our first reception last Thursday for forty-three Canadians here for an international conference of cooperatives being held for the first time in a socialist country. Most of them were Québécois, la Caisse Populaire being one of the most successful of cooperative enterprises, or at least so they told me, and all of them were jolly. We had a rather moving speech about how they had burst into cheers as they rounded the corner in their bus and saw the Canadian flag waving. They are the first large group of Canadians to come to Moscow in a long time.

But we are in Russia, after all, so let me describe a couple of last week's events as we set out to explore our new environment. On Saturday we decided to walk to Red Square and to see something of the Kremlin. The weekend crowds in Moscow are vast and remind one of nothing so much as a flowing river. People are always moving (except when they are in long lineups, which they frequently are) because "loitering" is not allowed and there is not a great deal to stop and look at in the windows anyway. And they seem to be going somewhere with purpose. They are remarkably quiet but determined. Most of them seemed headed to Red Square, or at least to its edges; the only ones allowed onto the main square were those headed for the lineup for Lenin's tomb. Among the crowd outside the Kremlin were many bridal parties, the brides in long, white dresses and veils, carrying cellophane-wrapped gladioli and hanging onto the arms of their square-faced grooms. They flowed forward as regularly as the waves of the sea, to lay a few blossoms on the Tomb of the Unknown Soldier, then back to their flower-bedecked cars surmounted by two large entwined golden rings and with a bright plastic doll tied to the radiator (a fertility symbol). Then, they drove off (so we were told) to have their photographs taken on Lenin Hills overlooking the city.

When we went to Zagorsk on Sunday I was struck with the ritualistic nature of the Russian Orthodox Church. Zagorsk is the heart of Russian orthodoxy, and has been for many centuries, almost since its founding in the fourteenth century. It is about sixty kilometres from Moscow and we drove out with Geoffrey's secretary and one of the interpreters. It is a fascinating place. The monastery is very extensive and in remarkably good condition. There are blue and golden domes surmounting white walls everywhere you look—and masses of people. Many of them were obviously very devout, making their obeisance to our guide, a handsome, full-bearded, blue-eyed priest who would respond to them in a perfunctory manner as he continued telling us about the tomb of Boris Godunov and about Ivan the Terrible who repented on his deathbed and donated vast amounts of money to the church for the good of his soul. Having killed his son in a fit of rage and sent six of his seven wives to convents, to say nothing of all his other nasty deeds, he obviously had a great deal to repent of. The church in Russia has never been known to refuse goodies from sinners, and they aren't starting now. It is quite obvious that this whole monastery and the seminary that trains new priests every year could not possibly be maintained in its present style without the offerings of the believers being considerably augmented by the state.

Perhaps going on a Sunday and being received in an official capacity is the worst possible way to see the true spirit of this great monastery. Or perhaps my spirit just rebels at unwavering orthodoxy, whatever form it takes. But I saw a great deal of similarity between the ritual of waiting in line for the sight of Lenin's body and the crowds waiting in line to kiss the reliquary of St. Sergius; between the brides and their new good luck rituals and the people waiting to take home little buckets of water from the holy spring of Zagorsk. The difference seems primarily to be one of aesthetics, and from what I have seen so far, on that score the Orthodox Church wins hands down.

Geoffrey comments that the Russians seem to be a very law-abiding people and one could say that of course they are, because the penalty of not being so is so great. And naturally that is a factor. But another factor that I had not realized before is this centuries-long tradition of Orthodoxy, that saying and doing things in a certain strict form is the Truth itself. There may have been Revolutions in Russia, but there was no Reformation.

LETTER NUMBER 2

October 28, 1980

Tomorrow Geoffrey will present his credentials and become a properly accredited ambassador. This has not stopped him from acting as head-of-post; he was not, for example, able to excuse himself from meeting the Ethiopian president yesterday at the Kremlin although the Bulgarian, who is at present Dean of the diplomatic corps, has refused to receive him until he is properly accredited. Anyway he will set off tomorrow with his senior officers (although not his wife because spouses are not invited) and the chief of protocol from the Foreign Ministry to deliver his document from Governor General Ed. Schreyer recommending to the attention of Mr. Brezhnev Geoffrey A.H. Pearson "in the character of Ambassador Extraordinary and Plenipotentiary of Canada" and requesting "that You will give entire credence to all that he shall say to You in My name, more especially when he shall convey to You the assurances of the lively interest which I take in everything that affects the welfare and the prosperity of Your country." I am quoting from the document because I have never actually seen "Letters of Credence" before. I suppose all ambassadors present the same piece of paper but in some cases the wording has a slightly ironic ring to it! Anyway there is apparently always a certain fear that one of the senior officers will have forgotten to bring the document to the actual ceremony. Naturally, Mr. Brezhnev will not himself be present to receive Geoffrey's credentials but the vice-president of the month, representing one of the Soviet Republics, will stand in for him. I will tell you next week who it was. After a rather stiff exchange of formalities and one or two lines of Russian by Geoffrey the officials will all return here for a *coupe de champagne* and I will be allowed to join them! Then in the afternoon we will have the entire Embassy staff including the Soviets into the Residence for a reception. After all, the first new Canadian ambassador to Russia in seventeen years is an occasion worth celebrating!

The presentation of credentials follows by six days Geoffrey's call on Mr. Gromyko. That was basically a courtesy call although it is not habitual for Mr. Gromyko to receive new ambassadors. We are told that there are many who come and leave after three years without ever being able to call on him at all. We are assuming that the Russians want to turn over a new leaf with the departure of Mr. Ford and the termination of the Olympics and all that that entailed. Also, there was no question, according to Geoffrey, that Mr. Gromyko remembered with some warmth experiences he had shared with LBP when they were both ambassadors in Washington in 1942–43. He also devoted several minutes of the meeting to discussing how he had heard the word "discombobulate" from Mr. Roosevelt and how he had to look it up in his dictionary.

We have started in on the round of our official calls. Actually it has been a very pleasant experience so far and a very good way to get to know people. Did I mention last week that we had been to the Australians? That was followed by lunch on Friday with the British, yesterday with the Norwegians, and today with the Dutch, Frans and Elspeth Van Agt. She is a Canadian, the daughter of Fred MacGregor, who was Mackenzie King's Private Secretary (in the British sense) if I recall correctly. She was in Moscow twenty-seven or twenty-eight years ago as secretary to our then Ambassador, John Watkins (whom she liked enormously), when she met her husband, who was then a third secretary at the Dutch Embassy. She is very lively and was able to give me a lot of advice. They have been here since March and they made seventy calls together. Well, sometimes the wives were not there and the Ambassador went alone, but generally it was a joint effort, which is the accepted practice. I have not yet heard whether there are any female ambassadors here but, on the whole, we have been told, the diplomatic corps is an interesting one. Tom Watson, the American, was at the Norwegians' and I found him quite delightful. An old man with nothing to lose, he is both shrewd and amusing and astonishingly frank. Well, you don't get to be president of IBM if you are not exceptional. His wife has gone back to the States to vote. Geoffrey is wondering what to get me for my fiftieth birthday. Mr. Watson told him that he had bought his wife an island in the Bahamas for hers.

One of the great interests of our "calls" is seeing the Residences that other Embassies have. As we enter each one we wonder whether it was a sugar merchant or a cotton merchant who had built it to set up a mistress in elegance. Occasionally it was a member of the minor nobility. The British have the best location, on the other side of the river directly across from the Kremlin. We sat at lunch and had a splendid view of golden domes and white palaces seen above a high red brick wall. Apparently the Swedes have a modern Embassy but most of the rest of us are housed in roomy nineteenth-century mansions. And what about the Soviet élite? Ah well, that I don't yet know.

It appears that Soviet authorities have a surprising interest in the restoration and preservation of old buildings. Last Saturday we went out with one of the other Embassy families to a beautiful site called Kolomenskoye. This was once a village and a monastery, built on a height of land overlooking the Moscow River south of the city. Most of the buildings have vanished, of course, but there remains a singularly handsome church built for the birth of Ivan the Terrible in 1532 and constructed in an elongated pyramidal shape (no onion dome) with graceful elliptical gables and porticoes. Judging by old photographs there has been a great deal of recent reconstruction although the basic form had never been destroyed. A Russian word I have learned very quickly is *remont*, which means "under repair," because everything always is. But in the case of Kolomenskoye and many other sites around Moscow the "repair" is a very serious affair, faithfully done according to old drawings, documents, and designs. Perhaps the money is being made available for ideological reasons, i.e., enhanced pride in their past will tie Soviet citizenry even closer to their motherland and with more passion than can now be evoked by political slogans—the ubiquitous banners and posters no longer seem to pack much of an emotional punch for the average Russian. However, whatever the reason that funds are being poured into this work, the whole world can benefit because there is great beauty as well as interest in the Russian past. Last Thursday I went to the Tretyakov Gallery to see an exhibition of paintings of Moscow since the sixteenth century, which was fascinating. And while I was there we came across a four-room exhibition of the works of Venetsianov, an early-nineteenth-century painter, which was superb—mostly portraits and some genre paintings of peasant, rural life. His handling of paint was masterly and his sense of colour wonderful. Perhaps some of you art historians had heard of him but I never had. Visually, Moscow is proving to be a whole new world for me, and one that really appeals to my eye.

We have started our Russian lessons with Natasha, who seems to be the Embassy teacher. She is very amiable if not demanding. However, she can keep us focused and correct us and we do have texts to work from. I will try to take five lessons a week (though Geoffrey will only have time for three) because I feel a tremendous need to communicate with my domestic world. You can imagine how frustrated I am to be cut off from chats in my kitchen!

I will add another paragraph for some of you who might be interested and to help clarify my own thoughts. The moral issue posed for me in Russia is quite different from the one I faced during our posting to India. The question in India was, how does a country like Canada relate in a useful way to a country like India with all its enormous problems? What can Canada offer India? How should we offer it? All the well-known problems of the relations between rich and poor countries ... India posed other cultural and social questions for us, personally, which have not been very easy to resolve, if, in fact, we have resolved them. But we all learned a lot from living in India. The question in Russia is also one of relationship. In this case, how does a free country like Canada relate in a useful way to a controlled country like Russia? The terms may be relative but you don't have to be here very long before you realize that the difference between our system and theirs is very real indeed and it has to do with degrees of freedom. Also, of course, the power of Russia is immense. How will they use it? Can we, Canada, make the slightest difference in the equation? and so on ... But the way the problem arises for me personally is, is there anything I can do on a personal level when I am here, in addition to my diplomatic duties? I think the answer is probably going to be no. On Sunday I read a copy of *Les Cahiers de Samizdat*, a publication produced in Brussels with articles and letters from dissenters inside Russia. There was a particularly moving section on women in the resistance movement and, honestly, it is easier for me to imagine living as one of Mother Theresa's Sisters of Charity than as one of these women, these extraordinary, ordinary women risking death and receiving years of hard labour and separation from families and friends in order to support the cause of human rights in this country. I would never have the courage.

I am also in the middle of reading *Babi Yar* by Anatoly Kuznetzov in an English translation (Dial Press, N.Y., 1967). It is a documentary "novel" about the German occupation of Kiev in 1941-42. Kuznetzov was twelve when the Germans arrived and he writes about his grandfather and his grandmother and his friends and how some of them managed to survive, including his cat Titus. There were 900,000 people in Kiev before the war. When the Germans left there were only 180,000. The whole story is told through his twelve- and thirteen-year-old eyes and it is a tour de force, beautifully written with some of the same quality as Satyajit Ray's film *Distant Thunder*, in which events that are almost unbearable are presented in such human terms that we are able to bear them and learn. It was published in the Soviet Union in a youth magazine. There is nothing in Canadian history that remotely resembles the kinds of experiences that the Russians have had. There is this tragic dimension to Russian life that fills me with awe. I can abhor policies, I can condemn a system, I can be horrified at the atrocities committed during the Stalinist period in particular but I cannot possibly judge a whole people. And I think that the whole time I am here I will find myself buffeted by the contradictions of this country.

One thing to be said for their system—they certainly can produce a new prime minister fast! No messy leadership conventions here! We watched the whole thing on a ten-minute TV slot. All the old men ... Some day they will die, and then what? The Revolution recedes further and further in time—Mr. Gromyko told Geoffrey he would like to retire but there was no one to succeed him ... He has been Foreign Minister for more than a quarter of a century—!

LETTER NUMBER 3
November 4, 1980

Now, let me tell you about the presentation of credentials, which was the big event of last week. It was supposed to be last Wednesday at 11:00 a.m. and then it was postponed at the last minute to four in the afternoon, which threw everything out because the ceremony had to be followed by a *coupe de champagne* for the Russian officials and we were also planning to have a big reception that evening at five for all the staff, Canadian and Russian, and that meant a lot of people. So I told Tamara and Nikolai that I would have to postpone the reception until the next day and they just laughed! *Nichevo*, they said, "It doesn't matter." And apparently people really do get used to these last-minute changes and do not worry about them because they happen all the time. Anyway, Geoffrey is now an "ambassador extraordinary and plenipotentiary" properly accredited. They tell me that the ceremony was quite impressive. Geoffrey and his officers all looked extremely proper in their pin-striped suits, except for Ann Leahy, who rejected pin stripes in favour of a dark blue knit. The rest of the Embassy staff crowded around to see them off to the Kremlin in the official cars ... Geoffrey looked very distinguished. There was some comment because he had at least five minutes longer with Mr. Kuznetzov (the deputy chairman of the Praesidium to whom he actually made his presentation because he accepts most of the ceremonial tasks of Chief of State) in private conversation than the American

Ambassador had had ... and that's what people speculate about in Moscow, a sort of reading of the entrails, as it were, in the absence of other more solid information. There was even a little article in *Izvestia*, which shows that the "truth" occasionally appears in that newspaper (*izvestia* means "truth" in Russian). In fact, we at the Embassy sometimes get checked for accuracy. They sent Geoffrey's biography over to protocol, who sent back a correction. The Embassy had given his birthdate as December 27 and they knew better. Anyway, after the *coupe de champagne*, to which I was invited because it was in the Embassy and at which we met quite a few Soviet officials, we went off to the Turkish National Day able to fly the flag on our car for the first

The weekend brought reminders of Hallowe'en. No trick or treating, which is no loss at all, but a rather jolly Hallowe'en party downstairs at the Canadian Club where everyone dressed up and we had some lively dancing as well as very good food. Sunday we slept in for practically the first time since we arrived—perhaps we are finally beginning to feel more relaxed. And then we drove out to Archangelskoye, a country estate built during the first years of the nineteenth century in a pine forest overlooking the Moscow River. Handsome, Italianate, and yet, not quite ... The great chandelier in the central rotunda was made of papier maché by the estate craftsmen in order to imitate bronze, the carved manes of the lions fall into gentle, mournful eyes, the squirrels leaping about on the pathways have pointed rabbit's ears, and the stone nymphs all the way down to the river are wrapped in capes of clear plastic to protect them from the rain and the snow!

LETTER NUMBER 4

November 11, 1980

For those of us living in Moscow, last week was marked by two major events, the American election and the National Holiday of the USSR. I won't comment on the former. Looking on the bright side I am saying to myself that in spite of campaign rhetoric, international events and the exercise of power have a way of transforming presidential behaviour or moderating it or something. Of course like most of you I imagine, I was rather surprised at the extent of the victory for Reagan and depressed at the defeat of liberal senators by the deplorable tactics of the single-issue lobbyists. I also find it depressing that so many people in the US feel so alienated from the political system that they won't even vote. Fifty-three percent of eligible voters seems like a very small percentage to me in a so-called democracy. Of course, here it is 99 percent and that's a statistic that has its own depressing meaning!

Anyway, the Sixty-third Anniversary of the Great October Revolution turned out to be a fascinating event for us new arrivals. Western European and North American ambassadors did not attend the parade (nor did the Chinese, not surprisingly) so we were able to watch it in warm comfort with the wives of those officers in the Embassy who did go. On November 6 the flags, banners, and decorations began to go up and they stayed in place until Sunday. I found the visual effect of the decorations very attractive, both by daylight and at night. Red is the Russian colour in a much more profound sense than I had ever realized. The word for "red" and the word for "beautiful" were once one and the same, although now they are slightly different—*krasniy* and *krasiviy*. Almost all the decorations are pure red. Even the huge portraits of Lenin and the slightly smaller ones of Marx and Engels (looking for all the world like Old Testament prophets) are in red on a buff background. The fourteen idealized portraits of the members of the Politburo (Kosygin's was missing although he has not officially resigned from the Politburo itself; he has just been left out) were also sometimes to be found in red although more frequently they were black on a buff background with a red border. The portraits were a bit much, perhaps, but I found the rest of the decorations, even the glorious steel worker and the muscled agricultural lass, to be executed in a handsome and sober style and with a certain genuine flair. And the lights at night were really beautiful. The Russians have found a way of lighting up buildings that is both subtle and mysterious. No one could ever forget the sight of Moscow University lit up when seen from a bridge over the river below. And the fireworks sent up simultaneously from each of Stalin's seven wedding-cake buildings were simply magnificent.

But back to the parade. It was much more interesting than I had expected. The Politburo and the Generals were all there on top of Lenin's tomb taking the salute, of course, wrapped in their mufflers and fur hats. The first massed group of passing soldiers looked like stern babies with their chins up, their heads turned right, but their eyes cast down. They were the conscripts, one gathers, because the more experienced soldiers came later with the hardware. The military section of the parade lasted about thirty minutes and then the remaining two-and-a-half hours was devoted to the "people" in their various activities: the factories with individual floats, representatives of various Republics, schoolchildren, athletes, and finally just masses and masses of ordinary people, some arm-in-arm, some with small children on their shoulders, all of them carrying paper flowers or balloons or flags. I thought they looked as if they were having a good time, and why not? Most people enjoy a parade with lots of music and colour when it is a holiday and their national pride is involved. Of course, it was extremely well organized and while some people may have wished that they had been able to stay at home and watch it on TV, others were probably sincerely happy to be part of the whole thing. The symbols used to evoke patriotic sentiment seem strange to us ... but the emotion evoked is a recognizably human one.

At one o'clock Geoffrey and I went to the Kremlin, to the Palace of the Congress (which is the one modern building within the Kremlin walls), to a reception to meet Mr. Brezhnev, the members of the Politburo, assorted generals, and other important Soviet citizens. There must have been two thousand of us in one huge room at the top of the building, with a hundred or so long tables laden with every imaginable form of Russian delicacy. And people standing at the tables, crowded together, eating and eating and eating. What an extraordinary sight! And it's not as if any of them look as though they were fading away! The heads of mission (and their wives) were introduced to the "portraits," some of whom (including Mr. Brezhnev) looked surprisingly human when seen in the flesh and all of whom had handshakes like iron! Afterwards they all sat down in a row with their backs to us and watched what passes for a Russian cabaret show while being handed plates of food. And I wandered around and tried to have a taste of everything, particularly any caviar that had not already been devoured. Geoffrey was less curious about the food so he did not suffer the stomach pains that afflicted me for the next two days!

If we knew Russian we would no doubt have found ourselves being inundated with propaganda, with messages about the Revolution and about the lamentable state of sin we are all in, particularly the Westerners. But as we don't, the whole thing could only be perceived visually as an event of great human interest. Next year we will be able to understand more and may wish we couldn't.

LETTER NUMBER 5

November 18, 1980

Bag day today! Our days are so full of interest and activity that a week flies by almost before I know it. Everybody here says that time passes very quickly and I can well believe it. Almost too quickly to catch my breath. Three mornings a week Geoffrey and I have a Russian lesson and then I have another one on my own as well as try to spend at least one extra hour a day working on it as well as immerse myself in Russian (and Soviet) literature, in English translations of course. And then twice a week I have a gymnastics class with a number of other foreign women, some of whom are even older than I am, which is taught by the most elegant thirty-eight-year-old I have ever seen (a Russian), who really makes us work hard. Geoffrey has been getting his exercise by swimming in the Bassein, a huge heated outdoor pool not very far from the Embassy. Because all of Moscow is heated from a few central boiler plants the warm water in this pool (which will accommodate two thousand swimmers) is part of that system and so it is always a comfortable temperature as long as you don't poke your head too far above the surface. Bathing caps must be worn and Geoffrey looks rather quaint in the red polka-dot head cover he had to buy there ...

We should be able to start skating soon. We have already seen lots of children out on every available scrap of ice. It has been cold for a couple of weeks now and I have an idea that winter is going to be even longer here than it is in Ottawa. No cross-country skiing yet, but apparently it is all the rage and I can see why. One badly wants to get out into the fresh air outside the city. From the Old Arbat, which is the area of the city in which we are living, we do not have too far to go.

We are also kept busy and fascinated by the two or three diplomatic calls we do a day when Geoffrey does not have to go to greet the President of Finland or the something or other of Mozambique. We have now met with all our European colleagues, western European, that is, and the Ambassadors from both China and Japan. Kenya we have also visited, because he is the senior African here, and they are a very attractive couple with nine daughters! The Bulgarian is the dean and a stickler for protocol so Geoffrey did not get to see him till after he had presented his credentials but found him very cordial when he did go. And today we have been to both the Czechs and the Poles in their enormous embassies, where we were greeted with smiles, vodka, and French translators. I find each encounter quite different and extremely interesting but a little hard on my waistline and my liver! In Moscow this time-consuming process is absolutely essential because knowledge of what is really going on and what may happen can only be arrived at by putting together many little pieces of information from a number of sources ... and also by knowing the right questions to ask. Observing Geoffrey I have decided he is very good indeed at the task. And, of course, aside from these calls and the ones he is making on the Soviets, he is also trying to read over Embassy files and find out as much as he possibly can, as well as deal with the daily business that comes from the Embassy itself or from Canada. One of the basic requirements for this post is the capacity for hard work. It is a very, very demanding job. And as the Polish Ambassador said today (he is not a career diplomat but comes from the industrial sector of Polish life and is therefore used to seeing concrete results), you are never really able to see the results of what you are doing as a diplomat, though you do have history to remind you of what happens when diplomacy fails!

Two special events last week might interest you. One night we went to see *Porgy and Bess*. It was a strange performance. If you can imagine Gershwin and the steamy south without a trace of sensuality, that's what we saw! The actors were all in blackface, but even the makeup betrayed them! The orchestra was excellent and the singing very good but the whole thing was directed like a grand opera. It made no kind of theatrical sense at all, and whereas in Canada you might have left in the intermission, here you remained riveted to your seat wondering what on earth they would do next! All the way through the opening number we thought the woman was singing "Summertime" to a watermelon until it occurred to us that the Russians just cannot imagine a baby who is not totally bound up. (They say a baby's hands must be bound to its sides until it is at least six months, or it may frighten itself with its own fingers!)

The other event of importance, of course, was my fiftieth birthday! I could never have imagined that I would find myself on the evening of the day I turned fifty dancing in the Praga restaurant in Moscow to the lively strains of "When the Saints Go Marching In" with the Dutch Ambassador! I mentioned the Van Agts in an earlier letter. We spent some time with them after the reception on November 7 and told them about my upcoming special occasion. Elspeth had recently turned fifty herself and said that it is a great event in Holland because you get to meet the prophet Abraham, a custom of obscure origins but much enjoyed today because it includes presentations of clay figurines of the prophet and special food and all that kind of thing. Early in the week we got an engraved invitation "to meet the prophet Abraham" at 7:00 p.m. on Sunday. So we went and I wore the new marten hat that Geoffrey has given me to replace the one he gave me fourteen years ago after his trip to Russia with Paul Martin, who was then our minister of External Affairs, and the Van Agts took us to the Praga restaurant to dine and dance and drink champagne and we had an altogether delightful evening. Built at the turn of the century, the Praga is considered to be one of the best restaurants in town. It has four floors and twelve separate dining rooms. We went right to the top, to the "winter garden," where we found a few scraggly potted palms surrounded by a dance floor, about twenty tables, and a live orchestra that was really very good. The food was not memorable except for the caviar but everyone in the room was having such a good time it would have been impossible not to enjoy oneself. Anybody can ask anyone else to dance in such a place and they do, in the most extraordinary combinations of two girls and one man or two women or three men and one girl. We watched groups come together and drink wine and dance and laugh and flirt and then shake hands formally and go their separate ways. Given the housing conditions and the climate there is nothing else they can do! Anyway we had a wonderful evening and I felt younger at the end of it than I did at the beginning—a good start to my second half-century.

LETTER NUMBER 6

November 25, 1980

I have just been to the outskirts of Moscow to buy a bright blue Zhiguli, commonly called a Lada when it gets to the Canadian market. First I had to go to the protocol section of the State Trading Corporation to get a stamped letter permitting me to buy the car and then we went to the huge government car and accessory store, jammed with people buying both new and second-hand cars, where we handed over my letter of permission and got another form permitting me to go and choose a car at a lot fifteen minutes away. When we came out of the sales office we found the Embassy car, which is seven years old and has been 75,000 miles but which still looks pretty impressive, surrounded three-deep by curious buyers who hoped, just remotely, that perhaps it might be coming on the market (they sell non-Russian second-hand cars there as well) but whom we had to disappoint as we drove off to select my rather ordinary vehicle. Everybody was in remarkably good humour and wanted to know what was Canadian for "blue" and "gasoline" and how was Mr. Trudeau? So Ilya (our extremely amiable driver who has worked for the Canadian Embassy for twenty-five years and has one of the twenty-five-year plaques signed by Mr. Trudeau, exactly the same as Geoffrey has, and who has never learned a word of English because all former ambassadors spoke Russian) and Helen, the translator (who is a graduate of the prestigious Institute for Foreign Relations and helps us move through the intricacies of the Russian system), and I all moved around the car lot and kicked at wheels and rubbed off the dust to look for scratches and finally selected one that looked just the same as all the others. And then we had to drive all the way back to the office, fifteen minutes' drive, and then I could pull out my great packet of D-coupons and watch them being carefully counted for several minutes and then I got the receipt and then ... but I won't go on. By that time it was too late to go back to the lot again for the car, so someone will go back tomorrow morning to pick it up. And by Friday I should have my insurance (which costs about the same as it does in Canada) and my diplomatic plates and be able to take off and drive around the city on my own. Actually, except for the fact that you are rarely permitted to make a left-hand turn, driving here looks to be very easy. There are many more cars than there used to be but traffic is still relatively light and well-behaved, owing to the ever-present "milimen" (the Embassy term for the Soviet police).

With the purchase of the car and the arrival last Friday of our second shipment, containing our library and assorted files, we have completed our physical settling-in process. The emotional and intellectual processes will take somewhat longer. I think I will only acquire a tolerable sense of psychic comfort after those of you who are coming for Christmas have all arrived. Your letters are now beginning to arrive regularly so I feel connected and my birthday phone call from Mom made me feel absolutely marvellous. But Canada still seems a long way away on those dark November mornings when we find it so hard to get out of bed!

Last week I gave my first large official lunch, for the Wheat Board, fourteen people in all. Geoffrey couldn't understand why I should feel so nervous but that's because he doesn't know about all the things that can go wrong. But it went beautifully. Tamara has no problem with quantities. She produced a *solyanka* to begin with, which is an excellent Russian soup with ham and cabbage and black olives, and then chicken Kiev and then a red currant soufflé made with frozen currants still available, for the moment, in the Polish frozen food shop. One is surprised that they are still sending any food whatsoever out of Poland. There was an equal number of men from the Wheat Board and from *Export Khleb* and they have all negotiated together for so many years that they are old friends. Mr. Jarvis from the Board gave me a long and complicated description of the difference between the Polish way of raising wheat and the Russian, with a quick pass through the Canadian West.

The other eating event of last week was at the Chinese Embassy. We had been invited to view some documentary movies, to be followed by supper, and I expected some large reception as we had experienced at the Chinese Embassy in New Delhi. However, as we passed through the huge portals we discovered a small coat rack with perhaps a dozen coats and, following our guide through a vast hall decorated with dragon columns, our footsteps echoing in a hollow fashion, we came upon a small group of huddled diplomats. We were all shown into a large movie theatre where, surrounded by empty seats, we watched *China Today* and *Chinese Stone Carving* and *How to Cook in the Suchong Way*, this last whetting our appetite for the feast to follow. Which was in fact very good but odd. I do not care for thousand-year-old eggs but the Peking Hungarian duck was absolutely delicious and the paper-thin slices of lamb cooked in great brass pots on the table had a distinctive and appetizing flavour. I apologize for going on so but one does find, as we had been warned, that the difficulty of obtaining foodstuffs in North American abundance does make one unusually interested in food and what can be done with it. Tomorrow night we are going to the French Embassy for dinner and are looking forward to what is reputed to be the best table in Moscow!

On Sunday we had our first opportunity to see the Bolshoi Ballet and found it to be absolutely wonderful, beyond all expectation. The ballet was *Don Quixote*, with splendid costumes, well-designed if not particularly imaginative sets, stars full of personality and grace, an excellent orchestra, and last but not least, gaiety, humour, and wit. All that for five dollars a ticket! The only problem is, well ... no one is barred from seeing the Bolshoi by cost ... but the tickets are almost impossible to get unless you stand in line for hours, or know someone with whom you can barter, or have some kind of "special standing." Nevertheless, I intend to take full advantage of our "special standing." No one will be impressed if I decide to stand in line with the rest!

December 2, 1980

The courier is late tonight so I have decided to go ahead and give you our news while awaiting yours. And next week, the same plane that brings the courier will also bring Anne and Michael. Fantastic! I find that the whole Pearson family is the subject of a considerable degree of good-natured curiosity so I hope all who are coming are prepared to be exposed to a certain amount of scrutiny. Living in a Residence that is part of the Chancery building is rather like living in a goldfish bowl. Of course, the Residence itself is public property and sometimes its inhabitants feel as if they were too, what with domestic staff and all kinds of repairmen and what have you appearing at unexpected times. That, combined with the underlying awareness that one is being observed by one's hosts as well as one's compatriots, though for somewhat different reasons, keeps one rather on the *qui vive* as we used to say. Those who know me well, which is all of you, will be impressed to learn that I am up and dressed and tidy every morning by 8:30 at least! So far we don't really find the situation oppressive because it is only behaviour and appearances that are of interest. No one seems to be particularly interested in what goes on in my mind and not at all in what lies at the heart's core. So common sense and a little decorum are all that are really required for "peaceful co-existence" when you are here! And when I drive around all alone in my little blue Zhiguli I let the windows steam up and feel happy and independent.

Last weekend we had our first out-of-town trip. We went overnight to the ancient town of Suzdal, about 240 km due east of Moscow. We set off in terrible weather with another couple from the Embassy and Ilya, our cheerful driver. It had snowed and been very cold during the week but Saturday brought icy rain and slippery roads and we almost cancelled the trip. However, it is almost as hard to change plans here as it is to make them so we persevered. You have to file a travel plan when you go any distance outside of Moscow and we were advised to fly the flag for instant recognition but it was soon almost unrecognizable with the slush. Our first stop was Vladimir, which has a magnificent twelfth-century cathedral and a fascinating smaller church of about the same period with the same austere and harmonious lines and, unusually, some delightful carving on each of its four façades, reminiscent, in the naturalness and humour of the human and animal figures, of the carving on Romanesque capitals, a refreshing change from the stylization of so much of the icon painting.

We arrived in Suzdal after dark and stayed in a "motel" that was designed by the Finns and then taken over by Intourist, with all kinds of odd results, the worst being the extraordinary expense and the best being the swimming pool, which you are only allowed to enter after you've had a sauna. So I have had my first experience, quite unexpectedly, of the Russia *banya*. I was on my own because the other woman in our group did not want to swim, and all of a sudden I found myself sitting on wooden slats with eight or nine other ladies, all of us more than ample of flesh. They were quite unabashed and chatted and laughed and pounded one another all around me as I stared at the floor! They were very friendly but my Russian has not advanced far enough to enter into any kind of real conversation, even though I am now communicating quite effectively with my staff without the use of the interpreter. I must admit I was fascinated as I watched them bundle into their woollies after sauna and shower, woollies like I haven't seen since the war, transforming them from charming, rosy young nudes into rather ordinary, plump young women. The dinner at the motel wasn't bad either with quite a good orchestra and lots of dancing and table singing, obviously a Russian custom.

The next morning the weather had improved immensely and we spent several hours exploring Suzdal, essentially a museum town and very charming. The earliest buildings date from the twelfth century and there are examples of all styles of architecture up to the nineteenth century. Monasteries and churches, large houses, and small peasant huts made of logs and decorated with characteristic carved wooden shutters and window frames painted white on blue or green or brown. Ours was the only private car and group. Every other group was a tour huddled around a guide, bundled up in warm wool or fur and everyone wearing a fur hat. They were all Russians, apparently very interested in the monasteries, to which Tsars regu-

larly sent wives they wished to dispose of, and to which, in the nineteenth century, they sent political prisoners. No churches seemed to
be functioning but when we drove back through Vladimir we went
into the cathedral to find a service taking place. The elaborate
Russian Baroque interior contrasted somewhat unfavourably to my
eye with the handsome, austere exterior but the service was curiously moving; destitute old women stood at the door and begged.

The diplomatic calls continue. Geoffrey has to work long hours to
make up for the time he spends out. Much is going on these days that
has to be recorded and reported. Many of our colleagues are experienced observers. The Polish situation is unstable ... The latest five-
year plan is cautious ... The food situation is problematic ... Mr.
Brezhnev is going to India ... And ordinary people go on living ordinary lives as best they can.

LETTER NUMBER 8

December 9, 1980

This will be the last letter to reach you before Christmas so it
comes with all our very best wishes for the holiday season and for the
new year to come. Who knows what that year will bring? One can
only hope for the best possible. We are looking with some unease at
the present situation in Poland and find it very difficult to predict
what will happen next. Much of the last week has been taken up with
speculation, discussions with other diplomats met with at the two
National Days we attended (Finland and Thailand), conversations
with some members of the foreign press, regular listening to the BBC,
which is our main source of up-to-the-minute information, at least
from the Western perspective, reading of telegrams and dispatches,
etc. etc. Of course I don't have access to the latter so try to assess
things from the little information I do have access to and am forced
to the conclusion that there is no way I can possibly know enough to
predict anything, so all I can do is hope that the Poles can arrive at
some workable solution to their present difficulties without the unde-
sirable intervention of others. I must say, though, it is very interest-

ing to be here and observe events as they unfold from the several points of view with which we are presented. Our vantage point is a perfectly safe one, no problem about that! And I still have hopes that 1981 will not be marred by excessive tension! We'll see. Anyway, Merry Christmas to all!

This evening Anne and Michael will be here and that will do a lot to bring joy to the holiday season. Moscow looks beautiful for their arrival. Winter has definitely come. There was an unusual amount of snow last week and now the weather is cold and bright with a fresh dusting of snow each evening. On Sunday we went for a long walk through the Kremlin and delighted in the sight of the golden domes partly snow-covered against the clear blue sky. Muscovites are proud of the fact that they have a low pollution level and possibly their pride is legitimate. Aside from the generating stations where the central heating is created, there are few smoke stacks and the air seems fresh. The snow has laid the dust that was omnipresent in November and at night the stars are brilliant. As we walked back to the Embassy we came across groups of children sliding on whatever slope they could find with shouts of laughter. Near the Embassy is a boulevard that goes on for miles, two lanes of traffic separated by a park of paths and trees, benches, and children's play areas. On Sunday the children were out in force, some of them with their sleighs, some with cross-country skis, little ones all wrapped up in furs being pulled along on their sleds by parents or grandparents, the rosiest of cheeks and brightest of eyes. Not many older children and not much rough-housing but a lot of tolerance of the whooshing sleds from the passers-by. Most people were walking briskly but the cold weather did not stop the old men from their eternal games of chess and dominoes on the benches nor the younger ones from stopping to read the newspapers that are posted up on boards all along the paths. One also sees the occasional dog, the big ones bounding along on their leashes and the little ones, fully protected by little red coats, picking their way delicately on the ice. Because ice abounds. Salt is not used here. In the great square of the Kremlin that is surrounded by cathedrals, the old women wheel their barrows of sand and throw it on the ground by toy-shovelsful. On the sidewalks the apartment-dwellers shovel and sweep and occasionally chip away at the ice with spiked poles and toss it into the road. On the road the snowclearing machines creep along with two alternating brush-like arms with which they pull the snow toward their great maws like huge snow-gobbling monsters. What happens to it eventually I don't know but it does disappear.

With so many people walking about I am surprised that I have not yet seen anyone fall but they appear to be as sure-footed as so many mountain goats—and I must say that my boots are in much better condition than they ever were in the salty slush of Ottawa. Some of our colleagues have already been skiing in the Lenin Hills but we are waiting for the kids. The arrival of winter has its disadvantages of course, one of them being the realization that the Residence does not heat up very well, it's too big and the pipes are too old, so we depend on little heaters for our comfort. My colleague from Iceland, who is a journalist when she is not on duty, tells me that she has a little electric foot-warming zipper bag that she bought in Norway and I think I will see if I can find one. Also, yesterday morning water started dripping from the ceiling in the entrance hall and, of course, a pipe had broken in the attic. Welcome to the Moscow winter, they told me as they repaired it for the time being ... Oh well, we are much better off than our African colleagues (we visited the Senegalese yesterday afternoon and sympathized with their discomfort), because we are used to this kind of happening!

One other thing I will write about this week is music in Moscow. Three quite different evenings since I last wrote provided us with musical treats. The first was a delightful dance at the Swedish Embassy where we were entertained by a troupe of gypsies. They have a theatre in Moscow so they are tolerated by the State but they are unquestionably gypsies in manner, appearance, and talent. The women were beautiful and reminded me of their Rajasthani roots, dark in complexion, soulful in expression, and colourful in dress. They sang with great feeling and danced with passion. I tried to find out something about how they live and how many they are, etc., but no one seemed to know so I just enjoyed their performance. Another night we went to the Conservatory to listen to Leonid Kogan play the Beethoven violin concerto superbly with the State Orchestra of the USSR, conducted by his son Pavel, who then proceeded to a powerful rendition of the Schubert C major symphony. I have never heard a finer concert. And lastly we went to the Norwegian Embassy to hear a young Norwegian pianist who is studying here (and living in a residence with a thousand others and competing every morning for the sixty practise pianos in the basement) play Grieg (of course) and Rachmaninoff and Prokofiev on a piano that Prokofiev himself used to play on. There is something rather old-fashioned about this side of diplomatic life in Moscow—but I am enjoying every minute of it! This part, that is ...

LETTER NUMBER 9

January 6, 1981

Katharine and Patricia will be leaving first thing Thursday morning and will take this letter back with them so it will reach you much quicker than if I sent in through the bag. You have not heard from me for quite a long time but I am sure that you have all been as busy with Christmas occupations as we have, although in a very different context. The departure of the last two will bring to an end four intense weeks of being a family again with all the emotional ups and downs of family interaction and we will feel very flat and very sad for a little while. Some of you will have heard directly from some of them accounts of our various activities and their personal reactions. I will try to describe our Russian Christmas from my own point of view. Having them here made it very special for Geoffrey and me and gave us some new insights into the country in which we are living. It has also made me feel more "at home" because they have left and will be leaving something of themselves behind. We sorely missed Hilary.

I last wrote on the day that Anne and Michael arrived. We hardly gave them time to catch their breath before taking them to Leningrad for three days. We booked a "deluxe" tour with Intourist that worked out very well, although we didn't really have a very good idea of what to expect. We went by train, which is probably the surest way of travelling in Russia in the winter and is also very comfortable (provided the sleeping car is not overheated as it was on the way there).

It was pitch dark when we arrived in the morning and it was still pitch dark when we set out on our first sightseeing tour after ten o'clock. The famous white nights of Leningrad in late spring have their counterpart in the dark days of December.

However, although the light was dim in Leningrad, we found it a fascinating city and thoroughly enjoyed our visit. We did all the tours we could, with a guide in a large, lumbering car called a Chaika. The general city tour was enormously satisfying to the eye with the combination of river, canals, palaces, churches, fine vistas of street and building, superb statues, etc., etc., but it left us with a rather jumbled impression of Tsars and revolutionaries. The one thing that comes through loud and clear is the significance and meaning for the city's residents of the Siege of Leningrad. To see the memorial cemetery, as we did, with its 500,000 massed graves covered in hoar frost was incredibly moving and perhaps helped us to appreciate more than we would have on a bright summer afternoon the extraordinary suffering and the extraordinary courage of these ordinary citizens. Would we survive in Toronto, in Montreal, for 900 days and never give in? How did they manage? I am constantly struck by the enormity of Russian history. Muscovites say that Leningrad is more of a monument than a real city, and perhaps it is, though there is a lot of industrial activity there and apparently a very active intellectual life. The theatre, we are told, is better there because the audiences are more critical, the writing more creative ... But it is true that you can't move an inch in the city without being reminded of its past and witnessing its careful restoration.

Catherine the Great's palace at Pushkin, which we visited with a delightful guide (who'd taken some B.C. foresters to visit logging camps near Lake Baikal in 1978 and remembers Canadians with great pleasure) in an Intourist bus that we had all to ourselves because English-speaking tourists are not too frequent this year, is an outstanding example of historical restoration. It was occupied by the Germans during the siege and then quite gratuitously burnt by them and yet it is now reappearing in all its former splendour of gilt and crystal, parquet flooring, walls panelled in amber or hung with silk. It is really very beautiful and, of course, a great tourist attraction but there is something else at stake here that I don't quite understand.

The Hermitage is a great museum with some of the world's most wonderful art so naturally it must be preserved, but Pushkin and the other palaces around Leningrad are something else again ... Well, we'll go back again and again to Leningrad. Our appetite was just whetted by this visit. I am very glad we made the first one there with some of our children. That experience will enhance the next one.

And then Patricia and Katharine arrived, the latter twenty-four hours late having missed her connection in Frankfurt. She had a peaceful night in a hotel thinking that we had been informed but of course the airline had not been able to reach us (if it even tried) and we didn't sleep very well for wondering where she was. So, when all four were safely under our roof we heaved a sigh of relief and pleasure and set about to enjoy the festivities. Those Canadians who had not gone off on holiday did their very best to make the season a jolly one for the whole Embassy community. Several people had Christmas parties to which everyone was invited no matter how small the apartment. Geoffrey played Santa Claus to the local staff in the club. Someone else played Santa Claus to the whole group here in the Residence (in the beard and red suit that the Embassy keeps in stock), which was a great success. Even his daughter didn't recognize him! Everyone sat on his knee including the Ambassador ... who received a Lenin cap that is too big for him. Afterwards we sang Christmas carols and ate and danced. That was Christmas Eve. On Christmas Day we opened stockings and other presents, went to church downstairs in the Red Room with a motley crew of Protestant English-speaking foreigners resident in Moscow, and then ate our Danish turkey and drank to all of you in French champagne! We had a really beautiful twelve-foot tree covered with familiar treasures and the Residence was decorated with all those *lares* and *penates* we have carried around for so many years, the crèche from Provence augmented by figurines from India, the Mexican animals we hang on the tree, the three kings that Hilary made in Mrs. Rahman's class at A.I.S. in New Delhi with new crowns produced this year by Patricia and so on. Christmas is an emotional time even in the most stable of environments so no one will be surprised to learn that some of us were rather worn out by the end of the afternoon. However, we went out to the Kremlin Palace theatre to see the Bolshoi dance a bal-

let called *The Legend of Love*, in which two royal sisters fall in love
with a working man who renounces them both for the people. It dis-
tracted us completely from our own discomfort and sent us to bed in
a happy mood.

The day after Christmas we drove north for two hours to
Zavidova, where UPDK looks after the diplomatic community when
we want to get away from it all. We stayed for four days in a small
dacha that was simple but warm and comfortable and enjoyed ourselves very much away from the pressures of Moscow. Our dacha
was set with a number of others on a point where the Volga joins
another smaller river and although the whole property is enclosed
behind a fence the river is wide and open and one can ski along it
quite freely for long distances. The weather was not too bad, cold
enough to keep the river frozen and retain enough snow on its surface for skiing. We also skated a bit and slid around on the ice that
covered all paths and took a delicious sauna in a special bathhouse
that could be rented for three hours at a time and where one could
pour tea from a samovar when one became dehydrated. It burned
down two days after we left. There was also a restaurant that was
not bad so that we didn't have to do all our own cooking. It has been
a very long time since so many of us have been able to spend so
much time with one another without interruptions and it was very
good even if the radiator sprang a leak and the bed in the living
room was too small and the gas stove nearly blew Patricia out of the
kitchen and Katharine's feet kept sliding out from under her whenever she walked outside!

Back in Moscow we tried to see as much as we possibly could,
museums, galleries, the fabulous Metro. We went to Zagorsk one
rainy day leaving Geoffrey to attend Kosygin's funeral. We had a
party for some of our diplomatic colleagues and their young people
at which we played charades and watched old Norman McLaren
movies. We went to a New Year's Eve party at the club, where we met
a Canadian film crew here to do a documentary about the puppet
theatre. One young member of the crew attached himself to us and
we have seen quite a lot of him ... We went to concerts, to the New
Circus where the clowns were among the funniest any of us has ever
seen, to the puppet theatre to see *Don Juan 1980*, which was delight-

ful and witty and sophisticated. We saw the ballet *Macbeth* at the Bolshoi Theatre, which is probably the best ballet I have ever seen of its kind, a powerful psychological drama beautifully and movingly performed. We walked the streets and talked and talked. I am sure it will take a long time for everyone to digest all that has happened during the last four weeks. I know it has made a tremendous difference to me to have had them here.

LETTER NUMBER 10

January 20, 1981

When I lift my head from my desk as I am writing this I can still see the same wheeling flock of birds I saw in October. The building crane is still there as well but there have been some changes in the three months we have been here. The branches directly in front of me are mantled with snow, the roofs are white, and icicles hang from every possible corner and cornice. Yesterday, I went skating with Elspeth Van Agt in Gorky Park. Sasha, the driver, took us because Ilya is on holiday, and he promptly got stuck, much to his embarrassment. He was horrified when we got out to push, not realizing how extensive our collective experience is, so we left him to extract himself with the help of some young boys and went off along the alleyways of the Park. The ice was not very good and Elspeth, who remembers skating at the Minto Club with Barbara Ann Scott, felt very uncomfortable in her Russian hockey skates. We weren't too keen, either, about the vintage rock-and-roll music that poured out of the loudspeakers. However, as the day faded and the soft lights came on along the paths and the snow shone faintly in the bushes and on the children's playground, we felt glad to be there among all the young people with whom we shared the ice.

We have also had our first cross-country ski, at Peredelkino. Last Sunday a whole expedition of Canadians, at least twenty of us, set off from the Embassy in a caravan of cars. Once there we split up a bit because some of us were on skis for the first time and some, like Geoffrey, had to go back to work, and the rest of us felt like some real exercise. It was delightful. Peredelkino is a little village not far from Moscow where writers and artists have dachas and where Boris Pasternak lived and is buried. It is one of the prettiest spots near the city because it has hills, pine woods, birches, fields, and streams, all within a small radius of the picturesque old village. There are lots of trails crossing and recrossing one another and one can ski for several hours without repeating a path, although one does not really go very far. At one point there is a great toboggan hill that was covered by youngsters going up and down with sleds and toboggans, and the occasional beginning skier doing a snow-plough down the slope. I will go back there tomorrow and every Wednesday thereafter, as long as the snow lasts, in order to ski with a group of women belonging to the International Women's Club and have tea with an Englishwoman married to a Russian, who lives there.

My writing has been interrupted for a couple of hours and now it is dark and I have closed the curtains. My head is aching. My brain is not as flexible as it once was so I find that several hours of struggling with a foreign language literally makes my head ache. Today I spent nearly two hours with Tamara giving her recipes from a French cookbook for a lunch that we are giving on Thursday and then going with her to the gastronome to do the shopping as well as to the market to get parsley and dill. The price of anything else in the farmer's market is now out of sight. Nine roubles a kilo for tomatoes (about $15) and a rouble and a half for each fading carnation blossom. And yet people buy and not just foreigners, and the sellers, the old women with their heads wrapped in innumerable scarves and the good-looking dark-haired young Georgian men, do not appear despondent. Apart from the prices I like the market. It's nice to find oneself in the familiar role of a customer whose business is being sought, an experience that is exceedingly rare here! Anyway, Tamara is convinced that my Russian has improved so much that she can talk away about all sorts of things. Since I can still barely remember the words for "carrot" and "boil" communication with her is a constant struggle for my poor head and my unaccustomed tongue. The language fatigue was compounded today by a courtesy call from the Colombian Ambassador, who speaks only Spanish and is very eloquent, being a politician rather than a diplomat. As soon as he left I had my Russian lesson with Natasha and now I have come back to my typewriter. If the rest of this letter comes out garbled I am sure you will understand why! Seriously, we are finding that learning Russian requires a great deal of physical effort and while I think we will be able to acquire a certain ability in it within the next few months I would prefer not to contemplate ever learning another difficult language.

All day of course we have been waiting to hear that the hostages have left Teheran, but as I write this we still don't know. And there is Mr. Reagan being sworn in with all the usual hoopla. It is a bizarre situation. Our BBC reception is unusually poor today but perhaps something will come through before I seal the envelopes. Ten days from now, when you read this, everything will be changed (and I will have just come back from four days in Helsinki). What will happen to international relations during the Reagan regime? Like everyone else today I find myself wishing him the best of luck because we will all need it! Mr. Watson gave a pessimistic interview to Kevin Klose of *The Washington Post* before he left last week and I think he was glad to be moving on, flying home in a little plane across the Atlantic with his son. But we will miss him and his wife.

LETTER NUMBER 11

February 3, 1981

The sky is blue, we have just come back from a long weekend in Helsinki, I am wearing my new Marimekko dress, Geoffrey finally has a new shower in the bathroom, my Russian is improving, and I am altogether feeling more comfortable than I have for a long time. I don't much care for what I hear on the radio or read in the newspapers. The political climate is chilly and will no doubt remain so for some time and, of course, that affects the atmosphere in which we live. But if you are dressed warmly and comfortably it is surprising how well you can withstand the vagaries of the temperature! I must say though that it would be a great relief if just occasionally the political rhetoric of either side would hint, by a small touch of humour, that, perhaps states fall away from virtue just as the men and women who live in them do. I think it is possible to make comparative judgments about states but never absolute ones. Individually, Russians can be very humorous and even without knowing the language I am beginning to make a small collection of jokes. Also, at the moment I am reading a very funny book called *The Twelve Chairs*, by Ilf and Petrov, which was published in 1928 and republished between 1953 and 1957 and which is, apparently, much cherished by all Russians who are lucky enough to possess a copy. The humour I am discovering about me is one of the things that is contributing to my greater sense of personal ease. I'll never feel at home here of course, because I'm not, but at least I can go about my daily life with growing anticipation and pleasure, as well as the interest I have always had.

I did not type a letter last week because we were too busy on bag day. I need to keep all of Tuesday free so that I can write a letter and copy it before the mail arrives and then answer those from whom I have received mail on your individual copies. Since our life is becoming more and more involved I think I will only be able to write at length every two weeks. The business of running the Residence itself is time-consuming, more than I would have thought. There is not much physical work of course, but lots of administration, much of it on paper, ordering, filling in forms, keeping records. The Residence and its contents are public property and have to be looked after as a public trust. And our representational activity is public too, and has to be properly recorded and justified. There are far more regulations about all this than there used to be, and quite rightly so because there is no point in doing something if it is not useful and relevant to the objectives of the Mission, but there is no question that it is a "job" and it does take time and energy.

Of course, there are lots of compensations for our status and the responsibilities it has brought. For one thing, we can invite a poet like Andrey Voznesensky to lunch and have him accept. He is one of the Russian declamatory poets who hold public readings that are attended by thousands and thousands. He is supposed to be charismatic, which was hard to determine at a small lunch. However, he was unquestionably charming and literate, as was his wife, who is a novelist, and I will go to hear him when he gives his next public performance in April. We can also get the nearly impossible-to-obtain tickets to *Boris Godunov,* which was splendid and which I was able to follow because I took the libretto. Without it I would have been lost because it is a very complicated story. The male singers were marvellous. Geoffrey did not go this time but has said he would like to go with Hilary when she comes in May. He did go, however, to *The Seagull,* which is also extremely popular although its modern staging is not welcomed by the more traditional Russians. The acting was superb although we had great difficulty understanding the Russian words. We took our teacher with us, which helped, and we reread the play before going. For the time being we will concentrate on plays that we can read in an English version. Sometimes I forget that we have scarcely been here four months and can hardly expect to understand very much! Those of our colleagues who speak better Russian tell us that the theatre is remarkably interesting if not particularly innovative so I would like to be able to understand more. My impression is that Russian writers are fascinated by the human heart and its desires and that they are extremely good at delineating it and its illusions, and its illusions are universal. Those of us who visited the Tretyakov Gallery at Christmas to look at Russian painting all agreed that the most successful paintings were those that had a powerful psychological dimension. Where psychological truth is sacrificed to Socialist Realism artistic vitality vanishes. Some modern short stories I have read seem to combine both and really work. Apparently some contemporary plays do too but I'll have to wait and see.

LETTER NUMBER 12

February 16, 1981

I have just walked with Geoffrey to the Bassein for his twice-weekly swim. The sky is perfectly clear, the sun is shining, there is fresh snow on the ground and about three degrees of frost. Walking back to the Embassy alone across the square and along the snowy tree-lined boulevard, I saw groups of young women at the Kropotkinskaya Metro Stop chatting with one another, smoking their cigarettes in sudden puffs; pairs of young men buying their ice cream bars or their sausages-on-sticks from the babushkas in the kiosks and striding off together along the path past the old men cheerfully arguing over their games of dominoes (I have described the old men before; they are always there, even at night, under the pale lamplight). Before coming down from the boulevard path through the gate onto the street in front of my rather seedy hair-dressing establishment, I had to jump out of the way of a number of school-aged children (they must be having a midwinter break because it is only 2:00 p.m.) swooshing on skis from the slight rise on one side of the boulevard across all thirty feet of packed snow to the iron railing on the other side! Seeing all this on the first day of sun for I don't know how long I suddenly felt lighthearted. In the midst of dire international events and portentous posturings to say nothing of wickedness and sin, ordinary people live not very extraordinary lives full of recognizable activities and genuine pleasures. I know that I can only see the outside of people's lives here but I still think that outside is worth describing. All those people I have just seen hardly noticed me pass. They weren't "performing." They were Muscovites enjoying, like me, a brief respite from Moscow's dreary winter weather, and having a good time with friends. The newspapers often convey an image of what is going on that is very one-dimensional. Except under extreme conditions we all live lives full of minor activities of a more or less routine nature, some of them pleasant, some disagreeable or painful. As a child I remember being fascinated by a book called *Daily Life in Mesopotamia*. It made ancient history real for me. And ever since I have always wanted to know how people were actually living during such-and-such a period of history, not only the unusual people but all the others. Well, some of the "others" here, on a bright sunny day in February, are enjoying themselves in the street. And when I came back to the Residence just now I found Tamara (whose cheek was swollen like a chipmunk's all last week from toothache and from whom I learned how to say "I'm afraid" in Russian because she wouldn't go to the dentist) singing like a lark! And *that's* good because we are having thirty people to dinner tomorrow night ...

Two events last week are worth recording for you. Last Thursday the diplomats were all invited to have a Troika ride at the Park of Economic Achievement. To "pay" for our ride we listened to a few speeches and toured one of the exhibition halls that showed what the collectives produce in the way of handicrafts during the long winter months when they are not ploughing and harvesting and so on. There is an attempt now to revive some of the traditional handwork that was lost as a result of collectivization for, one can assume, a variety of social and economic reasons. And, since a decree of January 16, individuals on collectives are *also* being encouraged to raise as many livestock on their own plots as possible by being offered all kinds of assistance—a major change in agricultural policy! Anyway a lot of handwork is being done now throughout the country and some of it is very attractive ... After looking at wooden boxes and purple pots we were taken to the troikas and though each ride only lasted twelve minutes and we were not chased by wolves we did ride through birch trees and the horses were magnificent! We also had a ride on a sleigh drawn by reindeer and driven by native peoples from northern Russia. None of the ambassadors fell off but that was *before* we went into the restaurant to have blinis and caviar and vodka ...

On Sunday a number of us from the Embassy went out to Leninskiye Gorky to visit the estate where Lenin spent the last part of his life. About twenty miles south of the city, it is beautifully situated on a wooded knoll overlooking the river. The house is large and classical in style but not ostentatious and most of us found the tour very interesting. We were not lectured or preached at. In fact, we were exposed to the *personality* of the man rather than his ideas. We saw a movie made up of old footage, some of it showing him at formal occasions and making speeches, but the rest of it rather like a home movie, very informal, very personal. And the house has been left as it was, bright, comfortable, not particularly luxurious. The room where he died of a stroke in January 1924 is exactly as it was and it is very affecting, somehow, to see it like that with his glasses and his book. There is no doubt that he was a *very* charismatic figure. Seeing the movie we could feel the pull of his personality. The movie was silent. I still haven't actually heard anything that he said ... But what power! More of him later, *no* doubt.

LETTER NUMBER 13

March 10, 1981

Ten days of cold clear weather have suddenly given way to a mild spell and I'm looking out my window at pouring rain and melting snow. But last weekend we went to Zavidova and had a marvellous, healthy, relaxing time on a couple of bright, sunshiny Canadian-style winter days. The dacha the Canadians have rented there for five months is bigger and more comfortable than the one we stayed in at Christmas except that it was impossible to turn off the heat at night and we found it hot and dry. However, we spent a lot of time out-of-doors so we got plenty of fresh air. We went across the Volga to ski on the island on the other side. I didn't know it was an island until after many twists and turns through the spruce and birch woods we suddenly found ourselves facing that village with its old church that we all skied to through the fog at Christmas. We had supper one night at the restaurant with our Cypriot colleagues, who were also relaxing for the weekend, but otherwise fended for ourselves with the help of Tamara's prepared goodies. We read the *New Yorkers* and the *New York Review of Books* that have now begun to arrive from time to time. And I also read all about Catherine the Great in order to prepare myself for our history discussion group that is coming up tomorrow. By the time we returned to Moscow with Ilya on Monday morning I was ready to launch into a week of heavy diplomatic activity.

Three black tie dinners and a dance with Mrs. Gromyko! The best of the dinners was at the Japanese because it happened to be on March 3, the day of the traditional Doll's Festival. Looking at the display that was set up in the salon I remembered all those times I read Rumer Godden's *Miss Flower and Miss Plum* to Patricia. Anyway, there they all were, The Emperor and The Empress on the top shelf and the maidservants and the musicians on the shelves below with all the miniature furniture, flowers, and food. The food we were served was also traditional Japanese and absolutely delicious. But, of course, the highlight of the week was the party given for all the wives of heads of post by Mrs. Brezhnev in order to celebrate International Women's Day. We met at 2:00 p.m. in a splendid reception house in the Lenin Hills, full of ladies and streaming sunlight. Brezhnev's daughter, Galina, a formidable woman, the image of her father except that she was wearing peach chiffon, received us along with other distinguished Russian women whose names I was unable to remember as I went through the receiving line. There were many Russians there, more altogether than foreigners, and they included Ulanova and Plisetskaya and the female cosmonaut and possibly the heroine of Soviet Labour, a modern milkmaid (she led production in a milk processing factory) whom I heard give what appeared to be a really amusing speech at the formal celebration at the Bolshoi the following evening. Anyway, nobody quite knew who anyone else was but it didn't matter in the least.

After we had all foregathered the doors were thrown open onto a magnificent buffet, which we were allowed to get at after we had heard a few not too heavy speeches in three languages and had drunk a toast or two to all the women of the world. After our pheasant and crab and *petit fours* the orchestra tuned up and we all danced. And we danced and danced and it was tremendous fun! Mrs. Gromyko asked me to dance and others joined us. We danced in twos and fours and round circles and conga lines and hardly stopped to draw breath for an hour and a half. Apparently Russian women started dancing together during the war and the custom has continued. No one has to wait to be asked, no one who wants to enjoy the music is excluded, everyone can join in and mix with everyone else. I have rarely experienced such good humour and lack of inhibition at a formal occasion and I seriously doubt whether the husbands and fathers and brothers and sons of all the women present would have been able to abandon themselves with the same energy and enthusiasm if they had found themselves in a similar situation. And then, when we were just about exhausted, we were given big glasses of fruit juice and escorted downstairs to watch a short, lively entertainment, leaving at last with bouquets of flowers in one hand and gifts of Russian handicrafts in the other. I can hardly wait till next year!

The formal occasion at the Bolshoi the following evening was an anticlimax in spite of the presence of Brezhnev and Tikhonov and altogether too many men offering up their rhetoric of equality. As far as I can see the last woman to hold any real power in Russia was

Catherine the Great, and her neglected son took his revenge by insti-
tuting the principle of primogeniture in the Succession with the
female to be excluded from the right to inherit! Sunday, March 8, was
the actual holiday when *all* Russian men celebrated women, some of
them to excess. Nikolai gave me a record of *Swan Lake*, and the drivers presented me with a red and white apron and head scarf. Now
what kind of message was that?

To continue with diplomatic activity. On Friday Geoffrey had a
lunch for some Russian foresters, and today, to mark Commonwealth
Day, he had eighteen Commonwealth ambassadors. Tamara and
Zhenya and Nikolai are really doing extremely well now as a team
and we are certainly keeping them busy. We also had the Canadian
students who are here for four months at the Pushkin Institute in for
supper on Sunday evening. Tamara prepared the quiches (which get
better all the time) but the students washed the dishes. And so it goes
... more next week.

LETTER NUMBER 14

March 17, 1981

Geoffrey has found out the explanation for the wheeling birds I
am watching, as usual, from my desk as I write this. Apparently they
are homing pigeons and what I am watching is their daily exercise.
With that mystery cleared up, the new mystery is whether or not
their owner uses them for any special purpose ... I am also looking
out my window at masses of snow. The mild spell I wrote about last
week only lasted a day and was succeeded by the coldest weather we
have had all winter, down to -28° C. So I have not had to put away
my skis and skates. Last Wednesday I skied in the Lenin Hills with
Liza Klose. We parked at the bottom and skied along the Moscow
River and then took an enclosed escalator up to the top near the
University. There is also a small ski tow on the Hills (which are very
steep but not very high) to which we watched children attach themselves with hooks to get to the top. To get to the top of any of the four
ski jumps, however, the youngsters had to climb by foot carrying

their long, long skis. We paused in the wind to watch them before sliding off ourselves very gently down through the woods to the river and my blue Zhiguli. Saturday I went to Gorky Park with Liz Heatherington and had a marvellous skate. The paths had been reflooded the night before and were as smooth as glass and all kinds of people were out, many of them with children. At the side of one of the main skating rinks there are several narrow rows of low parallel wooden bars where children and other novices can acquire the sense of confidence that will send them out onto the open ice. They are such a good idea that I would like to see them set up somewhere along the Rideau Canal. Tomorrow I will go back to Peredelkino again. All this helps to offset the diplomatic dinners and should get me to April in reasonable shape. And, psychologically, the lengthening days help. At the end of the afternoon we now get a brief, glorious burst of sunshine in both our private sitting room and the dining room. On April 1 the Russians are going on to daylight-saving time for the first time in history. I presume it has something to do with the new thrust to improve agriculture but I look forward to the long, light evenings it will give us. What I don't really look forward to is the messy spring. No one has much good to say about it. Nevertheless both lettuce and cucumbers have appeared in the Russian shops so it must be on its way. And I bought some freesia last week that is still perfuming the Residence, as well as daffodils, which are available in all the shops. There are a lot of flower shops in Moscow and the window ledges of most apartment buildings are green with plants.

Yesterday we visited the Ambassador of the Cameroons and his wife and with them we have come to the end of our official calls. Geoffrey thinks that altogether we made about sixty and I accompanied him to most of them. Now we are on the receiving end. The new Australian Ambassador, David Evans, and his wife came for lunch last Friday. They have been here only two weeks. I recognize how she feels and thank God that that first very difficult part is over. Like us, they have come with no previous experience of Russia or Eastern Europe and no knowledge of the language. However valuable a fresh approach or other qualities may be, it is extremely difficult for a foreign service officer to take on the responsibilities of running an embassy, establish official as well as diplomatic contacts, learn to understand both his political and physical environment, keep up with what is going on in Canada, and learn a difficult new language all at the same time. On Sunday we went out to have lunch at the American dacha with Jack and Rebecca Matlock, who are here to take charge until Reagan appoints a new ambassador. Jack has been here twice before, speaks fluent Russian, and knows the ropes. They are intelligent, pleasant, and comfortable. We had a delightful and relaxing day although the wind was blowing bitter cold across the steppes. Contrasting the two encounters made me appreciate what tremendous stress is placed on people like Geoffrey and David Evans when they begin their work here. For us, the last diplomatic call marks the end of the first stage. No doubt there will continue to be stresses, but of a different order. I would not like to envisage starting all over again!

This morning I went with a few of the Embassy wives to visit the Museum of Oriental Art. We had phoned ahead to see if we could get a guide but had not anticipated the wonderful hospitality with which we were received. We were led up the stairs to the office of the director, who was young and good-looking, talkative and enthusiastic, and who plied us with tea and tooth-breaking biscuits and all kinds of information about the museum and its contacts around the world. Elena had come with us to translate so we managed, in fact, to learn a fair amount about how a state museum like this one operates. The babushkas were as grumpy as usual but the three or four other museum employees that talked to us and showed us around were knowledgeable and interested and delighted to show off their treasures and discuss all their plans. The museum is small at the moment, only able to display one percent of its items, but they will be moving shortly into bigger premises. I don't know enough about most Asian art to assess quality but the small Indian collection had some superb pieces, particularly South Indian wooden sculpture, some twelfth-century bronzes from Bihar, and Mughal miniatures from the sixteenth century. The few Mongolian artifacts that were on display whetted my appetite for our May visit to Ulan Bator. We ended up in a room devoted (and "devoted" is the operative word judging by the glow emanating from the face of the woman who showed us this part of the museum) to the work and memory of an artist and collector called Nicholas Roerich. He painted masses of Lawren Harris-in-his-theosophic-phase-like pictures of the snow mountains, having spent most of his life in India looking like a mystic (judging from the photographs). Most of his paintings have temples or Buddha figures and a couple even have Christ-like figures. He preached universal brotherhood and peace through beauty (very Platonic) and his ideas are very popular in Bulgaria (according to his admirer), where many factories have set up Roerich art, music, and dance appreciation groups in order to improve harmony and increase production ... His works are part of the permanent collection of the Museum of Oriental Art and are treated with great veneration by all the people there. My visit last week to the Pushkin Museum to see two excellent small exhibitions did not hold as much human interest for me as my encounter with Roerich, but their artistic merit was greater. The first was a delightful display of decorative art of the ninth to the sixteenth century from both the Cluny and the Louvre Museums, featuring, among other enchanting pieces, several of the *mille-fleurs* tapestries I remember so well from my visits to the Cluny Museum when we were living in Paris. The other exhibition contained thirty or forty pieces of ancient Greek art from the islands of the Aegean. So there is a lot of art to see in Moscow. Unfortunately none of the exhibitions that come from the West are of contemporary art and the effect that isolation from trends in the visual arts has on a young painter was to be seen sadly in the show of new work by twenty non-official Soviet artists I saw on Saturday. Melancholic fantasy is the dominant theme, surrealism the dominant mode and green the dominant colour.

LETTER NUMBER 15

March 24, 1981

On March 21, appropriately enough, spring arrived in Moscow. What a contrast to last week! The temperatures shot up and the clouds vanished. Daytime temperatures have stayed around 14 or 15 degrees and the clouds have stayed away. The snow is disappearing rapidly, revealing layer after layer of grime and soot and all the other sordid remains of a city winter where garbage does not go out in plastic bags and no one has to clean up after a dog. However, Lenin's birthday is coming up early in April and apparently all the neighbourhood citizens' groups devote a weekend to cleaning the whole city. In the meantime one walks with care and keeps one's eyes on the buildings and on the bright blue sky. I think Moscow will look lovely in a few weeks when the pale leaves of early spring-time complement the delicate pastel colours of the old houses and slightly newer buildings in the Arbat, the area in which we live. Throughout the winter we have explored most of the streets in our surrounding environment and been constantly delighted by the discovery of old mansions and small churches tucked away in back lanes. There are trees everywhere and many gardens and play-grounds. At first sight Moscow is not particularly striking but I am beginning to realize that parts of it, at least, are really very beautiful. On Saturday we walked inside the Kremlin walls and, finding that two of the cathedrals we had not yet visited were open, we waited in line with other individual tourists to buy our tickets from a miraculously cheerful cashier. What a difference spring makes to tempers the world over! We saw the Cathedral of the Archangel, where the Moscow Tsars are all buried, including Ivan the Terrible and his poor son. And then we visited the Cathedral of the Annunciation, which is much more intimate and features some sin-gularly beautiful paintings. It was built in the fifteenth century and its marvellous iconostasis is made up of haunting paintings of the prophets by Theophanes the Greek and seven lovely "festival" paintings by Andrei Rublyov. We still have not seen the inside of the Assumption Cathedral, which is the largest of the three in the Square and which is where the coronations took place.

The whole Square was reconstructed on the stage of the Bolshoi Theatre for the performance of *Boris Godunov* that I saw a couple of months ago. I don't know how the Russians manage to produce such grandiose sets when all the theatres are repertory and the same play or ballet or opera is never put on twice in a row. They are very clever at changing sets rapidly and the design conceptions are often interesting even if the execution is usually, at least to my mind, rather disappointing. On Sunday evening we went to see

Anna Karenina, a ballet created for Maya Plisetskaya by her husband, the composer Rodion Schedrin. She was born in 1925 and is, apparently, reluctant to retire. At the end of the performance she was showered with flowers from every tier of the theatre, to say nothing of the baskets and bouquets that were brought up to her from the floor and the bravos and endless applause. I can well understand how hard it would be to retire to private life after you've known all that. Actually, the part suited her dramatic and lyric expressiveness and was not all that demanding technically, and the ballet itself was very well directed, especially the last scene where she throws herself in front of the train. However, Vronsky was a great disappointment. It was hard to imagine that she could have developed such a passion for a man with such a weak chin, even though he was a very good dancer. Karenin was excellent. That is such a good role!

In fact, last week was very cultural altogether, mostly thanks to other countries. On Monday I (because half the time Geoffrey stays at home to work) went to the Tchaikovsky Hall to hear a Vietnamese pianist who had just won first prize in Warsaw at the International Chopin Competition and who played Chopin as I have never heard him played before, brilliantly and totally without romantic sweetness. On Wednesday we went to the Hungarian Embassy to hear a concert to celebrate the hundredth anniversary of the birth of Bartók and to see an exhibition of Hungarian graphics that was stunning. The Bartók was difficult though I liked most of it, particularly the pianist. There is no doubt that Hungary has some qualities of imagination and style that are lacking here. I understand that their economic system is much more flexible than the Soviet model. I would like to visit. In fact I hope we may be able to visit all the Soviet bloc countries in order to compare. On Thursday we missed the Danish quartet because we had a previous engagement, but on Saturday evening I went to the Chinese Embassy to watch a movie of the Peking Opera performing the story of the female marshal during the Sung Dynasty who had to condemn her husband to forty lashes in order to maintain discipline since, as her vanguard general, he had disobeyed orders. The quality of the film was good although the sights and sounds were very strange to the Western eye and ear.

Very stylized, not too unlike Kathakali although with the addition of singing and a great deal of humour. This week we go to hear a Japanese cellist ... Well, when we have our next formal dinner, on April 7, *we'll* show some Norman McLaren films. The Russian cultural event of last week was our visit to the fashion show at the *Dom Modeley*, the House of Fashion. A group of us from the Embassy went to see one of the thrice-daily shows featuring the spring fashions. It wasn't exactly Christian Dior but actually we were pleasantly surprised. The models were attractive, tall and slim, elegant without being arrogant. The "safari-style" sportswear was smashing as were the pure silk afternoon dresses with blocked shoulders, long waistlines, and short pleated skirts. The ramp was slightly shabby and the PA system broke down a couple of times, but the interest shown by the audience of a hundred and fifty or so women was intense and there are shows every day all year round. The women, most of whom seemed in their thirties and forties and none of whom resembled the models, all drew madly in notebooks and then went downstairs to study the mannequins and to buy paper patterns. There appears to be quite a lot of cloth available in the shops although it is rather expensive and many *ateliers* where you can get things made up, but there is a shortage of goods for finishing—zippers, interlining, good thread, that sort of thing—and there is no tradition among Russian women of sewing for themselves. However, the desire to be fashionable is unquestionably there. *Vogue* magazine (brought in from the West) circulates in separate pages all over Moscow! The men appear to be totally uninterested in clothes although this show did have a male model. The evening dresses were disastrous.

This morning we heard Mr. Trudeau on the BBC. I wish him well. I want the constitution in Canada. I see no point now in arguing any more about methods or we'll never get it back. Let's hope the British will focus on the vital event of marrying off Prince Charles and not interfere in our national affairs. We hope other countries will restrain their desire to interfere in other places also ...

My niece Annabel arrived safely from London last night and Hilary phoned this morning to discuss wedding dates and it's Patricia's birthday and Michael's birthday will be on Friday and altogether I have spent most of the day thinking about you all and feeling connected. Tonight I hope there will be a good package of mail that will top it all off. This letter will be a little on the short side because we are having thirty-three for dinner (and hoping that a couple will drop out as they usually do at the last minute because otherwise my tables will be a little crowded) and although I do not have to do any cooking, I do have to have special instructions on the use of the projector that I fouled up last time and do all the other small things that fall to my lot, such as arranging the flowers and figuring out the protocol. I know it doesn't sound very onerous but I still get a bit nervous. I can assure all those who remember me at Christmas that things are much better under control now and I do learn from my mistakes. Tamara is *always* under control, I have come to realize. It is only a question of making sure that we have decided on the appropriate menu for the occasion. The improvement in Nikolai's confidence and competence is such that Geoffrey has only muttered once under his breath in the last two weeks.

We are having a good mix of people—diplomats, journalists, business people, and three Russian couples—and we plan to entertain them after dinner with a trip up the Inside Passage from Vancouver to Alaska (a splendid new film we have just received), a look through Kurelek's eyes at his father's life as a Ukrainian immigrant to Canada, which I have just checked in order to find out why and when he left Russia (no problem, all he really wanted was land!), and a Norman McLaren short (of course) featuring Oscar Peterson. Depending on what Mr. Brezhnev says this afternoon, an evening that relaxes tensions may be most welcome to one and all. (Although it may have to go on without Kevin Klose of *The Washington Post*. The print journalists are much less likely to appear at dinner parties than the radio or TV people. Hal Jones assures us that he will be able to come.) Actually, Annabel and I went to hear Kevin this morning sharing a panel with Geoffrey's number two, Peter Hancock, a man from the American Embassy, and a Brit, on the subject of East–West relations. The Americans came on considerably stronger than Peter and his British colleague and the discussion was very lively. Annabel was rather struck by the sight of these high-powered individuals sharing coffee and cookies with women and the grade nine students of the Anglo-American school but in Moscow one does live differently! It is marvellous having someone young here again, as it was having those of you here who came at Christmas. Your perspective is quite different. So are your experiences. Annabel just walked back from the Bassein, to which she had accompanied Geoffrey for his swim, and was approached by a Hungarian who made the kind of remark in Hungarian that Hungarians make to young women and was stopped in his tracks by her response in Hungarian to "get lost"! Even though the trees have barely begun to bud she still finds Moscow more attractive and much less formidable than she had expected and is settling in to enjoy herself. Let's hope that none of the things that the Americans like to predict with foreboding will actually come to pass.

Now a word about our upcoming plans so that you can follow us in your imagination in the next weeks and also understand why my letters will be a little irregular in coming. Next Monday night we will take the train to Kiev, where we will make a three-day official visit (April 14–16). Then Annabel will come back to Moscow with Ron Halpin and we will take the night train to Odessa. On Saturday we will board the MV *Adjaria* and sail down through the Black Sea and the Aegean to Piraeus. The trip only takes two days and should be very interesting. Then we have three days in Athens before the start of the Eastern European Heads of Mission meeting, which will last through the long Greek Orthodox Easter weekend. Then we will fly back to Moscow for a week before taking off again to Ulan Bator and the presentation of credentials. We will fly there directly but take the train back to Irkutsk, where we will stay for a couple of days before flying back to Moscow. Then Hilary will come and we will go to Leningrad and perhaps Novgorod and then on June 11 we'll leave to return to Canada. So the next couple of

months will be really busy and interesting as long as nothing happens to oblige Geoffrey to stay here. I hope not for all kinds of reasons, not the least of which is the fact that he needs a break, which
he has not had since we have been here except for our weekend in
Helsinki, and he also needs the opportunity to talk to his Canadian
colleagues at the senior level.

I have now established contact with the Institute of General and
Paedagogical Psychology. This Institute falls under the aegis of the
Academy of Paedagogical Sciences, which is ultimately responsible
for all educational research in the USSR. I find that work is going on
in many of the areas in which I am interested and in which I have
some experience. I have been invited to come back and meet with
many of the associates of the Institute and observe their work both
within the Institute itself and in the schools, which I hope to be able
to visit beginning in September. In the meantime I am trying to read
what I can on the Soviet system of education and some of the papers
of Institute researchers published in a language I can read. My spoken Russian is improving but I doubt if I will ever be able to read
Russian with any ease. However, a fair amount of the Institute's
work is being translated into Spanish for use in Cuba and I could
deal with that. Anyway, the people I met were very friendly and
interesting and I look forward very much to learning more about
what they are doing.

Last week, in pursuit of Russian history, I went with Elena to a
small Boyar Museum near the Rossiya Hotel. We were taken around
by the director, who speaks a limited and lilting English and who has
a fund of anecdote and fact about life in the sixteenth and seventeenth centuries. The Boyar Museum is in one of the few houses left
standing from what the Russians call mediaeval times (which appear
to be somewhat later than what we call the Middle Ages). Of course,
Russia never experienced a Reformation or a Renaissance so in some
ways the Middle Ages have just gone on and on and on ... Anyway,
back in the sixteenth century life was pretty difficult for noble-
women, who were forbidden to learn to read and were kept in seclu-
sion as a result of the Mongol influence and had to spend all their
time doing embroidery in small, cramped rooms as we could tell
from this old house. Worse even than being a female in a Boyar's

household was being the daughter of a tsar. Nobody was good enough to marry you so you had to spend your life in a monastery, also, no doubt, doing embroidery! And you always had to have your head completely covered in the presence of men. Having shown us a headdress our guide proceeded to tell us the real story of Ivan the Terrible's murder of his son. It was all his daughter-in-law's fault. Ivan came upon her with her hair loose and was so enraged at the sight that he struck her with his famous stick. She was nine months pregnant and her husband rushed to her defence, perhaps to the defence of the son she might be carrying. Anyway, Ivan struck him down but unlike the bloody image we saw in Ilya Repin's painting in the Tretyakov, he only died eleven days later of a fever, thrown into despair by the news that his son was stillborn. Our guide told us the story with relish and colour. The Russians can't read about today's murders in high (or low) places. They have to rely for a good scandal on the ancient past...

LETTER NUMBER 17

April 29, 1981

We arrived back in Moscow at four o'clock last Saturday morning to find Ilya waiting cheerfully for us with his fur hat back on and two inches of snow on the ground! The buds are scarcely any fatter than they were when we left two weeks ago and there is no green anywhere. They say that when in fact it does come to Russia it comes overnight and one wakes up one morning to find the world transformed. We'll see. We chased the spring to Kiev and found a snowstorm. We went on to Odessa and shivered in an unheated hotel. Only when we entered the Bosphorus did the sunshine break forth. The weather in Greece was perfect!

In spite of grey skies and chilly winds we thoroughly enjoyed our trip to the Ukraine. Kiev is situated on seven hills high above the Dnieper River and spreading beyond its banks. Coming in by train from Moscow you cross the river on a high trestle bridge and see trees and parkland and golden domes. Kiev will be 1,500 years old next year and has a thousand parks. It is a lovely city. It is softer and more graceful than Moscow and not as European as Leningrad. Much of it was damaged or destroyed during the war but you would never know it now. There are many modern buildings of course, but it doesn't look like a contemporary city. I wonder if any city in Russia does? It will be interesting to see some of the brand-new cities in Siberia if we ever manage to get out there. Anyway, the streets of Kiev are wide and spacious and people walk about them in a normal fashion, not flowing in an endless stream as they do in Moscow. The men are often very tall and dark and quite handsome and the Ukrainian women are admired for their vivaciousness and their dark eyes, as we were told by one who is small and dark and lively. The blue-eyed blondes, of whom there are so many in the Canadian West, descend from a relatively small blonde population along the Polish border whose ancestors are, probably, the Vikings who were summoned into the Ukraine in the ninth century to bring order to the warring Slav tribes or, at least, so the chronicles say. We were most hospitably treated by the people we met whatever their origins and we liked them very much. Geoffrey called on the Foreign Minister and the Mayor and the rector of the university, and Annabel and I were taken to visit a Pioneer Palace and a wonderful children's library. We were escorted by two very interesting women from the Ministry of Foreign Affairs, one of whom spoke excellent English, and after three mornings of doing things together we found ourselves discussing all kinds of topics.

On the last morning they took us to Babi Yar, the place where so many thousands of Jews had been lined up, stripped, and mowed down during the German occupation. And other people as well. Partisans, gypsies, people who resisted ... Now, all the bodies that were thrown into the ravine have been covered by tons of soil and green grass and a haunting monument has been raised, designed, we were told, by a group of young people who were not even born when the terrible events of Babi Yar took place. It depicts people of all kinds crowding up to the edge of the ravine and tumbling over it. A profound and moving work of art. Obviously a deeply felt and collectively held sense of outrage can occasionally transform Socialist Realism and committee decisions into an authentic and universal work of art. As we drove back into the centre of the city we talked about war and peace and Annabel asked Irena and Galina, both of whom are in their fifties, how they felt about the Germans. They said they held the Nazis responsible for what had happened, not the German people. And I am sure that Anne and Michael remember that in Leningrad the guides were careful to talk about the Nazis when they discussed the siege and the destruction. I wish that when we talk about the Russians and their presumed intentions we would be a little more careful to separate out who is responsible for what. In the Pioneer Palace and in the enchanting children's library there is a great sense of light and warmth, human involvement, and child-scaled activity. The people who work there like what they are doing and they obviously like children. In neither place is the environment spartan or the atmosphere punitive. The younger children appeared cheerful and slightly disorderly. The older ones are more serious and regimented. In the library there is a whole room devoted to fairy tales, surrounded by a delightful ceramic wall with images of Cinderella and Scheherezade, Pippi Longstocking, Dr. Doolittle, and Tom Thumb. I have seen fairy tales shown on Soviet television. They are told straight, witches, princesses, and all. Of course the children are also given lots of moral tales, but it is worth remembering the uses of enchantment ... If Churchill said that Russia is a mystery wrapped in an enigma he surely meant that one doesn't know what to expect next from this country and its people. So why should one, by always expecting the worst, contribute one's little bit to making the worst happen? There are other forces acting on the Russians in addition to Marxist-Leninist ideology, human forces that are universally understandable. The five-year-old pointing her toe with concentration in the ballet class in the Palace reminded me for all the world of Katharine in Mexico ...

When Geoffrey wasn't doing official things we all went sightseeing. The Saint Sophia church was constructed in the town of Yaroslavl the Wise in 1037. The exterior was restored in the eighteenth century but the interior is ancient and marvellous. The mosaics of the eleventh century are as fresh as if they were made yesterday, and full of wonder. The original frescoes were often painted over but they are now being uncovered where possible and are lovely if much faded.

When we left we were given a woodcut of the church. We were told that Mr. Trudeau had been given one too. Mention Canada and the response is Trudeau, wheat, or Guy Lafleur. Great disappointment at his short appearance in the recent hockey tournament. Not much of a show on our part.

We also went to see the Pecherskaya Lavra. A *lavra* is a great monastery. There are four in Russia. Zagorsk is, I think, the only active one. The monastery in Kiev was founded in 1051 and has many handsome buildings but the twelfth-century church that was its masterpiece was quite gratuitously destroyed by the Nazis. Still, there is lots to see, mummified monks with their holy faces covered by gold cloth in the caves below the hill, a flea with golden shoes (I'm not kidding—you look at it through a microscope). Also a portrait of Ernest Hemingway on a pear seed painted by a modern Ukrainian master. Annabel and I got the giggles at this stage and had to be moved along! A marvellous collection in another of the monastery buildings of Scythian gold: diadems and necklaces, breastplates and scabbards, dress ornaments and belts, all from the tombs around the Ukraine that have been excavated in recent years. We were taken around by a French-speaking guide who had almost as much gold in her teeth as was in the display cases! Being guided around churches and monasteries in Russia is a curious experience. Our guides are full of respect, admiration, and even knowledge of what they are describing to us but they haven't the faintest sense of the numinous quality emanating from the sites we are visiting. Easter is celebrated in Russia and there are obviously still many believers even among the young but it would be a delusion to think that they represent any significant percentage of the population. For the average Russian now Christianity seems to hold only a mild historical interest. Perhaps I am wrong. Who knows? But that is the way it appears to a visiting observer. Which is not to say that they don't have faith in something beyond themselves. That is another whole issue.

After three days in Kiev Annabel flew back to Moscow with Ron Halpin, the young officer who had come with us, and we took the overnight train to Odessa. The spring was further advanced there but it was still very chilly and I caught a cold. Odessa was designed by Catherine the Great in a fanciful mood. She laid her fan on the table and said that the streets should be designed to fan back from the waterfront. And the city does have a great deal of charm. All port cities do, I guess, but Odessa has a real southern quality with its wide avenues and plane trees and great chestnut trees coming into leaf. And the 192 steps leading down to the sea from the promenade above are extremely handsome as well as being redolent with history. They were built around 1840 but naturally they are known now as the Potëmkin steps and I found that Eisenstein's image of the baby carriage tumbling down them came vividly to my mind as I looked at them, although it is many, many years since I saw *The Battleship Potëmkin*. We had a day and a half in Odessa and saw as much as we could, including the vast extent of sandy beaches being spruced up for the summer onslaught. Our guide seemed to be particularly proud of the champagne factory, for some reason, and told us that the French were *very* interested in the new process the Ukrainians have developed to hurry up the aging process ... ! Actually, there is a Ukrainian wine called "the Pearl of the Steppes" (white) that is really delicious but the Georgians seem to have cornered the diplomatic market in Moscow and I don't know whether I will be able to get it here. We called on the Mayor, which was very interesting. Vancouver and Odessa are twin cities and have been since 1944 at the request of Vancouver in sympathy for the terrible suffering of Odessa during the war. Visits have been exchanged on a regular basis since, except last year when an Odessan delegation was put off. Odessa also twins with Marseilles, Genoa, Liverpool, and Yokohama, and has excellent relations with all those ports. Almost all our wheat is delivered to Russia through the port at Odessa and we have lots of common interests. The black fields of the Ukrainian Steppes stretching back from Odessa certainly look like Manitoba. I know that any action any of us ever takes is political but on balance I would rather weigh in on the side of common interests and common humanity, except in the most obvious situations.

We boarded the *Adjaria* on Saturday at noon. We had spent the morning visiting the archaeological museum because I am fascinated by the evidence of the Greek settlement of the Black Sea and by the Scythians and the other tribes that left their mark on Russian territory into the Middle Ages. We had also walked quite a lot, watching the

Subbotniks contribute their yearly work. Once a year, just before Lenin's birthday (the Saturday preceding it, actually) all over Russia people give a day's work to the community. Some of them spend the day, as we saw, sweeping the streets and raking the debris of winter, washing windows, or painting railings. Others apparently work at their normal job but contribute the day's pay to some worthy project such as a children's hospital or a bridge in Siberia. The Mayor was going to be digging in one of the new parks, planting trees with the assistance of the senior people in his office. He himself is a dynamic and attractive man, young and apparently able. He probably got a lot of trees into the ground! Some, no doubt, are a little more reluctant than others to do their part, but we saw all kinds of people, young and able-bodied, children, and the elderly, out on the streets cleaning up. It's not such a bad idea.

The weather was still grey all the way across the Black Sea and a little choppy but we had a very comfortable suite with windows facing port and starboard and a good deal of red furniture. More Ukrainian borscht for dinner (not nearly as good as Tamara's) and a good night's sleep. The next morning the sun shone and we stood on the bridge with the captain for two hours as we travelled through the Bosphorus, Topkapi, the Blue Mosque, the Saint Sophia. Sailing past Byzantium. The spine tingled. It was really thrilling! …

LETTER NUMBER 18

May 3, 1981

There has been no more snow in the week we have been back but the spring is taking forever to come. Perhaps it will have burst forth by the time we come back from Mongolia. We are off tomorrow and will be back May 12. I will send you all postcards, which will probably take ages to reach you but should be worth it for the Mongolian stamps. My next letter, which will be in two weeks, will be all about that. It is bound to be a fascinating trip. In the meantime we have had a very interesting week here much enhanced by the visit of Blair Seaborn on his way back from the Far East. He has a great deal of energy and managed to crowd a lot into his short stay here. We were able to entertain some of his Russian friends and Geoffrey took advantage of his presence to call on the ministry concerned with the environment. But it was primarily a private visit, to see Moscow again and to see us. He brought us Jack Granatstein's book on Norman Robertson, which we are glad to have, and a fair amount of news from Ottawa. He and Annabel went to the Tretyakov and walked around the city a lot. He and I went to hear Glinka's opera, *Ruslan and Ludmila*, and rather disgraced ourselves by giggling at some of the more outrageous moments so that the army officer sitting in front of us turned around and glared. *Ruslan and Ludmila* is a very Russian blend of the sublime and ridiculous but it was more than made up for for our houseguests the next evening when Blair and Annabel saw Prokofiev's ballet of *Romeo and Juliet*, which they both thought was marvellous. Geoffrey and I had dinner with the Irish and saw a film on W.B. Yeats.

Blair left on the morning of May Day and Annabel and I wandered up to Kalinin Prospket to see what we could of the parade. The weather was sunny and the people looked cheerful. It was curiously silent, though, because all the traffic was blocked and the cheering crowds were centred in Red Square. Children had balloons and there were masses of paper flowers and all the red banners and the portraits were on display. Although the Scandinavian countries, Turkey, and Iceland went, Canada sticks with the other NATO countries so we were not allowed to attend officially. We came back and watched the end of it on TV and decided we hadn't missed too much. However, we did miss the fireworks, much to our annoyance, because the Russians responsible paid no attention to daylight saving time and set them off at nine o'clock as they always do. It wasn't exactly broad daylight, but very nearly.

Yesterday, Annabel and I went out to Peredelkino to walk in the woods and visit the grave of Pasternak. The graveyard is full of Easter remnants, coloured eggs broken on the graves and Easter bread and masses of flowers, mostly of the plastic variety. While we were in Greece Annabel went to the wedding palace to assist at a wedding and now she is curious, as I am, to learn more about funeral ceremonies. Her curiosity about Russia is boundless. She has already seen more and walked more around the city than I have. Her daily swim at the Bassein gives her a special opportunity to observe and she is a marvellous observer. It is a treat having her here.

LETTER NUMBER 19

May 18, 1981

Ever since we went to Kiev we have been expecting the arrival of the Russian spring. We finally found it in Irkutsk, in Siberia! Then, we when returned to Moscow last week after our trip to Mongolia, we found the city transformed. Spring must be Moscow's most beautiful season, because the city is full of trees and parks and the pastel shades and crumbling stucco of so many of the buildings are likely to be enhanced more by the delicate, fresh green of spring than the dusty leaves of summer. Certainly the drive in from Domodevo airport last Monday in the late afternoon sunlight through long avenues of newly-leaved birches, past the park of Kolomenskoye, down along the river under the golden domes of the Kremlin to the door of our handsome Embassy was particularly lovely and we felt almost as if we were coming home! Well, we have been able to establish our presence in the living part of the Residence now so it really is home, at least for the time being.

There were only the faintest signs of spring, however, in Mongolia, enough to make the bare hills seem alive rather than dead, but only just. Flying in from Irkutsk after a three-hour unexplained wait in the airport we first of all saw nothing but range after range of low brown hills, outlined by the remnants of the winter snow and only the barest hint here and there of pale green. Then, all of a sudden, in a valley, we could see the city of Ulan Bator with modern grey and pink buildings, factories, and smokestacks, and surrounded by extended areas of closely packed yurts, the large, round, white felt tents that so many of the Mongolians still inhabit. And then we were on the tarmac being greeted, along with our Swedish colleagues who were also on the plane, by the chief of protocol, who looked, with his aquiline nose and Mongoloid eyes, exactly like one of the handsome

Mayan princes depicted at Palenque or Bonampak, and the resident British Ambassador who looked, well, British! We discovered that our delay in Irkutsk had been caused by the arrival in Mongolia two hours before us of the Mongolian cosmonaut and his Russian companion, who had just completed a space flight. Naturally all the welcoming ceremonies for them had to be completed before they could turn to visiting ambassadors who had come to present credentials. Ambassadors come and go, but for a country like Mongolia that only sixty years ago had a literacy rate of barely one percent and a society that was backward in most other respects, the arrival back from space of one of their compatriots, the son of simple herdspeople, was an event of overwhelming significance. In fact, we were lucky that our visit coincided with theirs because we were able to participate in some of the activities organized for them and to see a part of Mongolian pride that we might otherwise have missed.

For the Mongolians have a great deal of national pride, for all that they are so closely associated with their neighbour to the north. After all, the Mongolians knew great glory in the past and made a tremendous impact on world history. It was from High Karakorum (about 400 km south of Ulan Bator and where all that remains in the desert, shades of Ozymandias, is a gigantic carved stone turtle) that early in the thirteenth century Genghis Khan set out to conquer the world and very nearly succeeded. The Russians have never forgotten the "Tartar Yoke" that was laid on them for 250 years starting with the winter campaign of 1237–38 (the only successful winter campaign that has ever been conducted against Russia) and that profoundly affected their social and political development. If Batu, Genghis Khan's grandson, had not had to return to Karakorum following the death of the Great Khan Ogedir, that yoke would have extended much further into Europe. Kublai Khan built his pleasure palace in Peking and Tamerlane led the Golden Horde from Samarkand, but after his death the Mongolian strength waned and Russia and China moved in to contain once and for all the "recalcitrant herdsmen of the Steppes." And the Russians and Chinese have been involved in the history of Mongolia ever since. But there have been other connections. Mongolia is part of what is known as Inner Asia along with Tibet and the Central Asian Turkic areas, most of which are now part of Russia, lying on the northern flanks of the Himalayas and the Hindu Khush. And, on the whole, the Mongolians remind me very much of the Tibetans I saw in India and Nepal, both physically and temperamentally. They seem to be a lively and attractive people with high colour and wide smiles. At least half of them wear the national costume, the *del*, which has the wraparound characteristic of the Tibetan dress but is only knee-length and has sleeves. The dress ones are made of beautiful Chinese silk in royal blue or jade green or purple and the ordinary ones are lined cotton, navy blue, beige, or brown with silk belts folded and twisted double around the waist. Both men and women wear the same dress with boots and bowler hats! The Tibetan similarity was reinforced for me when we visited the one remaining "working" monastery in Ulan Bator, the Gandang. Tibetan Lamaism came to Mongolia at the end of the fifteenth century. It took a form that appears to have emphasized the demonic in quite frightening ways, to judge by the masks and figures and wall paintings on display in the seventeenth-century summer palace of the "living Buddha" and an early twentieth-century monastery in the centre of town, which has been turned into a cultural museum. It also had a strong Tantric component the evidence of which is modestly displayed in unlighted cabinets. The Russian influence is really very Victorian. Even symbolic sex must be carefully veiled, at least in public.

Ulan Bator (which means "red hero") used to be called Urga and was the residence of the "God-king," the living Buddha, the head of a theocratic state, for some 400 years until the revolution and the founding of the People's Republic of Mongolia in 1921. At that time, for a population of less than half a million, there were 100,000 monks, who were, at least nominally, celibate. One has the impression that the Lamaism of that period was decadent but it is hard to know how powerful a spiritual force it was in earlier days. The Indian Ambassador told us that right after the Revolution and the closing of the lamaseries there was a destruction of books and manuscripts that is presently regretted by the authorities. Nevertheless, some things were preserved and are now being studied in the archives slowly but surely. There are even some Sanskrit manuscripts that no longer exist in India. Lamaism is now tolerated by the regime and we saw a great deal of activity at the Gandang, including a service with the blowing of the conch shell and the burning of incense. The prayer wheels were being continually spun but it was quite clear to me that the holy link between form and meaning has been broken forever for the vast majority of the Mongolian people and that Buddhism will have to take on a new form if it is to reach the hearts and souls of the sons and daughters of the Revolution. Which is not to say that I think Mongolian culture has been destroyed now that it is no longer so picturesque. The Russian cultural influence is strong and recognizable in everything from the buildings to the ballet but still we all found the Mongolians and their activities distinctive and vital.

When Geoffrey had his private chat with President Tsendenbal after the formal presentation of his credentials he heard a lot from him about "the old days," not, of course, the old days of Chinese control (Mongolia declared independence from China in 1911 and has bitter memories of life under the Manchurian Overlords) but the old days of the birth pangs of the Republic. Although he is young by the standards of Russian (not to say American) leadership—he is only 65—he has been in continuous power longer than any other head of state, having become minister of finance at twenty-four! Still, he was not exactly present at the creation, nor was he paying very much attention during the extraordinary episode of the Mad Baron, which he described to Geoffrey with such intensity. The Mad Baron was a Russian of German origin named Baron Von Ungern Sternberg, an officer of the Russian Imperial Army, utterly reckless, incredibly brave, and quite insane, who after being cashiered twice and then decorated in 1916 went off to Mongolia with visions of becoming a new Genghis Khan. With the help of the Japanese he raised a regiment of lawless Cossacks and other mercenaries and committed almost indescribable atrocities on every victim who came his way. He captured Urga, ousting or killing the remaining Chinese, and, still supported by the Japanese (mainly financially), who had their own interest in the outcome, he entered Siberia, where, of course, he was defeated by the Red Army. The army pursued him back to Ulan Bator (Urga), where it remained after it had captured, tried, and executed him. The Baron (and the havoc he had created) was obviously a factor in bringing about the birth of the new People's Republic. I don't know what happened to the "living Buddha," but I do know that the

Dalai Lama visited Mongolia recently so there is clearly something left of the Buddhist connection ...

In July, Mongolia will celebrate its sixtieth anniversary as an independent republic. There will be all kinds of jolly events including archery, wrestling, and horse racing, which are the ancient and current national sports. There will also be all kinds of speeches, no doubt, about friendship and peace and our helpful northern brothers, about socialism and progress and Lenin. Yet it is hard to imagine what would have become of this country at the back of beyond without Russian assistance after the depredations of the Mad Baron, handicapped as it was by the economic stagnation of a theocracy that took two sons from every family and did not even teach them to read. Now everyone goes to school and increasing numbers are going into higher education. The two paleontologists whom we met in the National Museum setting up new displays in preparation for the July celebration had both been fully educated in Ulan Bator but they spoke with easy knowledge in broken English of the dinosaurs in Alberta and the skeletons on display in the American Museum of Natural History. They kept reaching into glass cases and hauling out clutches of ancient eggs or small reptilian skulls to show us while they described their expeditions to the Gobi Desert. I am sure you will be fascinated to know that more dinosaurs have been found in Mongolia than anywhere else in the world! Anyway, it is obvious that Mongolia is producing professional paleontologists as well as cosmonauts and is justifiably proud of their achievements. They have not yet been notably successful in taxidermy ...

The population of Mongolia seems very young in contrast to the population of Moscow. Naturally, the birth of children is encouraged, because there are only 1,600,000 people for all that big country (1,500 miles from east to west and 900 from north to south; desert and mountain but also good grazing land and arable soil too, once it's cultivated—the Wild East, where cowboys and Indians are one and the same). Most of the women work so they provide maternity leave, daycare, all-day school programs, and so on to make it easier to have families of two or three or four. They are also encouraging a Mongolian genetic propensity for multiple births by providing extra assistance to parents of twins and triplets. We drove past a school where all the little children looked so much alike in little groups of red or green or blue coats that I exclaimed and then I was told that this was a kindergarten for *les jumeaux*. The man assigned to us by protocol interpreted only into French, which was either a reflection of the shortage of English speakers or an appropriate recognition of Canada's bilingual nature. He looked after us pretty well except that somehow he managed to confuse our train reservations so that at the last minute we were informed there would be no train for us the next day and we had to spend an extra twenty-four hours in Ulan Bator. No matter, or *Nichevo*, as the Russians say. We were able to drive out into the country and see some wild and beautiful scenery as well as attend the Mongolian National Ballet performance of a Mongolian folk legend all about the friendship between a lion and a calf. The dancers were young, the scenery was imaginative, the prima ballerina was terrific, but we weren't too sure how all those mermaids got themselves into a landlocked country unless they dated from the time of the dinosaurs!

A few words about why we were there. Geoffrey presented his credentials on May 7 after the Swedish Ambassador and before the Portuguese. A busy day for the President and for the Mongolian Army band, who had to play three national anthems in a row. Christine Bell and I had to stand outside in the chilly damp shifting from foot to foot to keep warm and smiling occasionally at the band members who were doing the same thing, while Geoffrey and Mike Bell (the Minister-Counsellor for commercial affairs at the Embassy in Moscow and, along with his wife, *excellent* company) went inside the Presidential Mansion for the official ceremony. Rather a long time later they came out again wreathed in smiles, the band played a jaunty tune, and the Canadian flag waved alongside the Mongolian one above our heads. Even though I couldn't witness the actual ceremony I found the occasion moving. We share this planet with many countries in various states of repair. If we recognize them at all, then they all deserve equal respect on this symbolic level. To see those two flags flying together symbolizing two countries so distant from one another yet sharing a common humanity (as well as dinosaur bones) is a comforting reminder for me that there are real connections between peoples that somehow keep the whole world from falling into pieces. So these connections, however tenuous, must be drawn clearly and must be maintained, a web to preserve us. Also, I must say that when I saw that Maple Leaf fluttering in such a remote place I experienced some pretty strong feelings about it. It looks good! Mike Bell brought a great handful of Maple Leaf pins with him and I can tell you there are now so many sprinkled about Ulan Bator that it looks like the Gatineau in the fall.

We left Ulan Bator on Sunday May 10 for a twenty-four-hour ride on the trans-Siberian train to Irkutsk. I expect that it is the only segment of the trans-Siberian we will ever ride and luckily for us it must be the most spectacular. On the Mongolian side we climbed up through the mountains until we reached the divide and then followed a river valley that became greener and greener as we descended. After the short night and the long delay at the Russian border while the train was searched from stem to gudgeon we followed the shoreline of Lake Baikal for four hours in sparkling sunlight. On one side of the train rose snow mountains and on the other sometimes right beside us and sometimes seen through pale green birch groves stretched the ice-rimmed brilliant blue lake, the deepest in the world and one of the most beautiful. Nor was Irkutsk a disappointment when we arrived, although our stay there was curtailed by the train mix-up. It is a city with a sense of space and openness built on a great river reminding me in some ways of Saskatoon. Interspersed among the newer buildings are some delightful old wooden houses carved in the Russian style, which give a distinctive flavour to the place. Siberia now has a new meaning for me and we will plan to see much more of it when we return to pay our respects to Mongolia next year.

SOVIET UNION AND MONGOLIA 1980

ARCTIC OCEAN

FINLAND

RUSSIAN FEDERATION

SIBERIA

Tallinn
Riga
1
2
Leningrad
Pskov
Minsk
Zavidova
Moscow
BELARUS
4
3
POLAND
5
Kiev
Kishinov
UKRAINE
Odessa
Yalta
Black Sea
RIVER VOLGA
Volgograd

Bratsk

Ulan Ude

Lake Baykal

Irkutsk

Ulan Bator

MONGOLIA

CHINA

Alma Ata

Lake Balkhash

KAZAKHSTAN

KYRGYZSTAN

Samarkand

Dushanabe

TAJIKISTAN

UZBEKISTAN

Bukhara

Aral Sea

Khiva

TURKMENISTAN

Caspian Sea

Derbent
6
7 8
Tbilisi
9
10
Baku
Yerevan

TURKEY

1. ESTONIA
2. LATVIA
3. LITHUANIA
4. KALININGRAD
5. MOLDAVIA

6. GEORGIA
7. CHECHNYA
8. DAGESTAN
9. ARMENIA
10. AZERBAIJAN

PART II

August 10, 1981

For me, leaving Canada seemed like the end of summer and it would have seemed even more autumnal if I had not had Patricia with me, but in fact, when we arrived here, the July heat wave was still blazing and it continued for two or three more days while we struggled to adjust to the drastic time change and make the necessary cultural adaptation. Geoffrey had really been sweating it out in the two weeks he had been back. The temperature had hovered around 32 degrees and the Embassy is not air-conditioned. All the windows had to be opened wide to catch whatever breath of air there was along with hundreds of sticky black flies. We are sure there is some way to put screens on the Residence windows but no one has figured out how and anyway the carpenter is on holiday until the end of August. We have not yet managed seven at one swat but sometimes they are close enough together that we should be able to. Nor have we been able to locate a fly swatter so Geoffrey lashes out with a damp washcloth. Summer sounds in the Canadian Embassy: slap! swash! Anyway, by the time we had recovered from jet lag (Patricia and Julia still in bed at 10:30 in the morning has more to do, however, with their age and their nocturnal habits!) the weather had cooled off and the last few days have been perfectly beautiful. And we hope it will continue fine this weekend when we go up to Zavidova for four days. Having skated on the Volga we are anxious to discover what it is like for swimming and other aquatic activities.

The big outdoor pool where Geoffrey swam in the winter is closed now for cleaning—as is the whole hot water system for this district, so we haul hot water for our baths from the kitchen or, if brave, like Geoffrey, take a cold shower every morning (they promise to restore the hot water in a couple of weeks but the Bassein will be closed until the end of August). So to replace the lovely, cold Gatineau River, Geoffrey has obtained a pass to the Olympic Pool where he swims twice a week. He has a new blue rubber bathing cap and has to buy a new tight-fitting bathing suit because they don't like his boxer-style for some reason, so we will go in a day or two and see what we can find in a local store because he would prefer to continue swimming there all year as it is less crowded than the Bassein and there is more space for swimming lengths without colliding headlong into a fleshy military officer, as he did occasionally at the other pool! In the summer, of course, there are many places to swim in and around Moscow other than the Olympic Pool, indeed every stretch of water in the district, however green and questionable, is full of bathers in an astonishing variety of swimwear. However, the foreigners congregate at two spots: Serebrany Bor (the Silver Wood), where the Embassy will eventually have a permanent dacha (we hope), and a place that is known as the "diplomatic ditch," which is actually a stretch of pastureland on the Moscow River well above the city. We have been there a couple of times and it is much nicer that I had been led to expect in spite of the crowds. From the Embassy there is a very pleasant forty-minute drive to it out along Kutuzovsky Prospect past the handsome triumphal arch celebrating the victory over Napoleon that marks the beginning of the green belt, and then through birch and pinewood, rolling countryside, and past all the forbidden roads branching off to the dachas of the privileged. Yesterday, when Geoffrey drove us back to the city in our blue Zhiguli, we met five black Zils, several Chaikas, and innumerable Volgas (for the small fry) coming to pick up their VIPs. The whole length of the winding country road was strung with watchful *militsia*. The Moscow River is cold and refreshing at our diplomatic haven and the air is fresh (as well as fragrant with barbecue and loud with transistor). The current is fast but not dangerous so one plunges in at one end of the "beach" and swims effortlessly and rapidly down to the other. One gets a sense of power without exertion. That suits my athletic inclinations admirably! We will go as often as we can until it gets too cold ...

I must say I was happy to get back to the Residence. It looked lovely and peaceful and clean. And to greet our Russian staff after the holidays. Ilya had been busy working on his dacha, which he is constructing on land he bought twenty years ago in the country west of Moscow. He hopes it will be finished in September and he goes out there now every evening after work because it is only twenty-five minutes from his apartment, on the outskirts of the city. Zhenya had benefited greatly from the stay UPDK had provided for her in a sanatorium for high blood pressure problems, a hundred or so kilometres north of Moscow. She had a room to herself, something she had never experienced before, and was well away from the demands of her family. Tamara, who I am sure runs her family as effortlessly as she runs my kitchen, rested with them in their dacha to the east of the city. Nikolai stayed at home and resisted painting the rest of the apartment as his wife wanted him to because it was *too* hot ... They all seemed glad to welcome me back and I discovered, with some relief, that my hour or so of Russian a day throughout my time at home had actually brought about some improvement. Or maybe I just think that I know what they are telling me!

The Embassy itself is full of new Canadian faces. This summer there will be a sixty-percent turnover of Canadian-based employees. But it is easier to get to know them as they arrive over the next several weeks than it was to deal with them all at once as we had to last year. The atmosphere will be quite different this winter. There are many more francophones and lots more children. But I will miss those who have gone, particularly Liz Heatherington and Christine Bell. And Annabel ... Geoffrey is overworked because the Embassy is very short-staffed for the moment. People leave at the beginning of the summer and are not replaced for several weeks. Perhaps it doesn't matter but the ones who are left are putting in a lot of overtime and G. has to spend a lot of time planning the deployment of the resources he does have. Luckily the social life, aside from a few national days, is very quiet. In the evenings, that is. We continue to have people to lunch every day and will start up the dinners and receptions at the end of August.

In the meantime, it has been lovely for me having Patricia and Julia. They have installed themselves down at the far end of the apartment with a record player. The place is beginning to look really lived in! We have done lots of sightseeing, of course, including some places I hadn't been to before like Abramtsevo, an artists' colony near Zagorsk, and Kuskova, a fairy-tale estate on the eastern edge of the city where one can actually imagine grace and elegance. Most of the theatres are closed for the summer but we went to a very lively rock concert at the Olympic Village, a new spectacle at the New Circus, where there was a sinuous lady snake-tamer and a man who played with alligators, and a performance of *Romeo and Juliet* by the Kuibyshev Opera and Ballet Company, which was a bit too much opera and not enough ballet but which offered us such a Romeo as young girls dream of. Other evenings the girls go downstairs to the Red Room and watch movies on video. Sometimes they watch three in a row. No wonder I have trouble getting them up in the morning! They did get to the Marine bar at the American Embassy the other night with some of the Canadians but seem in no hurry to return.

We see Mr. Brezhnev smiling every night in the Crimea as he greets another Eastern European leader for the TV audience. There is a sense of uneasy calm here—who knows what the winter will bring? ... Canada seems far away again—but I think of you all often—and reflect on the pleasure I had seeing everyone and being restored by the time we had together.

LETTER NUMBER 21

August 23, 1981

Patricia leaves tomorrow. I will send this letter with her. There was no point in writing last week because no bag went out although a very small handful of mail came in—a letter from Hilary, and a bank statement! Yesterday we received the first *Globe and Mail* since the mail strike cut the Embassy off from all Canadian papers and periodicals. We were delighted. Without them we get no news from Canada except for the brief summary that comes by telex every morning. Nothing like living abroad to cut one down to size! Actually that is not quite true. Mr. Trudeau got a certain amount of coverage for his statements in Nairobi. And *The Moscow News* is beginning to publish a list of every single game the Russians and the

Canadians have ever played, with their outcomes! But otherwise we
can't compete with Mr. Haig and Mr. Reagan, the Poles, the Libyans,
and the IRA! Anyway, we hope this week's bag will bring us news of
some of you and any backlog of mail that accumulated during the
strike. And Patricia will have the latest thing from Moscow. I will be
sorry to see her go. She and Julia had such a positive attitude to
everything (except the rain at Zavidova, but more of that later) and
gave me an excuse to go to all kinds of places I wouldn't have gone
to otherwise, such as the Zoo, where Patricia and I went on Friday
with Elaine Mathys, whose husband François has come to replace
Peter Hancock, and two of her children. We all liked it. The animals
look healthy and well cared for in spite of the space limitations. (It is
a city zoo like Regent Park. They have nearly completed a new open
zoo in the woods outside the city but they are also reconstructing this
one so there will always be some place for city families to go to easily. And there were more children there than I have seen anywhere
else in the city since we have been back because so many of them
vanish during the summer, to summer camps or to dachas with their
grannies.) Most of the animals seem to be Asian and some of them I
was seeing for the first time. There were two enchanting polar bear
cubs in an ample enclosure being guarded fiercely by a tatterde-
malion husky dog from the crowding of eager onlookers. The handsome lioness in a much smaller cage bore with human curiosity as
long as she could and then, with great dignity, turned her back on the
pressing faces, lifted her tail, and let loose a powerful stream of liquid on the astonished group, producing yellow-stained shirts and
gales of laughter. One thing that can be said for the Russians: they
laugh heartily at themselves. Geoffrey and I and Patricia went to the
puppet theatre last night, which has just reopened its season, and,
while we enjoyed ourselves immensely, found ourselves regretful
that our Russian will probably never be good enough to understand
the satiric barbs that had our neighbours convulsed in their seats.

This afternoon (the weather is very fine indeed) we will go to join
the crowds in Gorky Park and this evening Patricia and I will sam-
ple another music group for the young, this time folk rock at the
October Cinema concert hall on Kalinin Prospect. Patricia's last
excursion tomorrow will be (it if is open) to Chekhov's house on the

Garden Ring. She read The Idiot earlier in the summer and now she
has just finished *Dr. Zhivago*, which she liked even better. Julia had
just enough trouble with customs control when she left to remind
her of the darker side of Russian life but I think both she and Patricia
have felt it to be a privilege to experience some of the richness of
Russia as well.

Yesterday UPDK came and seeded the back garden (and today
the sparrows came and ate it all up!). Patricia has been frustrated
because we have not been able to sit in it at all and enjoy the continual sunshine that has been brightening the city. And when we went
to Zavidova last weekend for four days it was rainy and cold almost
all the time. We drove up in a pelting downpour, stopping at Klin to
visit the house where Tchaikovsky spent his last year and where his
piano is kept among all the other late-nineteenth-century furniture
and memorabilia. Twice a year, on the anniversaries of his birth and
his death, famous performers come to play on it and every four
years the winner of the Tchaikovsky international piano competition
comes to play the winning piece. The house is large and made of
wood and the extensive, heavily shaded garden was dim and
romantic in the heavy rain. The rest of Klin is industrial and depressing. It is the only large town on the way to Zavidova from Moscow
so the whole trip is relatively quick as long as the highway is not
completely choked with trucks, as it often is. In the summer
Zavidova is just as beautiful as it is in the winter and it yields a
whole new set of pleasures. One can rent rowboats and paddleboats,
even motorboats to go waterskiing, as well as bicycles and tennis
racquets. In the rowboat we went into the bays of the Shosha, where
we had all gone skiing in the winter and where now the waterfowl
glide by, fat and sleek, or else nest in among the reeds. The hunting
season opens this week and my heart sinks for all those sitting
ducks. With the reeds and the willows and the cattle standing in the
shallows flicking away flies, a place that reminded us of Canada in
the snows of winter becomes European in summer.

We walked a lot. I went out alone after the rain stopped and the
sky began to lighten in the late afternoon. An old river steamer was
puffing down the Volga followed by a couple of huge barges. I
crossed a stubbled field from the riverbank and skirted a very thick

grove of trees. Glimpsing an old building I penetrated the wet under-growth and came, quite unexpectedly, upon a graveyard surround-ing the ruins of an old chapel. Many of the graves were from the nine-teenth century and scarcely visible through the tangled brush but others were very new, the mounded grave freshly raked, the photo-graph of the deceased smiling under a plastic cover, flowers turning brown amid the artificial roses and on one, at least, half a banana, a tomato, a cucumber, and some bread carefully laid out in ritualistic fashion. Almost every grave was surmounted by the Russian Orthodox cross and had a little bench and a table within a small fenced enclosure. I was very moved by this sight that I had stumbled upon by chance. It's hard (though probably misleading!) not to see such a place as symbolic of the secret soul of Russia surviving hidden in the secular state. Particularly after visiting the Tchaikovsky house. On the other hand, when you compare the new houses constructed along the road for the state farm workers with the charming but decaying wooden village cottages, you see some of the advantages of modern times. I spent the rest of the weekend reading Turgenev's *Fathers and Sons*, whose fine ironic style puts "old" Russia into per-spective and made me wonder what conflicts were going on in Russian families between parents and children now and also made me hope that some gifted contemporary writer is exploring the theme in a novel that may one day be published.

With the arrival of the new administrator, Maurice Hebert, and the commercial counsellor, George Hazen, and the return of those who have been away on holiday (Anne Leahy went back to Quebec for her mother's wedding), the Embassy will soon be up to full strength. We had a big cocktail party last week to introduce the Mathys to the diplomatic community and some of the official Russians and on Tuesday we have a delegation of Canadian foresters coming to lunch and then we give a reception for the Russian scien-tists who are going to the Pugwash Conference on Disarmament in Banff. I am teaching Tamara the recipes from Craig Claiborne's Gourmet Diet cookbook ... So diplomatic life resumes in full force.

LETTER NUMBER 22

Today is the first day of September. The weather is cool but the sun is bright and the sky is clear. This morning we heard a tremendous chattering of people outside the Embassy. We went to the window and saw the most marvellous sight! Across the street from the Residence children were going to school for the very first time. First they arrived with their parents wearing their new uniforms, the girls with white starched pinafores and huge stiff bows in their hair, with their new satchels on their backs, and carrying, in the hand that was not clutching tightly onto the reassuring hand of father or mother, a large bouquet of flowers. They went into the school with their families, presumably to register, and then came out again into the street where each small child was entrusted to an older child lined up along the sidewalk. Every little separation was a personal event to those of us who were watching. The child was embraced and the hand was released and given into the hand of the senior student and they stood there waiting together for the signal to enter the building. Parents and grandparents milled about in the street talking and laughing and taking photographs. Some monitors with small loudspeakers and a look of importance were moving around trying to keep a semblance of order. The little children looked about them at the crowd and then up into the faces of their new protectors. And then off they went in an uneven procession waving their red gladioli and their yellow and white asters and their pink and purple phlox. What a warm and cheerful sight! Everything is done to allay the apprehension of these seven-year-olds who have every right to be nervous. Most of them will already have been to kindergarten, 57 percent of them throughout the Soviet Union according to the latest statistics. But kindergarten in the USSR is, on the whole, a comfortable and undemanding place where the emphasis is on physical health, games, dancing and singing, and other forms of group activity suitable to the very young who are expected to grow up as useful contributors to a collective society. Now they have to confront the challenges of learning to read, write, and figure as well as study, each and every one of them, as stated in a recent Soviet Press article—the documents of the Twenty-sixth Congress of the Communist Party of the Soviet Union! Never mind, we would do well to emulate the ceremony, the sense of family support, and the warmth with which the little Russian child is brought into the school system. I don't know what is happening inside to those children at this very moment but the classrooms must look delightful, full of flowers and fresh faces!

Patricia left last Monday and the Kilbourns arrived on Tuesday. Each set of visitors provides us with an opportunity to see something different, and those who are old friends like the Kilbourns add quality to our lives. Betty Kilbourn, who is on her way tomorrow to Poland to an international conference on pastoral education (which is why she and Bill came at this time), was here for a while some years ago so they have been able to get around quite a lot on their own but I always like the chance to see things again as well as to walk about in streets that I usually only get to see from the window of a car.

The weekend before last, when Patricia was still here, we drove 60 km northwest of Moscow to Istra for the day with Col. Macneil, the amiable new military attaché. The New Jerusalem Monastery at Istra was founded by the Patriarch Nikon in 1656. He was a man of grandiose ideas and excessive ambition (for which he and the Orthodox Church eventually paid and from which the Church never really recovered in terms of political power). With the construction of this monastery his idea was to prove the greatness of the Russian Church and justify its claim to be the true centre of Christianity, the third Rome. The result is that the Cathedral at Istra is more impressive and has a much greater sense of space and height than any other I have seen in Russia, with the exception of the Imperial St. Isaac's in Leningrad. It is also in a terrible state of repair. It was occupied by the Germans during the war and quite gratuitously blown up when they retreated. It is now being restored. The power of the Russian Church, when Nikon was setting himself up as a temporal rival to the Tsar, is also reflected in Rostov, where we went last weekend with the Kilbourns. It is the most beautiful of all the ancient towns of Russia that we have visited so far, and was the highlight of our trip, which included Zagorsk, Pereyaslavl-Zalessky, and Yaroslavl, where we spent the night.

There is no need to describe Zagorsk again but Rostov is a wonder. A small town built beside a lake some 120 km north of Zagorsk, it dates from the ninth century and has known several periods of great importance, politically in the twelfth and thirteenth centuries, and as a religious centre in the seventeenth. The *kremlin*, which dates from the latter period, is an extraordinarily harmonious ensemble of whitewashed walls, towers, and grey-tiled and golden domes surmounted by crosses and weathervanes and banners. The thirteen great bells in the bell tower seldom ring now but the whole effect is so enchanting that you expect them to peal out at any moment across the lake and for the gates to open and the clergy and boyars and soldiers to pour out across the plain, full of colour and purpose. The huge flagstones of the Cathedral Square in the Moscow Kremlin are now beginning to convey this sense of authenticity to me as I read more history and visit them more often. But Rostov presupposes almost no knowledge to have its impact. The metropolitan's residence now houses an international youth movement, its rooms full of banked beds. In the inner garden, under the clustered trees and beside the little pond, young people are talking and reading. Betty and I decided we would shed thirty years (each) and settle down to live there if we could ...

Yaroslavl does not present the same temptation, although it is a pleasant city with open, broad avenues and a handsome embankment along the Volga and many beaches and parks as well as churches and monasteries. It is said to have been founded by Yaroslav the Wise (whom you last met in Kiev) in 1010 and is thus more than a century older than Moscow but it doesn't feel like such an old city for some reason, perhaps because it is laid out in such an orderly fashion. We hired an Intourist guide for the morning to show us around, who insisted on recounting all the bible stories painted on the walls in the Church of the Prophet Elijah and the Reverend Kilbourn held her tongue with great restraint! On the way back to Moscow we stopped at Pereslavl-Zalessky from the citadel of which Prince Alexander Nevsky set out to do battle with the Swedes in the Neva Estuary (present-day Leningrad) in 1240. And on the lake below the citadel Peter the Great began to sail as a boy when he summered there with his maternal grandfather and later built his first boats, which were the forerunners of the Russian Navy. There is one in a little museum on a hill that he apparently built himself and which I found fascinating while Geoffrey muttered! And all the way to Yaroslavl and all the way back the woods were full of mushroom hunters carrying pails of fungi back to their cars. Pavel was our driver this weekend because Ilya was out at his nearly completed dacha indulging in the national pastime! I guess they know what they are doing. I bought some in the market yesterday from the tables and tables of mushrooms on sale and they were delicious.

On Thursday we are off to Moldavia for three days with an airplane full of ambassadors. We will visit two factories and a *Kolkhoz*. I only hope that one of them turns out to be a vineyard!

Mr. Brezhnev is back from the Crimea and the Russian fleet is about to start exercises in the Baltic. A new school year has begun. What will we all learn?

LETTER NUMBER 23

September 8, 1981

When I went out to the airport with Bill Kilbourn today it was cold and foggy and I thought that the good weather had come to an end for sure. And today was the day when those in charge must have decided to make things particularly difficult for all outgoing passengers, so we shifted uneasily from one line to another where, each time, travellers in front of us had to spread out all their possessions on the counter, including in one case the plastic machine gun that some person had been so unwise as to purchase at the Detsky Mir, the children's shop where war toys are just as available as they are in the West! Bill finally made it through all the hurdles with five minutes to spare before his plane took off. And when I came back out through the terminal door, I found that the fog had lifted and the sun was shining and it was a fine autumn day. So I went to the farmers' market and bought lots of fresh vegetables to serve at tonight's cocktail party to introduce our new commercial counsellor George Hazen and his wife to the "commercial" community of Moscow. The women in the market were cheerful and friendly and we had a long conversation about the price of cauliflower. Russia is so unpredictable. Bill was, no doubt, glad to finally take off for London, and I was glad to find myself still in Moscow. Except I would like to hear from some of you. The courier has just come in and there are only two letters, one from Hilary and one from Jane. What are the rest of you up to? As I read Jane's letter describing how she waited in line for tickets to the Canada Cup and finally got some for the Canada–Sweden game, we were actually watching the third period on television so at least I knew where *she* was at that very moment! To say the least, the Russians are enormously interested in what is going on. The big game between Russia and Canada is Thursday and we have to go out to the Philippine Embassy for dinner, but it starts at 7:00 so we can watch the first period and then ask the waiters during dinner how it is going because they are sure to be listening in the kitchen! Canada has had more publicity in this country in the last week or so than at any other time since we have been here. There have been several TV programs about our country, one on Canadian history and another showing some of the cities where the games are being played. Everyone knows the name of Wayne Gretzky. In Kishinev last week we found that they also know about Winnipeg. I am not sure that many people in Winnipeg have ever heard of Kishinev unless they are descendants of victims of the pogroms in Moldavia in 1903. But all over the Soviet Union you can be sure that at least half the population, over 100,000,000 people, have their eyes on the hockey nights in Canada! Most of the games are being televised, at least in part, and certainly the semi-finals and finals will be shown in their entirety. By the time you get this it will be all over. I hope we will have performed as we should...

We had a marvellous trip to Moldavia last week. Annabel will read this with interest because she went there last May. She tasted the wine, but we were also able to taste the grapes, and the apples and the pears and the nectarines, which are new in the Soviet Union and which fascinated Tamara and Nikolai and Zhenya when I brought some back for them to taste. Alas, not much of the absolutely gorgeous Moldavian fruit finds its way to the Moscow shops. And it is hard to get Moldavian wine here too although I think it is better than the Georgian wine that is available everywhere. Moldavia at this time of year reminds one of the Niagara Peninsula. The weather is similar. The soil is excellent and there are lovely trees as well as vineyards and apple orchards stretching to the horizon. And there are masses of beautiful roses. What is missing, of course, are the roadside stands and the carloads of people driving into the countryside to enjoy the early autumn sunlight and stock up on their supplies of fruit for the winter.

Every year the protocol department of the ministry of Foreign Affairs organizes ambassadorial excursions to the various republics of the Union. This is the first time we have taken advantage of the opportunity and we certainly will do so again because the experience is not to be missed. A passel of "Posols" (ambassadors) and their "charmingwives" (all one word) were loaded into a special plane at Sheremetyevo airport and flown into the sunny southwest corner of the USSR where they were greeted by schoolchildren with flowers and curiosity (the Nigerian Ambassador is particularly striking in his African robes and they haven't seen a Chinese for so long that the Chinese Ambassador's wife was asked if she were Vietnamese) and by many local officials exceedingly friendly and hospitable and loaded with statistics. Do you know (do you really want to know?) how many taxicabs there are in the city of Kishinev or how many tomatoes are processed each day in the canning factories along the Dniester River?

The men met with the Prime Minister and the Mayor and many other dignitaries and the New Zealand *chargé d'affaires* started off an endless discourse by asking about sheep. The ladies were taken to a kindergarten where the enthusiastic director showed us several bright and tidy rooms full of dolls sitting at toy tea tables and where the only real children we saw were those who met us at the door with bunches of asters wrapped in cellophane or those who performed for us, singing *Savez-vous Planter les Choux?* and *Jack and Jill* to show their knowledge of other languages, as well as Moldavian and Russian folk songs. The atmosphere was so warm and cheerful, the teachers so serious and kind, and the absence of anything to stimulate the imagination or intellect so obvious, that I was reminded of the comment of a Canadian primary school teacher, quoted as saying enthusiastically, "Whenever I see a spark of creativity, I water it!" The wife of the Romanian Ambassador, who is a very interesting woman, spoke to several children in the native language of Moldavia, which is actually Romanian except that it is now written in the Cyrillic alphabet, but she discovered that most of the children were Russian-speaking in spite of the fact that, we were told, ethnically over 65 percent of the population of Moldavia are "Moldavian," another significant percent are Ukrainian, and not very many are Russian ...

The ladies were also taken to a furniture display centre where some of the items shown could be ordered by shoppers and would be delivered within a year. The furniture industry is expanding as housing improves and the designs would have looked very well on the floors of Simpson-Sears. They told us, in fact, that some pieces were being exported to Canada and I was not surprised. The Nigerian Ambassador, who is actually a businessman, was prepared to buy the whole lot on the spot but this threw everyone into confusion! The men had joined us there after another of their official sessions and some of them seemed even more interested in the furniture than their wives! Our first day ended with a reception given for us by the Prime Minister, where we ate delicious Moldavian delicacies and drank a great deal of Moldavian wine, and at the end of which he said "and may you dream in colour." On the second day of our stay we drove out into the countryside in three buses (French, English, and Spanish) preceded by two flashing *militsia* cars who made all the traffic on the highway pull over to the side. We went to Tiraspol, the second largest city in Moldavia, where we visited a clothing factory. Actually it was fascinating. The director, a powerful lady in her sixties with a row of gold teeth and sure convictions, gave us a long talk about the marvellous qualities of her domain (6,000 workers, looked after from womb to tomb ... we were shown the marriage room but not the undertaking establishment) and then we visited the factory floor and felt we were in an authentic place ... rows and rows of women cutting and sewing and ironing and packaging ... not much automation but loads of light and colour. And then we all participated in a Moldavian folk dance of greeting where the Ambassador of Jordan knelt on a brightly embroidered handkerchief and embraced the beaming Valentina Sergeyevna and everyone else stamped and clapped hands. On the way back to Kishinev we had long lectures about the difference between collective and state farms and the new combined agri-industrial enterprises. And we stopped in the middle of a laden apple orchard to refresh ourselves at long tables brilliant with autumn fruit and later in the middle of the tomato fields where we watched the harvesting. Then, donning white coveralls, we splashed our way through the canning factory to yet another feast of the fruit of garden and tree (and vine). By the time we were poured onto the special plane on Saturday for our return flight to Moscow after yet another feast, this time at the technical institute of winemaking near Kishinev, we were all feeling extremely jolly and pleased with our trip and with one another. It was only the next day that our stomachs and our heads began to feel sore ...

LETTER NUMBER 24

October 6, 1981

The Whelans brought superb weather with them and then took it away again when they departed, leaving us with a series of damp, dark days that may go on until I don't know when. But they have also taken with them fine memories of Russia, of a golden autumn and superabundant hospitality, of Moscow, Leningrad, Kiev, and the Crimea, all aglow with warmth and sunlight. Of course, Mr. Whelan, being an experienced farmer and a shrewd man, knows quite well that the Soviet Union will have a disappointing harvest again this year owing to poor weather conditions and other factors. However, while they were here, we were shown the best of what the Russians *can* produce in the way of fruit and vegetable, wine, and horses. Would we do it any differently? Only it's a pity that all that gorgeous produce doesn't make its way in any quantity to Moscow ...

Mr. Whelan is the first Canadian minister to come to the Soviet Union in five years. He was an excellent person to start off what we hope will be a series of ministerial visits over the remaining time that we are here. We liked him and Mrs. Whelan very much indeed. They are both quite genuine people who responded with good humour and considerable interest to all the events on their packed schedule. And the five other members of their delegation, who came from the Minister's office as well as the Department of Agriculture, were like- able and interesting people. So there were no real problems except that we all ate and drank far more than was good for us. The Hong Kong tailor came today to measure me for a nice tweed suit and inquired mildly whether I expected to put on any more weight? Well, I certainly hope not but it's difficult not to when you have three seven-course meals a day, not including breakfast! Perhaps the Minister of Agriculture was served more than some other minister owing to his portfolio, but somehow I doubt it! By the way, the typi- cal meal served us during Mr. Whelan's visit started out with a plate of black and red caviar and smoked salmon to be followed by a plate of tomatoes and cucumbers cut in half. Then we might have mush- rooms in sour cream followed by borscht. Then sometimes a chicken dish followed in turn by beef fillet with potato and cabbage cutlets. Then ice cream or jelly and fruit and coffee, the whole accompanied by vodka and white wine and vodka and red wine and vodka and champagne and cognac! And fruit. Thank goodness for the fruit.

They arrived punctually at 3:30 on the afternoon of September 25 and we met them in the company of the Minister of Agriculture of the Soviet Union, Mr. Mesyats, and his very handsome, intelligent wife of whom we saw quite a lot during the visit. Naturally the women separated out from the men but that was all right because both Mrs. Mesyats and Mrs. Whelan had a lot to say. By the time we arrived at the hotel they had fortunately discovered a common knowledge of German because my Russian is not yet up to translating more than the most banal conversation. Although it improved a certain amount last week because I had so much practice both in speaking and in lis- tening. When speeches are being translated at least you know what the meaning of the words is *supposed* to be.

Mr. Whelan had come to the Soviet Union partly to sign an agri- cultural agreement for the exchange of knowledge and scientists that had been on hold for a long time. So, on Saturday morning the men went off to do that while the ladies went to the Tretyakov Gallery to admire nineteenth-century Russian psychological realism as well as the huge canvases of Slavic fantasy. I prefer the portraits, for which I think the Russians of the end of the last century had a special gift. Then we joined the men at the Praga Restaurant for the first of our many official meals. The interpreter was a little unsure how to translate "Whelanese" (Mr. Whelan was always saying that Canada has two official languages and he doesn't speak either), particularly some of Mr. Whelan's stories, which were sometimes a little bawdy and almost always funny. All during the trip the translator would stand with his hands behind him and his eyes on the ceiling and do his best. As the trip and the vodka progressed others would throw in their translations so that eventually the general sense if not the exact nuance would be conveyed! Actually, I liked Mr. Whelan's speeches because they were both earthy and idealistic if, inevitably, somewhat repetitive. He always talked about the responsibility of both Canada and the USSR as food-producing nations to contribute to the solution of world hunger, something that never got mentioned in the Russian speeches. And he talked a lot about what Canadians are, including all those hundreds of thousands who came from the Ukraine and other parts of what is now Russian territory, in terms that might sound banal if I put them on paper but sounded anything but when they came from his mouth. And he kept asking questions even though he did not always get the information he would have liked to obtain. He didn't put the Russians on the defensive and the atmosphere was quite open. It's just that some information is never given. Still I learned an awful lot about agriculture last week, both in Canada and in the USSR. I'll forget all the statistics but I'll remember the delicious taste of grapes in Yalta, the bread at the collective farm near Simferopol in the Crimea, and the button mushrooms being grown in the greenhouse enterprise near Moscow that we visited on the first afternoon of their stay, after lunch at 1:30 and before supper at 4:30. And then we all went to see *Swan Lake* at the Kremlin Palace of Congresses where I sat beside Mr. Whelan and explained the plot. It was beautifully done and had a happy ending, which I don't remember the last time I saw it performed by the National Ballet. Mr. Whelan referred to it during the rest of the trip as "this ballet about a man who falls in love with a bird."

On Sunday the delegation set off for Leningrad. We didn't go but joined them in Kiev the next day. What a beautiful city in the autumn!

We saw more of it this time including a visit to a delightful outdoor museum where old villages from all over the Ukraine have been moved to a couple of hundred acres of rolling countryside. It's rather like Upper Canada Village though at least in Canada in the nineteenth century you did not have to forgo a chimney and proper windows because of the tax imposed on them. The Whelans went to the Armoury Museum and the Diamond Exhibition at the Kremlin on the day they left, and Mrs. Whelan kept commenting to me about the contrast between the cottages we had seen in Kiev and the silver horseshoes of the Imperial Horses and the diamonds of the icon covers. Her response was very direct. The Russians are much more ambivalent about their imperial past.

From Kiev we went to the Crimea. The weather remained fine. It is not difficult to understand the attraction for Russians of its landscape and subtropical climate. Also it is resonant with history. One can visit the site of the Yalta conference but Sebastopol and Balaclava are closed to visitors from other countries. So we had to forgo the "Valley of Death" immortalized by Tennyson for *les caves de Massander* and the botanical gardens. At the former they have a collection of old wines, the most ancient being a bottle of port from 1775. Both Geoffrey and Mr. Whelan were presented with vintages from the year of their birth! The fact that Crimean wines don't travel has less to do with their delicacy than with lack of transport. Some of those that we tasted were excellent.

Back in Moscow Geoffrey and Mr. Whelan called on Mr. Gorbachev, the Politburo member who is responsible for agriculture, and apparently had a very good meeting and then the delegation came to our house for dinner, along with the Mesyats and the other Russians we had been travelling with or had got to know because of the visit. Mr. Mesyats and Mr. Whelan signed the protocol for the agreement on the coffee table in the salon, thus causing our soup to get cold. I have not yet learned to plan menus appropriate to this kind of occasion but I seemed to be the only one upset. It was a very jolly evening.

Before they left Saturday evening, taking the sun with them, we had a lovely visit to a horse farm near the Diplomatic Beach, admired the thoroughbreds, and rode a troika. At the airport very warm goodbyes. We saw them to the plane—and returned to the Embassy to find a couple of very distressed elderly Canadians, immigrants of course of several years ago, who were so hassled by customs they missed their flight back to Montreal.

This is a big country and has many levels—Mr. Whelan's visit was appreciated and it was important. For us and for them and for food.

LETTER NUMBER 25

October 20, 1981

As we drove back from Zavidova yesterday the damp fields I was watching slip by on either side of the road began to turn silver and Ilya said *"sneg"* (snow) and then *"pora"* (it's time) and I guess it is but the flurry stopped before we entered the outskirts of the city and with sunshine today we have been reprieved for a little while longer. We had had a lovely weekend at the dacha. The birches and the willows hang on to their golden leaves for a long time. The cow meadows are green and muddy because there has been so much rain. We took one of the flat-bottomed boats with Ron and Françoise Halpin and three-year-old Sarah and rowed up the Volga in the pale autumn sun. That was Saturday. On Sunday it rained but we walked and breathed the fresh country air and I finished reading *Dr. Zhivago*, which is a novel of great beauty and of passionate interest to anyone living here. It seems to me tragic that so many Russians are deprived of Pasternak's account of their common past because the book has never been published here. Pasternak is a revered name. Others of his works are available. Some of Dr. Zhivago's poems were published last year for the first time here but who knows how long it will be before the book itself is allowed to appear? Geoffrey read papers and periodicals and wrote some reflections on his first year here. We are very lucky to be able to stay at Zavidova. It is so peaceful. We hope to renew the lease for next year because the dacha that was promised to us last year nearer to town is still in the process of (desultory) negotiations with UPDK and the members of the Embassy are really quite happy with the present arrangement.

So we are beginning our second year in Russia. On October 10, which was the anniversary date of our arrival, we had all the foreign service officers (and their wives) in for drinks, as well as young François Cadieux, who had come to Moscow for a week from Leningrad where he is studying so that he can write the foreign service exams. He was staying with Ann Leahy whom he had known in Ottawa and she took him off that evening to the avant-garde theatre as she unquestionably knows more about what is going on in Moscow in that sense than all the rest of us put together. The others stayed behind and we talked over the last year. No one regrets coming on posting to Moscow because it is an experience unlike any other in the foreign service. On the other hand, none of us can quite figure out why the Fords stayed for seventeen years! I think the winter we are entering will be less difficult than last unless there is some major catastrophe in the outside world, which is certainly possible. The sense of community among the Canadians is already strong. We had a very jolly Thanksgiving celebration starting downstairs in the Red Room with an ecumenical service performed by the Baptist Rev. Lamprecht, whom some of you will remember from last Christmas, and Father Laplante, who is one of those New Englanders for whom the American-Canadian border is not very important. The service was bilingual as well because we now have a good admixture of francophones, including a Canadian mathematics scholar who is living with his wife and five children and mother-in-law in a small flat provided by the University of Moscow, and who is immensely excited by the research in pure mathematics that is taking place here. His family is quite happy with their experience but I think they were all glad to share the Thanksgiving holiday with the rest of us. We ended the service with a simultaneous rendering of O Canada, which the francophones sang with gusto while the anglophones were somewhat uncertain of the new English wording. And then we all went downstairs to the club to have turkey and all the trimmings, some fifty of us including lots of children, and all of us thankful, I think, in this country to be Canadians.

And last Wednesday there was another "Canadian" event in Moscow. I'll quote from the TASS report of October 14. "The Canadian Ambassador to the Soviet Union, Mr. Geoffrey Arthur

Holland Pearson, and the president of the Soviet Ice Hockey Federation, Nikolai Korolkov, today presented the 'cup of Canadians' to Soviet National Team captain Valery Vasiliev, Vladislav Tretyak, named the best player of the Canada Cup tournament, and Spartak captain, Sergei Kapustin, before one of the central games in the Soviet championship between Central Army Sports Club and Spartak. The 'cup of Canadians' is a replica of the official Canada Cup made by Canadian ice hockey fans with their own money. The organizers of the recent tournament kept the Canada Cup at home. Fourteen thousand spectators gathered at the sports palace of the Central Lenin Stadium and about a hundred million sports fans at the television sets watched the presentation ceremony. Vasiliev, speaking during the ceremony, said that the Soviet hockey players convey their heartfelt thanks to the Canadian sports fans for their good feelings for them and their country. The 'cup of Canadians' will be placed in the sports museum in Moscow." And the TASS report is factually accurate although of course there is more to the story! I'm sure the Canadian press must have recounted how Mr. Eagleson and others went into the Soviet dressing room in Montreal and removed the Canada Cup from the dunnage bag under the towels, where the Soviets had placed it in order to bring it back to Moscow, and how a Mr. Smith from Winnipeg had raised money to make a replica. The announcer in the arena described these events, which François Mathys, who was sitting beside me, translated for me. When he said "Eagleson" there was a big boo from the crowd and Mr. Smith got a big cheer. Then Geoffrey, down on the ice, found he could hardly lift the thing, which weighed about 30 kilos. We were sitting in the stands behind him so we couldn't see very well but Natasha came in the next day to tell us that her mother was all in a swoon about the *Posol* who had such a charming smile!

The game we watched was a little disappointing because the Army team was much stronger than Spartak and they had Tretyak in goal. The stands were full of army officers and Mr. Brezhnev was there too. Apparently he never misses an Army game when they are playing in Moscow. His doctor told him it was much better for his health to come out and watch the game than to see it on television. And it's true that he now looks rather frail. But then he really is an

old man. This was the first game that I have seen here and I enjoyed
being there. So did all the others, particularly the Army supporters,
although Spartak is a Moscow team and its two goals were ecstati-
cally cheered. The skates look like Bauers and the sticks are Finnish
as is the scoreboard although the letters that light up are in the
Cyrillic alphabet. But the icing machine is Russian and so are the
advertisements around the boards, including one, I discovered to my
surprise when I deciphered it, for a vacuum cleaner called
"Typhoon." Between periods we went to have a glass of champagne
and an incredibly sweet biscuit with various dignitaries such as Mr.
Pavlov, head of the Soviet Sports Committee, and the Soviet cosmonaut, Leonid, who had had the rendezvous with the Americans in
space back in 1974. They were both very jolly and there was a good
deal of joshing. I have never seen a lean and hungry-looking senior
military official in the Soviet Union. I don't know whether that's a
good sign or a bad sign.

The diplomatic season is in full swing. There seem to be endless
"formal" events of one sort or another: national days, dinners, receptions to "farewell" (as they say in diplomatese) departing ambassadors or to introduce newcomers. Concerts of visiting troupes (last
night we saw the Ghanaian Cultural Group, which has, as Geoffrey
says, a long way to go before it reaches Broadway), commercial dele-
gations, Commonwealth lunches ... And my own activities, the
International Women's Club, of which I am vice-president, the
Canadian Community Association, the Soviet history group ... It's
rather an odd life!

LETTER NUMBER 26

November 1, 1981
All Saints' Day

I hope all the malevolent spirits that were abroad last night have
gone up in smoke with our cottage at Burnett and that there are none
left around to get in the way of rebuilding. There is nothing like a
phone call from home announcing bad news to clarify one's priori-

ties. You realize that, compared to people, property has no value at all. Hilary had the good sense to start by announcing that something very unfortunate had happened. The choice of that particular word prevented my heart from sinking through the soles of my feet. Because a fire is a misfortune but when there are no injuries it is far from a tragedy. Particularly when there are no great works of art involved. Burnett was a pleasant cottage but I don't think any one would pretend that it had architectural merit. And the combination of many winters and many generations of mice had rendered the contents, well, a little shabby to say the least. Of course, Geoffrey may miss his tattered running shoes and his holey sweater, but I don't think I will. The photographs and cartoons are a loss, it's true, but Geoffrey says there are copies of most of the photos in the archives and the best cartoons are either at Laurier House or in our possession here. The new cottage that we will build will at last be our very own and we may finally do what we've been talking about for so many years, build on the other site with its beautiful view down the river. Because that is really what the best thing about Burnett has always been, its location. It would not be true to say that we felt no pangs at the loss of the cottage but surprisingly few considering all the memories it held. Perhaps that is because memories, themselves, do not burn up. They will always be around and in the meantime I can get on with planning the cottage I have always wanted, and then see whether we'll just have to settle for the one we can afford!

And while sparks were flying around across the water we were gallivanting with the Canadian Community in the basement of the Embassy. Three of us Embassy wives had gone down to the Central Children's Theatre on Sverdlov Square early in the week to borrow some costumes. The two cheerful women who led us up and down and around the backstage labyrinth to the room of discarded birds and princesses and soldiers and fools were fascinated by the idea of Hallowe'en and did their best to find costumes that would suit Vassiliki's dark, Mediterranean beauty, Elaine's slight and supple figure, or the children they were both describing. The excursion for costumes was almost more fun than the party itself, but perhaps that is a question of taste. The Ambassador was a little reluctant to descend for fun and games but the pretty ladies came to fetch him and he con-

sented to put on the Lenin cap that someone gave him at the
Christmas party last year. Hal Jones took a picture of us with his
Polaroid, which I will bring with me when I come home. I went as a
"mixed feeling."

We have had our last outings of the season. We will be going to
Minsk for a couple of days just before I leave but that's an official
visit, not an outing, so it won't matter what the weather is like.
Yesterday we went to Zvenigorod with Geoffrey's new secretary,
Betty Massey, and Audrey Kinnear, who works overtime in the consular section. Victoria, one of the local staff whom some of you know,
met us there with her mother, who is an architect, and her thirteen-
year-old daughter, who curtsies when being introduced and blushes
and watches everything that is going on with intense interest. We had
been there last year but there is always more to see because this is the
oldest town in the Moscow area, on the old Smolensk road, the way
to (and from) Poland. The town itself stretches out along the Moscow
River and the countryside is hilly. The whole area is what the guide-
books call "picturesque" and has been popular with many generations of good and bad painters, samples of whose works (the bad
ones, that is) we saw in the local museum. And Chekhov once
worked here in the town hospital. The two most-travelled fellows in
nineteenth-century Russia must have been Pushkin and Chekhov,
who turn up in some form (usually a bust or a statue) in virtually
every town we have visited. In Zvenigorod there is only the plaque
on the house where Chekhov stayed and a photograph of the house
of Pushkin's grandmother. I just want you to know that there are
other heroes in Russia besides Lenin, and a country that idealizes its
writers, albeit of the last century, has some sense of the proper order
of things.

After we had visited the Monastery and the charming whitewashed "working" church dating from the end of the fourteenth century that stands alone at the edge of field and wood and is reached
by climbing up a steep embankment and passing through a jumble of
old wooden houses, we went with Victoria and her family to have tea
at their dacha. Victoria's father was a naval historian and a member
of the prestigious Academy of Sciences, an institution that resembles
the French Academy more than anything else, though at the moment

its hundred and fifty members are more likely to be scientists than writers or historians, given the general state of things. Anyway, just after the war many members were given property in this beautiful countryside and dachas were constructed for them by German prisoners of war from a nearby camp. The property was given outright. It belongs to the families of the original owners if they have since died, as has Victoria's father. We had an excellent tea on the verandah (most dachas are really summer cottages although they sound more romantic when called dachas). It was a little chilly so we had a little cognac as well and returned to Moscow in a pleasant glow.

The week before, when we went to Tsaritsyno, the weather was better, not much warmer but sunny. Tsaritsyno is a magnificent folly, a whim of Catherine the Great who wanted something suitable in the countryside near Moscow and commissioned one of her architects to build her a palace. He constructed a strange building with ogival windows and high white pillars, a curious blend of Moorish and Gothic. She didn't like it. The roof was never put on and now it stands, a gigantic skeleton, dominating an artificial lake and lovely parkland, all of which is being enjoyed by the descendants of her unhappy peasants. The building itself was being clambered all over by a rock-climbing club with climbing boots and ropes and pitons, to say nothing of the little children who were playing hide-and-seek in the grass-filled halls. On the open parkland two fierce soccer games occasionally mixed up balls, the woodland paths were full of runners, and occasionally amid the trees you could see young girls doing gymnastics. The twelve-year-olds had cornered the stately alley descending to the lake and were swooping down in soap-box go-carts. The stream leading out of the lake was full of fishermen in hip-waders with rods and butterfly nets. The rest of us were just having a good time shuffling our feet through the fallen leaves. The whole area is now surrounded by city, huge apartment blocks and more coming up, but this place will always be there for them to relax in. One wonders what Catherine would have thought!

Two more events I would like to describe if I have time. The closing of the pouch is approaching and I have to photocopy and address so you probably won't find much in the way of personal notes this week and my typing will no doubt deteriorate! Anyway. Last Sunday night I went with several others from the English-speaking Protestant community to a service at the Russian Baptist Church, the only "working" Protestant Russian-language church in Moscow. What a marvellous experience! The congregation was welcoming and unafraid. It was young to middle-aged (the children attend at an earlier service). The people looked well dressed and vigorous, different from the congregations I have observed in the Orthodox Church. There was no liturgy but a great deal of music. The choir was splendid with all those deep bass voices that we never seem to be able to muster for our churches at home. The congregation sang lustily as well. And we had four short sermons by four different pastors, only one of whom I could follow as the others spoke too quickly. The whole ended with the Beatitudes, which were spoken by all with the emotions that you can imagine. You felt almost as if you were back in the early church, persecuted and despised, but joyful. I am not too sure of the history of the Baptists in Russia. I know there are not many although their number is said to be growing. But I am glad they exist. They are like a great breath of fresh air.

The other story I want to tell is particularly for my mother. I went for a long walk in the rain the other day at the foot of the Lenin Hills along the Moscow River with my friend Annette Yaker (the wife of the Algerian Ambassador). We did not bring her dogs because the youngest, a lovely grey male *Dogue* as the Russians call the breed and which she had bought at the pet market a couple of weeks ago, had just had his ears clipped and we had left him at her house with his bandaged head placed carefully on the stomach of their old brindled bitch. She told me as we walked that she had taken him to the veterinarian clinic the day before and had sat for a long time in the waiting room while they did the ear clipping with care and patience. Beside her was a woman who had brought in a little Japanese dog, rather like a Pekinese though smaller. The woman was furnished with hot water bottle and flannel cloths. Before very long one of the assistants came out with a little tiny puppy, which they both wrapped up in flannel and then the woman put it inside her blouse over her heart. Soon there was a second, which followed the first into the warm place, and that was all. Her little dog had had a successful Caesarean and was soon ready to go home. Annette offered to drive her but she said she had two hours to travel by electric train and she would be able to keep all three dogs warm with the hot water bottle. She was ecstatic with her new puppies and brought out some presents for the clinic staff. Annette says that the atmosphere at that clinic is marvellous. She has been there several times. Everyone is there because they like animals. It is totally non-political and the conversations in the waiting room are remarkably open even with a foreigner. What is important is how you feel about your dog or cat or whatever. Geoffrey thinks I might buy a whatever but he has put his foot down on a dog or cat ... The new American Ambassador has a parrot that is learning Russian ... Well, I'm not sure but maybe I'll go to the pet market soon.

LETTER NUMBER 27

November 10, 1981

The damp places in the backyard are turning to ice and there is snow on the tops of the cars. There are still a few yellow leaves on two of our garden trees but otherwise there is nothing to see but bare, black branches and big, ugly black birds. No one seems quite sure as to whether they are rooks or ravens or crows but they are raucous and unlovely and entirely too numerous. I think this is the worst time of the year here. The days are getting shorter and shorter and everything is grey and smudgy. No wonder the festivities of the seventh of November are so welcome and the red banners and propaganda posters look so good! Celebrations started early Friday afternoon in the drivers' room above the garage, where the pool table was covered by all kinds of *zakuski*, the plates of cold appetizers of which the Russians are so fond, and where vodka was being distributed by Gennady and Sasha to all the guests, Canadian and Russian alike. Around five in the afternoon Geoffrey and the drivers exchanged toasts to continued good relations between the Canadians and the locally engaged staff and to the sixty-fourth anniversary of the Glorious October Revolution, and then he and I left to watch the "pompous ceremonial" concert on television (a direct translation of

the Russian words on the invitation), which we were officially boycotting, to see what we were missing. Well, lots of pomp and ceremony for one thing and a long speech by General Ustinov, which we
wouldn't have been able to understand anyway. Then, at 9:30, as we
went out the back door to get our car we met the last of the
Canadians to leave the garage. At least they were still on their feet but
vodka certainly does have a glazing effect on the eyes! We drove ourselves (having decided that that was the safest thing to do) to the
Swedish Embassy for their annual ball. The incident of the Russian
nuclear submarine discovered spying in Swedish waters had a uni-
fying effect on all the western nations and we all felt particularly
warm to our Swedish hosts. It was an excellent party with a delicious
buffet, lots of dancing, and some good balalaika music while we rested up because none of us is as young as we once were, although some
of us still have illusions. Geoffrey says I am not to name names! The
fact that so many of us did not have to get up to go to the parade the
next day meant that we stayed rather late. The Cypriot Ambassador
is a fantastic dancer.

The parade had already begun when we woke up next morning
so we watched it in our dressing gowns drinking plenty of hot coffee.
The military section was shorter this year and it seemed to us that its
offensive nature was being downplayed. While there were not exactly flowers coming out of the gun barrels, that part of the parade was
followed so very closely by the "workers" with their gigantic paper
bouquets and balloons and floats saying *Nyet* to the neutron bomb
(the whole parade is carried on Eurovision) that the overall impression was one of sensible and disciplined defence rather than aggressive and fearsome power. So what is really going on? People speculate endlessly but who really knows for sure? I can say, though, that
the old men look tired. The official boycott of the parade does not
extend to the reception at the Kremlin Palace of Congresses, which
we attended along with all our other diplomatic colleagues (except
the Swedes) and two thousand members of the "Nomenklatura," the
Russian power élite. I am now used to these long tables laden with
food and drink and surrounded by people standing up to eat so I was
able to exercise more restraint and made straight for the crab, which
one only sees once a year! We also placed ourselves toward the front

of the line, so that we were greeted with some cordiality by the polit-buro portraits come to life and thawed out from their long stint on the reviewing stand and not yet worn out by shaking hands. When the Chief of Protocol introduced Geoffrey to Mr. Brezhnev his ruddy face lit up with a wintry smile as if the word "Canada" had pushed a button and he said "Trudeau." We had thought he might also mention hockey but although his face still retained the trace of a smile when I shook his hand he said no more. Not all the people present go through the line, only about five hundred, including the Patriarch of the Orthodox Church, large and resplendent in white and gold and long, grey beard, accompanied by four or five somewhat smaller but still impressive bishops (I presume). And then, as last year, the old men turned their backs to us and sat down, ate their lunch, drank their vodka, and watched the cabaret show. New this year were three blonde, plump, sinuous belly dancers. The attention from the front row was considerable! The ambassadors stopped exchanging confidences as well! Afterwards we came back to the Residence with our Danish and Dutch colleagues and had Black Diamond cheese and chocolate chip cookies and coffee!

In the evening Rick Kirby, one of our political officers, and I decided to go down to Red Square to watch the fireworks and take pictures so we went by the Metro and mingled with the crowds. There were hundreds and thousands of people all over the downtown area, which was closed to traffic. The weather was not very cold but damp and misty. The crowd was very cheerful. There were many families with little kids and a fair number of older people. But mostly, I think, the groups wandering around full of energy and high spirits were between fifteen and twenty-five years old. I only saw one person in all that vast crowd who was obviously drunk. We felt perfectly safe, of course. The crowd control was excellent and for once the milimen weren't the least bit officious with their fellow citizens. We went all over the place trying to take pictures but the crowd was so dense it was hard to see clearly. After walking around Red Square we went down past the Lenin Museum to the huge Square of the Revolution and across it to Gorky Street, which was lit up like Times Square (well, not quite, but everything is relative) and then back through the Alexander Gardens below the Kremlin wall to the bridge that crosses the Moscow River to the south. We thought that would be the best place from which to see the fireworks. While Rick set up his tripod under the curious gaze of a young boy and a bored soldier, we were entertained by a circle of young people who sang lively songs and swayed back and forth to the sound of a couple of guitars. Then the fireworks blazed up and burst into showers of light, spreading a crimson glow throughout the foggy night. And each one was accompanied by a long, drawn-out "hoo-oorah" from the crowd, which got louder and louder as the display went on. With a final swoosh from the terrace of the Kremlin itself the whole thing was over and the crowds streamed away from the centre into the dimmer streets that lead away in all directions from the heart of the city. We walked up past the Pushkin Museum and the Bassein (where I am discouraging Geoffrey from swimming till his nose stops running) to Kropotkinskaya and so back to the Embassy. Apparently after the fireworks people go to parties in one another's apartments and go on celebrating until early in the morning, but we just came home and had a hot drink!

The Russians clearly enjoy their national holiday but one can only guess at the feelings that are aroused in them by the speeches, exhortations, and propaganda with which their senses are bombarded. Their patriotism is genuine, of that I see plenty of evidence. But do they really believe in a "radiant future under Communism," to quote General Ustinov? Can anyone really believe in a "radiant future" under anything, anymore? Perhaps I'm just getting cynical in my old age. After all, I'll be a year older by the time you get this. But I'm sure I won't lapse into a depression like the hero of Chekhov's play *Ivanov*, which we saw on Sunday evening at the Moscow Arts Theatre. I don't know if it is ever played in the West. It preceded the great plays that we all know and is not on the same level as they are. It doesn't quite work as a play but as a study of clinical depression it is very contemporary and it was so well acted that I was in tears at the end like most of the rest of the audience. Not that I could have understood very much if I hadn't just read the text. How slowly my Russian progresses!

LETTER NO. 28

December 31, 1981

It is three o'clock on the afternoon of the last day of the year. What light there was is already going. It is snowing heavily; large, soft flakes. The Embassy is very quiet. The residence staff all left at two, as they are entitled to do under Soviet law on the day before a major holiday. The Canadian staff left too, not wanting to be less privileged than the locally engaged staff. Geoffrey has gone out on an official call. Michael and I are in the sitting room warming ourselves by the electric heater. Ever since I came back UPDK has been in the process of *remont*ing the Embassy heating system, changing all the piping and replacing all the radiators. There are great holes in ceiling and floor and horrid-looking pipes vertically and horizontally exposed on my elegant walls. They tell me it would have been worse if they had opened up the walls to take out the old pipes and they have promised to box the new ones in but it will probably be another couple of months before they are finished and in the meantime we will have to put up with ugly pipes and temperatures in the 50s. We warn our guests to come with sweaters and shawls!

We have spent the morning making last-minute preparations for Moscow's annual closedown, ploughing through the slush to the diplomatic gastronome to purchase the weekend's food as well as some champagne to share with all the young (and not so young) Russian women who work inside the Embassy: Victoria, Elena, Tanya, Irina, Lydia, Natasha, and all the others, of whom Geoffrey approves because they all show him the proper deference and appreciate his sense of humour, to say nothing of being indispensable to the working of the Embassy and of enormous assistance generally to the Canadian community as well as to visiting Canadians. So we drank to their health and our own and to a stable and peaceful 1982. But before we did that, Michael and I had other purchases to make and presents to wrap and deliver, and a brief moment of panic to suffer when we learned that his Aeroflot flight to Amsterdam on January 2 would be delayed for two hours, making, we were afraid, his flight connection problematic. However, we were then told that the change was made because that flight was no longer stopping in Warsaw and he should get there in plenty of time and we won't have to get up at 5:30 a.m. after all to get him to the airport! So, we hope, he will arrive back in Canada as scheduled, carrying this letter with him. From now on there is nothing more we can do because, as those of you who were here last year will remember, on New Year's Day *nothing* stirs! Michael has now gone off to think about his packing and the lights have come on in the apartment buildings all around us. I'll close the curtains and try to finish this before the year itself draws to an end. We are going to a party later and then to Red Square at midnight but now it is very peaceful and for the first time since I returned I have some time to reflect.

I arrived back from my visit home very tired, as you can imagine, and the stimulation that came from seeing you all was temporarily subdued by the fact that I was over thirty hours late, what with weather conditions in London and weather conditions here. And when my JAL flight finally set down at Scheremetyevo we had to wait *two* hours before there was space for the plane to park. So when I came into the lounge Geoffrey and Michael were already there, each having arrived separately on earlier flights, Michael via Frankfurt and Geoffrey from his meeting in Paris. On my delayed flight I met John Ziegler of the NHL with some companions and discovered that I had kindly invited them to lunch the following day, so there wasn't much time to relax when I got to Moscow. Luckily the Residence staff were already aware of this upcoming event and had made some of the necessary arrangements so the lunch, which was for Mr. Ziegler and Mr. Pavlov of the State Committee for Sports and Recreation, went off very well. Michael was fascinated by the speeches and comments exchanged among the various personalities, and by the contrast between the ways in which the two "systems" organize hockey, and by the frankness with which the problems were discussed. The NHL cannot, of course, afford to release a team to play in mid-season in the Izvestia Cup and the Russians are disappointed because they perceive the North American teams as their only real rivals. Michael went to three of the Izvestia Cup games and quite enjoyed them even though the Russians don't see the Finns or the Swedes or even the Czechs, now, as serious competitors. Geoffrey managed to get to only one of the games because we had other obligations, including reading one of the lessons in the annual Festival of Carols and Lessons at the British Embassy. This year he read the Magnificat.

After four or five nights I began to sleep properly again but there was no let-up in activity. Everyone entertains around Christmastime, including ourselves, so when we were not out for dinner or a reception or a National Day or a Canadian get-together we were having forty Russians to see Peter Ustinov's *Leningrad* and enjoy a buffet supper or seventy Canadians to the annual Christmas Eve party for children and their parents. This year Marcel Blagdon made a cheerful Santa Claus and Robin Metz from Newfoundland played beautifully for the carol singing. There were a lot more children than last year and eleven (!) good-looking young men came to visit their parents and altogether everyone seemed to have a good time in spite of the fact that Tamara had forgotten to add the rice to the casserole so that there wasn't quite enough food to go around. I went to bed brooding on my failures as a caterer but next morning was Christmas and with Michael's presence and signs of you all in parcels and cards we were as cheerful as we could be under the circumstances, and we ended up the day with a splendid Brahms concert at the Conservatory. And the *next* day we celebrated thirty years of marriage with some beautiful long-stemmed roses and at least one piece of evidence of the fruitfulness of our union! From all this you can gather how much it has meant to us to have Michael here and for me, at least, the pang of separation at such a festive time was much softened by having seen you all in your own spaces so recently.

Although there has been little sun, the weather is much more pleasantly wintry than it was last year so we have been skiing in Peredelkino and skating in Gorky Park and Michael has played a couple of games of broomball, once in the "League" on the slippery British ice and yesterday against the drivers and the *dvorniks*, our Embassy yardmen, on local ice around the corner from our building, watched by a derisive bunch of kids who were torn between the spectacle of grown men acting so foolishly and their desire to get on with their own serious game of pick-up hockey. Pavel played the whole time, which I thought was pretty impressive for a grandfather, but Ilya just laughed when I asked him why he didn't play! We have also done some sightseeing though not much because there isn't the same urgency the second time around. However, we did join the line to pay our respects to Lenin yesterday, which is a charged experience no matter what one's views may be about the occupant of the sanctuary, and we also went to see the panorama of the battle of Borodino. It's hard to say what the people here think about the possibility of war over Poland, although I am convinced that the average Soviet citizen finds it hard to view himself or herself as the Devil incarnate and does not really know what to make of American pronouncements, except to be increasingly afraid of the US. These are tense times but let's all hope that no one too powerful draws the wrong conclusions for us all in 1982.

LETTER NUMBER 29

January 10, 1982

I don't know what weather is like in your part of the world but, like the Germans and the French before them, I would retreat from Moscow if I could. It is bitterly cold now, far more snow than last winter, and an icy wind blowing in, presumably from the steppes. The snow removal equipment that seemed barely adequate last year is having a very hard time keeping up with the fresh snowfalls and even on the main roads the ruts toss the cars back and forth like ships on a frozen sea. In the summer we rejoice that no salt has rusted away our vehicles but right now the salt might be somewhat more effective than the sturdy old ladies out in their mufflers and felt boots and orange jackets hacking away with picks and shovels. However, contrary to what the western journalists report, a "real" Russian winter (which they keep telling us we are getting) brings out something very positive in the Russian character. Yesterday, Geoffrey and I made our way around the corner to the little museum about the poet, Pushkin, where the lady who sold us our tickets actually told us to keep our coats *on* because the rooms in the house were too cold.

After we had seen the autographed manuscripts and the portraits of his contemporaries and the death mask and the lock of hair, to say nothing of the very pen with which he had been writing the day before his fatal duel, we braved the wintry streets again to go and peer through the steam that almost totally obscures the water in the Bassein. We could hear voices and eventually could distinguish a few hardy swimmers but I am trying to discourage Geoffrey from returning until later in the spring. Earlier in the week, on an equally cold day, I went skating with Elaine Mathys and her children in Gorky Park. When we arrived the *Kassa* was temporarily shut for some reason and one of the babushkas who stands at the gates to take tickets came along and harangued the people inside with a great stream of invective for letting all these poor children on a school holiday stand outside and freeze while they were having hot tea and I don't know what else inside. And eventually they relented, laughing, and she turned to us full of triumph and stalked back to her position by the gate and we all applauded. And the changing houses are warm and cheerful, full of friendly comments and "we are all in this together, let's enjoy it as best we can" attitude. Being with children helps and speaking better Russian also helps but I'm sure this old, familiar enemy, this seasonal challenge, evokes a special spirit of camaraderie that expands to include everyone willing to be included, foreigners as well.

Since Michael left we have been very quiet. Actually, we are reluctant to ask people in owing to the massive *remont* of our heating system with the accompanying mess and considerably lowered indoor temperatures. So I have been focusing on things like Russian history; next month I will lead our history group in a discussion of Lenin, a continuation of the discussion led by Mrs. Ma at the Chinese Embassy last week. Although she is most certainly a Communist and claims to be a great admirer of Leninism she does admit to the same fascination the rest of us feel for psychological factors and gave us a pretty full account of Lenin's family background, his childhood, and the early influences that came to him from the Russian revolutionary tradition.

I have to pick up from the time that he was expelled from the University of Kazan for being mildly involved in student protests, but mostly for being the brother of an executed terrorist. So I have spent the last few days plunged into a biography that I found in the

Embassy library written by a professor at Harvard, Polish by nation-
ality, Geoffrey says, named Adam Ulam, a book that is so fascinating
I can hardly put it down. It's such an incredible story! Years ago I
read a short story by Stephen Bênet that impressed me very much. It
was about the life and family problems of a talented Corsican soldier
and it is only toward the end of the tale that I realized he was writing
about Napoleon as if he had been born thirty years earlier. Because,
of course, without the proper historical sequence of events, nothing
much happened. I get this feeling when reading Russian history, that
so much of it is accidental in somewhat the same way. Perhaps that is
because ultimate power was concentrated for so many centuries in
the hands of single individuals that their decisions, however irra-
tional, however petty, were able to have such enormous impact. And
there seem to have been so many times that their decisions were so
arbitrary that they could just as easily have been quite the opposite!
Or that a particular decision, five years later, would have had a completely different effect. I have found myself frequently saying to
myself as I've followed the fortunes of the Romanovs or their prede-
cessors "if only he had ..." or "if only she had not ..."

For me the story of Lenin has something of the same fortuitous
air and not just because there were so many chops and changes in
his recorded views, as well (although not with his family) as in his
relationships, with his political colleagues and other contemporaries, but also because there were so many occasions on which he
could have been removed from the scene. And yet he was always
being rescued by people who were "class enemies" if not worse!
Suppose, for example, that he had been interned in Germany during
the First World War as he very nearly was, because he was there
when hostilities broke out and actually spent a little time in a village
jail? Once he obtained power a certain inevitability appears to char-
acterize subsequent events. In the system that surrounds me now I
see the ripple effects of his own personal experiences as an exile and
as a member of the Russian Intelligentsia, much as he hated "them."
But I don't see anything inexorable about his road to power. It mattered that he was born when he was and not thirty years earlier, and
it mattered that certain conditions were present in the situation of
Russia in 1917. And it mattered that he had certain characteristics of

personality and intellect. But there were so many times between 1900 and 1917 when decisions, some of them quite minor, could have rewritten the whole scenario! Of course, I have never been a historical determinist. I believe that forces are set in motion by human decisions and the fact that they often get out of hand also has to do with human decisions. I guess the present state of world tension is making me particularly conscious of the potential impact of all the decisions being taken at this moment by people in power. And while I am optimistic by nature, experience is tempering me and rhetoric that always places the devil in the other camp frightens me. I personally find it harder and harder not to see that tail flicking out of sight behind my own door!

But I'll end on a more cheerful note. Last week I went to a concert at Spaso House given by an American baritone of Armenian descent, in Russia on a Fulbright fellowship, teaching and studying in Yerevan. He has a voice that is at once mellow and joyful and the last part of his program was devoted to Armenian drinking songs. At the very end he managed to get us all to join in the rousing refrains. Most of the audience were Russian, and when Donna Hartman, the Ambassador's wife, thanked the singer she said, with remarkable grace, that she wanted to congratulate him on being able to create in these times a Russo-American chorus! And we all laughed together, for a moment.

LETTER NUMBER 30

January 23, 1982

From where I sit I can see three little girls beside the main door of the school across the street standing together waiting for someone to come and fetch them. They are all bundled up in warm coats and fuzzy wool hats, two of them with bright blue satchels on their backs and the other clutching a short pair of wooden skis. Their heads are bent together and they are talking with great animation. Every minute or two they break apart to giggle! What do you suppose little girls can be talking about on the streets of Moscow in this January of

1982? A little earlier today I saw a troop of six-year-olds, twenty or so
strong, setting off accompanied by two or three teachers, each child
carrying one of those old-fashioned sleighs, the kind you sit upright
on with the curved metal bar at the back, painted in many colours.
They were going to Gogol's Boulevard nearby, which has a splendid
ice slide. Today is Saturday but children go to school here six days a
week. However, their school day is shorter than ours and on
Saturdays they seem to be as much outside as in.

The period of severe cold I described in my last letter didn't last
very long. Judging from the reports we have had from Canada we are
now better off than you. At least from the point of view of weather.
The ideological gusts swirling about us here continue to have a bitter
edge to them and the forces that keep them in motion show, alas, little sign of abating. I expect we feel the tension of events more here
than you do at home. We are only too aware of the tragic dimension
of what is taking place here and to the west of us but our everyday
experience frequently does not fit the stereotypes about Russia and
her people that are being created by the reports of Western journalists. So we cannot help but be rendered uneasy by an analysis of
events that seems to be so much based on those stereotypes. I have
just watched a young couple walk down the street swinging on each
other's arm, and a little boy run past with a large, friendly dog, and
a thin, nervous father move up the street carrying gingerly what
appears to be a large bundle of laundry tied with a blue ribbon but
which is, of course, his newborn baby hidden under layers of gar-
ments and blankets, enveloped in a white sheet. Beneath all these
East–West abstractions we are all members of the same species, and
an endangered one at that!

The *remont* of the heating system is proceeding apace. Only two
rooms remain to be fitted with new radiators and then the system will
be switched over. If all the welded corners hold and we don't have a
flood, then within a week or so we should find ourselves living in a
reasonable indoor temperature. Our guests have been coming well-
warned and no one has developed pneumonia yet, but it has been a
little trying. After the system has proved itself we will then have to
repair the aesthetic damage, which will require some ingenuity. The
plumbing is going to be changed too and we will get a new bathroom

but that will depend upon coordinating the work of UPDK with a Danish contractor, a feat we are not sure our resident Canadian building engineer is up to. And then spring will come and we will watch avidly to see if the new lawn has survived all the ice that keeps getting thrown off the roof and whether the tulips come up.

All this work has reduced our entertaining somewhat but we expect to make up for it during the next couple of months. In the meantime Tamara and I are having a chance to explore my cookbooks, particularly the Time-Life *Cooking of the World* series. Last week she made four varieties of Danish pastry, tournedos à la Bearnaise, and some Italian pizza. Unfortunately, the pictures that seem to attract her most are of desserts ... and it is hard to resist what she wants me to try!

Being a little bored with trying to memorize the dative case, I have taken to asking Natasha to accompany me to one of the local museums rather than have my afternoon lesson at the Embassy. Since I last wrote, we have been to both the Chekhov museum and the house of Alexander Herzen, which is just around the corner. The Chekhov museum is delightful. He lived there from 1886 till 1890 and although it is not furnished exactly as it was when he lived there, everything in it is authentic. The director who guided us through the house is as much in love with him as any of the other women in his life. She showed us photographs of the two who never quite managed to capture him and spoke with what appeared to me to be real jealousy of his wife! This is a museum about the man, not the writer, and her feeling for him, plus her knowledge of so many little details in his life, plus the personal quality of the objects gathered in the house— the woollen plaid on his bed that had covered him as he lay dying in Germany, his sister's nightcap on the pillow in her room, the photographs, the letters, the manuscripts—all combined to make the presence of the man so vivid that when, in the last room, I came upon the portrait that Valentin Serov painted of him in the last year of his life, I almost fell in love with him myself! The museum director is a guardian of his person, not his work, in which she did not, in fact, seem all that interested. But tomorrow night we are going to see *The Cherry Orchard* at the Maly Theatre with two young students from Canada and we are looking forward to it immensely. Herzen is my other favourite nineteenth-century Russian but his museum does not have quite the same personal charm, in spite of the fact he did live in it once before he went to Europe to spend all the rest of his life as an exile. Only a couple of rooms are furnished in period style with family portraits; the rest have prints and books and display cases of objects. And our guide, while informative and enthusiastic, as they all are in these small museums when they realize you are genuinely interested, had not become emotionally involved with Herzen. However I find him irresistible. He was obviously handsome, as I could tell from the paintings and photographs, and his cast of mind, as one discovers it in his writing, is particularly attractive to contemporary readers. Natasha tells me that although he is much admired in present-day Russia as a revolutionary thinker, he is not much studied in school. Perhaps his sense of irony would be misunderstood?

Elaine and François Mathys had a very successful party last week, which they focused around the screening of an excellent NFB film made last year called *For the Love of Dance*. One of the dancers featured is Kevin Pugh of the National Ballet, who was a great hit when the Canadians competed so successfully in the ballet competitions in Moscow last June. So Elaine, who took classes at the Bolshoi when they were posted here in the mid-seventies, invited a number of Bolshoi figures, including Ulanova and Valukin, who has taught at the National Ballet School in Toronto from time to time, and many of them came. I don't think the film, which shows seven dance companies in Canada including the Contemporary Dancers of Winnipeg and Anna Wyman's company in Vancouver, makes us look better than we are. The truth is, we are better than we think! Of course, we couldn't stage anything like *Prince Igor*, which we went to hear and see a few days ago. That kind of thing really isn't our style! Besides, only totally state-supported companies can afford the enormous expense of huge sets, rich costumes, and casts of thousands. But what a treat! Borodin's music is so beautiful, Prince Igor was extremely handsome, even in defeat, and the Polovtsian dances wildly exciting. And if you can't get tickets (although the Palace of Congresses holds six thousand) you can watch the full performance on TV. The story is full of drama, sex, and violence—though I expect the Soviet public would prefer to watch *Dallas* if they could!

LETTER NUMBER 31

February 7, 1982

The cold weather has returned. It is bright and sunny but the streets are empty. I hope that most people are somewhat warmer inside than we are. At this stage of our heating system *remont* the old system of radiators has been enclosed in cement and the new system has not yet been turned on. We are not quite sure what to expect next although we have been promised heat by the middle of next week when we are having a large dinner party. The workmen are all quite cheerful and as far as I can see they are efficient but I cannot tell where they are going to turn up next in the Residence. Ah, the pleasures of living in public property! Anyway, to cheer myself up I will tell you about my trip to Georgia and Armenia, which had its inconveniences too, but of quite a different order!

The lands of the Caucasus have a very special character and, as usual when we travel in the Soviet Union, I am dismayed by how little I know about the places we are visiting. The name of Armenia was fixed in my mind many years ago by my grandmother (Lala), who rebuked my stubborn refusal to eat everything on my plate by urging me to "remember the starving Armenians." At the time her admonition served only to make me reflect on the problems of distribution, how could my uneaten food possibly get to Armenia, wherever that was! But now, years later, I have been made aware of the dimensions of that particular tragedy and I finally stand rebuked. The geographical position of Armenia (and to a lesser extent Georgia) made it the meeting place of many influences and ideas from both East and West but also doomed it to be a two-thousand-year-old battlefield between dominant empires. In relatively brief periods of independence both nations flowered, Armenia in the Middle Ages, particularly in the tenth century, and Georgia somewhat later. While the history of Georgia has not been quite as tragic as that of Armenia, national feeling runs very high in both areas and a national identity will unquestionably survive no matter what the future brings. We were very attracted by both places, although most of us liked Georgia best. We all want to go back when the weather is better. The end of January is not really a sensible time to travel in the USSR but most of us knew what to expect and none of us regrets having gone.

Leaving Moscow was easy. We set off Monday morning, January 25, seventeen "International Ladies" and an eight-year-old boy! Four Indonesians, four Germans, Elaine Mathys and I, four Americans, a Mexican born in Hong Kong, a Philippine, and a gorgeous blonde Yugoslav and her good-natured son. The plane left more or less on time. We had some soda water in a brown paper cup and a wonderful view of the snow-covered Caucasus, and descended smoothly through the smog to Tbilisi airport. We never saw the mountains again but at least we know they are there! We spent three days in Georgia, quite a lot of it wandering around on our own because in the USSR you can never really plan anything until you arrive and then you learn that everything is closed on Monday or in *remont* or the roads through the mountains are blocked by snow. However, wandering around Tbilisi is delightful. To begin with, the Georgian people are very handsome, both men and women. They are usually tall and slim with dark hair, strong features and white skin. Sometimes they look rather fierce and they are certainly volatile (we witnessed a couple of fights within a very short time) but they were friendly to us everywhere we went. Also, the city has a great deal of natural charm. The old city is built in a narrow river valley with the ancient citadel high above and many of the newer buildings climbing halfway up the bordering hills. Traditional Georgian architecture is marked by balconies with tall, slender pillars surmounted by narrow, slightly pointed arches. The flavour is Eastern and there are enough of such buildings in the city to offset the bulk of Soviet-styled public edifices. Streets go up and down, there are many trees, there are courtyards with grape arbours, and elegant, ancient churches. Add the cypresses and you will see that the total effect is Eastern Mediterranean. In the summer, when it is very hot and people are living outside, it must be very pleasant indeed. Even in January daily living appears to be easier than in Moscow. Lineups were few and people's expressions were not as grim and heavy as they often are in Moscow in wintertime.

In the twelfth century Georgia knew peace from her constant invaders. Under David the Restorer and Queen Tamara there was a great artistic flowering. On the second day of our visit we saw the collection of icons, crosses, and other works of art from that period in the National Art Museum. The style is unique, linear without being too stylized, much more lively and vital than the works being produced in Russia at the same time. Of course Georgian culture is very ancient. It was to one of her Black Sea ports that Jason came in search of the golden fleece. One shouldn't be surprised, therefore, at the sophistication of her craftsmen. The cloisonné enamel work we saw in the museum was of great beauty; three stars, *vaut le voyage*. And that evening we had a very good time in a local restaurant where we went to watch some folk dancing. The women glide and the men dance on the upper part of their toes, they wear only black and white and silver and it's all quite romantic and elegant. Most of the ladies left after the performance but Elaine and I and two or three others stayed and then the real dancing began! There were very few other women in the restaurant and so we had the pick of the men who wanted to dance. The Georgians have a wonderful sense of rhythm and the orchestra played everything from tangos to disco. Every time we came back to the table we found another bottle of champagne and by the time the music stopped there were seven! We have no idea where they came from! We opened and drank two in the company of the only man who actually sat down with us, an Olympic champion bobsledder who became a little sentimental about his stops in Gander and showed us a photo of his thirteen-year-old son. The champansky was brut, the first I have drunk in the USSR, and *much* better than the semi-sweet stuff we usually get. I still had a headache in the morning, though.

The last day we spent in Georgia was full of contrasts. We went first to visit an astonishing fortress church built high on a hill overlooking the ancient capital of Georgia, Mtskheta, about 15 km from Tbilisi. It was built at the end of the sixth century and has resisted all the invasions. The lines of the church are sober and harmonious. There is no decoration on the inside. The original altar remains where it was first placed, in the middle of the church, on an ancient sacred site. Christianity came early to Georgia, in the fourth century, and Zoroastrianism had been strong here before. This wild, solemn place still feels very holy. From there we drove along the river valley to Gori, which evokes very different emotions indeed. Here, in the town where he was born, is the only museum to Stalin in the Soviet Union. Visiting it was a very strange experience. From the moment we arrived in Georgia we were cold; although it gets cold every winter, they make no allowance for it in the public places so we were constantly chilly, even in our coats. But nothing compared to the way we felt when we sat down to eat in the unheated Intourist restaurant after we had been through the Museum. In front of the Museum stands, in its original location, the two-room cottage where on December 21, 1879, Joseph Stalin was born. It is now protected from the elements by a pillared temple. I think that was done when he was still alive. No one would answer any direct questions so we don't really know for sure. Behind it stands a very large building that, while not exactly like Stalin's seven towers in Moscow, does nevertheless bear some family resemblance to them. I would call it Stalinesque Moorish, as opposed to Stalinesque Gothic.

Inside we went up a vast flight of marble stairs to a suite of lofty rooms devoted primarily to photographs of certain very selected events in the life of the "Man of Steel." Our own guide, who was very knowledgeable and pleasant, was not allowed to guide us. Instead we were taken around by a young woman who was fiercely proud. We saw pictures of Stalin's parents, his early school days, the seminary where he studied in Tbilisi, early revolutionary companions. We saw a model of the underground printing house in Tbilisi that you reached through a well. We were told that he was put in prison and escaped more times than any other Russian revolutionary. We saw one or two photographs of the Revolution, a picture of him signing some decree with respect to industrialization, another of him embracing a small child. Then nothing until the War. Lots of photos of the war and maps showing advances and retreats and a huge, grotesque bronze table lamp representing a charging tank. Photos of the conferences of Teheran and Yalta, of course, and the last photo taken before he died, by some American journalist. Finally, we saw the death mask in bronze on a red velvet dais surmounted by a canopy held up by slender pillars. Around the wall very carefully chosen quotations from world leaders, Roosevelt, Churchill ... And then, "Now, would you like to pose any questions ... ?" Well, where do you start? We trailed off to our inedible lunch ...

In the evening, in search of culture, we trouped off to *Carmen* at the State Opera House. The overture started with such a clang of cymbals that we practically leaped out of our seats. The opening scene was awkward and we watched the girls pouring out of the cigarette factory with some anxiety. No need—Carmen was gorgeous and had a fine voice. A burst of applause from the audience greeted their great tenor, a People's Artist of the Soviet Union, and he bowed to us as much as he could over his great girth. Well, he did have a fine voice but somehow the magic was gone, particularly when the toreador was only a trifle slimmer. I suppose one should concentrate on the music but once you've been to Spain that suspension of disbelief becomes just that much more difficult ... We had to leave before the last act anyway to catch our train to Yerevan, about which the less said the better. The fact that it was unheated was only one of its flaws ... But we were a good-natured crew and no one broke an ankle leaping down onto the track next morning, throwing our bags out before us.

Unfortunately the weather in Yerevan was very disappointing. The fog was so thick that when we had a city tour we had to take our guide's descriptions on hearsay. We are told that the city is dominated by Mount Ararat but we'll have to go back to find out. So we focused on ancient Armenia, visiting the historical museum with its artifacts from the thirteenth century BC when Armenia took shape, as Urartu between Lake Sevan in the Caucasus and Lake Van in Turkey, and then survived the Medes and the Persians, Alexander the Great, and a whole host of other powers and principalities. Armenia became Christian in 301 and we were told that it was the first country to recognize Christianity as the state religion. The most interesting museum we visited, the Matenadaran, testifies to the great role that Christianity has played in Armenia ever since. In this building, the visitor sees only a very small percentage of the vast number of books, manuscripts, and documents that are being preserved but that small taste fills one with wonder. Both Armenia and Georgia have their own scripts, a factor that goes a long way toward preserving both their languages and their national identities. Which is why the Armenian script was invented in the first place, in the early fifth century. The earliest manuscripts in the collection date from the same period and the miniatures from a little later. We also went to visit some ancient churches but the snow blocked our way to some of the most interesting places we had planned to visit. We went to the market instead, which was full of beautiful fruit, bought a golden pear, and thought about the summertime. If we liked Georgia better it was probably because of the weather so we'll have to visit both places again ... and we will.

LETTER NUMBER 32

February 23, 1982

Today is Soviet Army Day. Driving around the city this morning in search of flowers for tonight's reception Ilya and I kept coming across groups of young soldiers on outings. While they did not all look as if they were having a great old time, I'm sure it was better than whatever it is they do on an ordinary day. While I was at my hair salon, a client brought my hairdresser, Valentin, a box of cigars for the holiday. He says that efforts are being made to turn this day into a Men's Day to rival International Women's Day, which is coming up on March 8. After all, he says, almost all men are in the army at one time or another. Alas, in this country that is no doubt true. However, as yet only the members of the armed forces have a holiday today. All the others have to work. There will be a big concert on television for them tonight and fireworks at 9:00. Which we will miss because we are going to hear a Canadian group called the Hertz Trio play Brahms and the Canadian composer Violet Archer at 7:30 and bring them back to the Residence afterwards along with some Soviet musicians for a cold buffet. This prompted me to get hold of a piano tuner for Mrs. Ford's grand piano in the drawing room just in case somebody wants to try it out! You will be glad to hear that they will be warm. The new heating system has been functioning quite well since last week and I am really not depressed. The days are slowly getting longer and the weather has been pleasant, often sunny and not very cold. There has been no new snow for a while but in the parks it is still surprisingly white. Not in our backyard though. While we are now warm, they are still replacing the radiators downstairs.

Then they are going to start in on the plumbing as well as complete the necessary carpentry work to cover up all the new pipes. I expect they will still be at it when we return from Canada in May!

Also we are extremely busy, which keeps me from brooding too much. Our activities are mostly social and cultural, at least mine are, because there isn't too much movement in other areas these days for Canadians in Moscow, as you can well imagine. Except for broomball, the favourite winter game of the foreign community! While the ladies have had a rather ignominious season, the men's team is well on its way to the League Championship (we take this game *very* seriously, although it is sometimes hard to do so as a spectator!). The men haven't lost a single game and they are now in the semi-finals. The last game will be on Saturday against the Finns so the whole Embassy will turn out to cheer. But the men benefited greatly from the energy and skill of François Mathys and the addition for three weeks of two lively French-Canadian dentists who came from Montreal to look after our teeth during the day and have a good time at night. They worked extremely hard and after they had finished all the Canadians, including Geoffrey and me, they took on some Americans and Brits (the equipment is at the American Embassy) and even the Chinese Ambassador. They not only polished up our teeth but did a tremendous job for the Canadian image! Though sometimes, when they were playing broomball, their opponents accused them of trying to create work for themselves.

We seem to be in the middle of a diplomatic social season that is a mixed blessing. While our rather informal evening two weeks ago for ambassadors, at which we showed them some new and colourful NFB films and provided a buffet supper with tables but no protocol, seems to have been quite a success, we are rapidly building up more "debts" and what do you do for an encore? Sometimes we have delicious food as we did last week at the Malaysians but often we don't and protocol always gives us the same dinner partners. Yet the diplomatic corps needs to be cohesive and supportive in a post like this and there is more value than one suspects in these frequent dinner parties. I am not, however, losing any weight! For a change we went to have dinner the other night with the Canadian students at their hostel. They are a lively bunch, particularly the young women, and determined to get the best out of Moscow if not out of their formal studies. For those of you who saw *Moscow Doesn't Believe in Tears*, the foreign student hostel resembles the place where the girls lived when they first arrived in Moscow in 1958, although today's inhabitants look rather different! The kids managed to cook us a good dinner served on a variety of plates, all they could borrow; a beef curry and some rice that one of their Afghan friends prepared. It's *very* nice to spend an evening among the young!

We also enjoyed the recent visit of a Canadian film delegation, which included a fellow named Peter Pearson who turns out to be a not-too-distant cousin. The delegation brought a print of *Les Plouffes*, which we were able to watch downstairs in the club in place of the usual Friday night rerun and which all of us who were there and particularly our rather large contingent of French-Canadians enjoyed a great deal. We went with the group to spend a day at the Mosfilm studios, which was fascinating. The weather was very cold so we were not able to have much of a tour through the sets. But we saw the workshops where they create wigs and masks and makeup and one of the studios where they are constructing a replica of the Maryinsky Theatre in Leningrad for a British-Russian co-production about Anna Pavlova. They have asked us to come back in April when they are actually filming. We were shown some excerpts from Soviet films in order to admire their techniques and skills. Our delegation confirmed that Soviet filmmakers know what they are doing ... technically. We had lunch with a number of important people, some of whom made it quite clear that they were more important than others. The most interesting was Sergei Bondarchuk, the actor and director responsible for *War and Peace*, who specializes in mass scenes. He is in the process of completing a film about John Reed called *Red Bells*. Initially, Bondarchuk said, he and Warren Beatty had discussed a joint Russian-American co-production but for "various reasons" it was not possible. So *Red Bells* is a Mexican-Italian-Russian production. The Mexican part has been completed and reportedly the Mexicans are very pleased about it. Although I have never read John Reed's reports about the Mexican Revolution, I have recently re-read *Ten Days that Shook the World*. It conveys a remarkable sense of immediacy even though the language, like the author, gets a little overwrought.

LETTER NUMBER 33

March 1, 1982

I have decided to write you again this week because a lot of inter-esting things happened during the last few days that I would like to tell you about now rather than later, and as we are going up to Zavidova on Friday for several days' holiday I will not be able to post anything in next week's bag. So here goes with a week in my life.

When I wrote you last Tuesday, Soviet Army Day, I was preparing for the Hertz Trio. They turned out to be excellent and played to a small but extremely enthusiastic audience in one of the concert halls of the Conservatory. The violinist and cellist were sister and brother and the fine pianist was the only native-born Canadian, but all three made us feel proud. Geoffrey is not particularly keen on chamber music but he enjoyed the recital more than he had expected and we both enjoyed talking with them afterwards at the Residence about their experiences in the Soviet Union. When Yaela Hertz was last in the USSR ten years ago she gave a concert with David Oistrakh whom she admired to the point that she wept when she talked about him. But then everything about her was dramatic and she looked resplendent in a brilliant yellow brocade gown. I had spent part of Monday translating recipes for French pastries with Tamara and she had done wonders with them along with a cold *roulade de boeuf*. You will forgive these domestic details but they do account for rather a lot of my day as you can imagine! I'm not sure how many people came back after the concert but it was an interesting mixture of Russians and Canadians and some of them stayed rather late.

On Wednesday afternoon Elaine and I went to a Commonwealth Ladies Tea at the Cypriots' where the Ambassador's wife, Tina Angelides, treated us to honey cakes, and some Cypriot students from Patrice Lumumba University danced for us, some traditional dances and one splendid modern male one. In the evening Geoffrey and I went with Lydia and Irene from the commercial section of the Embassy to see a remarkable play about Lenin called *Blue Horses on a Red Field* at the Lenin Komsomol Theatre, where we saw the rock opera last fall. An imaginative and innovative production, the play

was an impressionistic study of Lenin in his later years by means of
the events of one day. Much of it was very funny and our two companions laughed and laughed. And some of it was obviously moving,
tragic in fact. The actor playing Lenin made no attempt to look like
him but his characterization was so human and so complete that you
were really convinced by it. All Russian theatre is repertory and this
seems to give the actors a vital connection to one another, which you
don't always feel in theatres that only do one play at a time. The play
lasted for two hours without a break but we weren't bored for a
moment in spite of our limited Russian. And afterwards Lydia did a
fine job of translating since she seems to have almost total recall! This
has given us the courage to go to more modern Russian theatre.

On Thursday I went with Margaret Keble, the wife of the British
Ambassador, a charming Scotswoman, to a baptism service in the
Russian Baptist Church. I think I wrote you about visiting the church
once before in the fall but this time we were invited back to attend a
group baptism, the event that is central to the life of the church. It was
astonishing. We could not get over the courage displayed by these
twenty-six adults, five men and twenty-one women, who descended
on a wintry night into the baptismal pool in their white hospital-like
gowns and stocking feet to call out *"veruyu"* (I believe) and *"obe-
shayu"* (I promise) before being blessed by the pastor shoulder-deep
in the water in his floating sky-blue robe and then bent over backwards by him for full immersion. Afterwards there was great rejoicing in the congregation, the young people brought them flowers and
everyone kissed everyone else, including us. We felt privileged to
witness such an act of faith in this country. I have never witnessed an
adult baptism in Canada. I am sure it, too, would be moving, but I
can't imagine that it would have the same flavour of bravery and
crowding and oversized emotion, unmistakably Russian.

On Friday we had lunch for some people from the Export
Development Corporation and a Canadian businessman and his wife
here about a contract that has been pursued for quite a long time.
Conversation was lively. In the afternoon I went out with Joyce Roy,
wife of our military attaché, to see exactly how long it would take us
to purchase the ingredients for supper, given the fact that many
newspaper stories seem to harp on the endless food lines in Moscow

as if that were the very sign and symbol of everything that is wrong. Anyway, we figured that within forty minutes of leaving the front door we would be able to return with the ingredients for the following dinner menu: borscht with sour cream, lamb chops, mashed potatoes and carrots, salad (lettuce and green onions), apple pie and ice cream. (And wine of course, and coffee, if we could afford it.) If we had spent another half-hour we could have purchased a canary in a cage, a pretty jade ring for twenty roubles, and a pair of Finnish pantyhose for seven. Now of course if you want a different menu or a pair of jade earrings or a velour dressing gown you'll have to wait for another day! But we did our best, and it wasn't so bad after all. In fact we were rather surprised because, of course, we don't go into the local shops all that often and we read the newspapers.

Then on Friday evening we went down the street to the Austrians' for a dinner dance. Some of us looked attractive but, alas, few of us are young. In the old Russian novels, when there were balls, possibly in these very same rooms, there was obviously a wonderful mix of ages and plenty of room for romance. Well, we are not a very fast crowd nor particularly elegant but many of us have become good friends and some of us are excellent dancers, including Geoffrey, so we managed to have a good time.

On Saturday we went skiing out on the Kaluga road with our Danish friends, Pol and Inger Steenberger, and then went back to their place for spiced herring and schnapps. The weather was very fine though cold when we left them after 3:00 to go to the British rink to watch the Canadians win the broomball championship against the Scandinavian team, 5-3. Iced champagne and *O Canada!* while the sun sank behind the golden domes of the Kremlin.

On Sunday Layachi Yaker and Bernardo Bermudez, the Venezuelan Ambassador, came for a long, leisurely, interesting lunch. Annette Yaker spends most of her time in Algiers now with two of their children pursuing her career in the Ministry of Health and Beatriz Bermudez is in Vienna arranging for the wedding of the eldest of their four beautiful daughters that will take place in May, so the two men appreciated a companionable Sunday lunch. And in the evening, at the invitation of the Embassy of Spain, we went to the Rossiya Theatre to watch a performance of *Zarzuela* by a troupe from

Granada. Alas, it was rather disappointing, too much light opera and not enough passion. However, the Russian audience loved it and it will play to full houses of two thousand or more for ten days here and another week in Leningrad.

Today we had some visiting Canadians for lunch and tonight we go to the Chinese Embassy for dinner to say farewell to the Japanese Ambassador. For tomorrow I have organized a men's lunch for eight while I plan to go with some women from the International Women's Club to the Central Baths for the first time. And so it goes. I must say it is a strange sort of life but not without interest! Yet, the longer I am here and the more I learn about this country the more fascinating it becomes. It's so enormous and complex. I continue with my language studies and read as much as I possibly can. My history group, which met here this morning, is helpful. At present we are trying to disentangle the story of Stalin's rise to power. The 1920s appear to have been a remarkably interesting period in Russian history. I am not looking forward to the 1930s. I wonder how interesting the 1980s will turn out to be in retrospect. Of course there is a great deal of tension at the moment but one senses that there are a lot of shifts and movements taking place below the surface of things. I hope I live long enough to be able to look back and see whether any of my hunches about the shape and direction of social change in this country prove to be correct. Not that I am any more likely than anyone else to be right but since I can't *act* here I am driven to observe and ponder …

LETTER NUMBER 34

March 15, 1982

When I made a comment to one of our Soviet guests at lunch today that March is the dirtiest time of the year he scolded me for saying anything negative about spring, but I told him it was a problem of rising expectations and that "April is the cruellest month." Oh, he said, in April spring will already be here, but I told him that I was a native of northern climes too, and I knew that was not true, not even in the Soviet Union. And, indeed, although the pussy willows I cut last week at Zavidova have come out since I brought them indoors and are just about to burst, outside the rotten snow is black and grimy and the skies are leaden. The best thing one can say is that it is now light when my alarm clock goes off in the morning and last week the first rays of late afternoon sunshine penetrated our yellow sitting room. On Sunday we take off for Central Asia for ten days, where we are sure to find blue skies and bright sun and flowering almond trees among the tombs of the great Khans (provided, of course, we make all the necessary air connections between Dushanbe and Tashkent and Samarkand and Bukhara and Khiva) and when we return we will find the *subbotniks* cleaning the streets and tidying up the parks in preparation for the birthday of great Lenin. And *then*, when we return from Bucharest, where we are planning to spend Easter with our Ambassador to Romania Peter Roberts and his wife, we might actually find some buds on the trees. My next letter will describe our trip East, which we are looking forward to very much indeed, and then there will only be time for one more letter before we return to Canada on April 30.

Since I last wrote we have celebrated International Women's Day and had a lovely long weekend at Zavidova. Mrs. Brezhnev's party was just as enjoyable this year as last, in fact even more so although it didn't have the charm of novelty. It took place in the midst of all kinds of rumours so husbands expected their wives to come back with information as to which politburo wife was there and where she was standing with respect to Mrs. B. and all that kind of thing, but most of us are not Kremlinologists and don't know who is who anyway as they don't wear labels, so we just decided to relax and have a good time. Mrs. Brezhnev herself was the hostess this year and welcomed us with a short, dignified speech about women and peace wearing a cream-coloured lace polyester suit. Then we all fell onto the blinis and caviar and the strawberry sherbet. Mrs. Gromyko came and chatted to us and we had some photographs taken before she was whisked off to another group of ladies and in general there was more mixing than last year, although it is hard to get a conversation going when you really don't know who you are talking to. But, of course, when we danced it didn't matter at all who we were. Pam Evans (Australia) and I did a smashing tango together and got a round of applause!

This morning in our Soviet History group we were talking about literature and the arts in the 1920s and the tremendous burst of activity that followed immediately after the Revolution, when a brand new world was abuilding ... In the visual arts the real revolution had taken place long before 1917 and what was really new was the changed relationship between artists, society, and the state, which carried them forward for a while in a state of enthusiasm until their autonomy was lost to political considerations. In literature, too, change was not really radical. Among the great writers perhaps only Mayakovsky created a style that was fully in tune with the new epoch. But the theatre, apparently, was something else and, taking advantage of the support and encouragement initially offered it by the Bolshevik government, it had a great flowering in the early 1920s. It was a director's theatre and Meyerhold was possibly the most innovative and exciting of them all. Apparently Zakharov, the man who staged the play about Lenin I wrote about in my last letter, is considered to be a descendant of that great tradition and there are a couple of others whose work we have not yet seen. Obraztsov started his theatrical career in that astonishing period and as the decade drew to an end began to work with puppets. Work with children's theatre was a refuge for many in those days and his puppet theatre dates from 1931. One can only imagine what his work was like in the 1930s but he survived with his creativity intact and he is still producing new pieces for his puppet theatre that are lively and imaginative and very funny.

We had a very good weekend at Zavidova, three days, because Monday March 8 was the state holiday for women so that they could stay home from work and cook meals for their husbands, who could also stay home to help them celebrate! When we drove up on Friday evening it was mild and raining a little and we were afraid there would be no skiing but overnight the weather changed, it became cold again and a fine dusting of snow made the cross-country trails slippery if somewhat crusty. So we spent a lot of time outdoors, following the paths on the other side of the Shosha through the birch woods and skiing down along the Volga to the village with the blue church where we all went a year ago Christmas when some of you were here. It was Sunday and there was a service in process so we went in as quietly as we could to join the ninety-year-old ladies and the slightly unkempt priest who were chanting morning prayers. Like the priest, the church interior looked well lived-in, a little untidy but full of beautiful objects, icons in fine silver frames and carved wooden screens and stands, and the handsome, sombre embroidered cloths of Lent. The place was sacred so we stayed for a while, and then tiptoed out, as best we could in our cross-country boots. Then we visited the village store where we found friendly people but not much to buy except big glass jars of pickled vegetables, some dry cookies, eggs, and 115 loaves of fresh black bread that had just been delivered. So we bought one for lunch and set off back up the river, past all the men huddled over the holes in the ice hoping to catch a few fresh fish for their supper and fortifying themselves from time to time from a shared bottle. Although it was not terribly cold the wind was blowing hard and next day long stretches of the river had been blown clear of snow so we skated for a couple of hours on the part of the river where it is widest before it turns south and where the skies seem vast and empty. This was a Nordic weekend that we shared with our colleagues from Norway and Denmark and Iceland and we plan to make a tradition of it because it was very relaxing and I guess that, on balance, it was healthy because although we did eat and drink rather a lot, we laughed even more.

LETTER NUMBER 35

April 4, 1982

We have just come back from a Sunday afternoon performance at the Bolshoi. We walked there through the April streets gritty with the dirt left behind by city snow retreating after its long winter siege. We had to pick our way carefully around piles of brick, loosely stacked lumber, lengths of metal tubing, and large concrete storm sewers waiting to be installed. I have never known such a city as Moscow for building and rebuilding, for repainting and repairing. As soon as construction is terminated there has to be a *remont*. The building where I have my hair done has Valentin in despair. He has worked there since it opened and it is now undergoing its third *remont* in seventeen years. He has stubbornly hung on to his corner of the second floor and his clients sit in lonely splendour under a single dryer surrounded by disconnected basins and dismantled shelves. He said it would take a year for the work to be completed and I would have laughed if we hadn't gone through this winter's *remont* in the Residence. The latest word is that they will complete the plumbing repairs (which involves the complete remodelling of our bathroom) when we are home in May. We have been promised auxiliary hot-water heaters to cope with the annual city hot-water pipe cleaning, which takes six weeks, and also screens throughout the Residence to keep out the innumerable summer flies. Well, at least they have stopped tearing down all the other buildings as they were doing some years ago. I would much rather continue to put up with untidy piles of building materials for reconstruction and repair than contemplate row upon row of Soviet Modern in the Old Arbat!

Anyway, at the Bolshoi we have just found that same uneasy juxtaposition of enchantment and propaganda that makes this country so fascinating and yet so disturbing, and which we met at every turn during our recent trip to Soviet Central Asia. The program at the Bolshoi was made up of two one-act ballets. The first was an inept fable featuring a young man who, on being released from prison, tries to turn his back on his wicked past as a city hooligan. The love of mother and collective farm worker (female) cannot preserve him from being done in by his former evil companions but nevertheless his soul goes off with some dancing birch trees and somehow turns into the spirit of Soviet agriculture. The other was a magical performance of *The Wooden Prince*, by Béla Bartók, staged with great imagination and superbly danced, and with no "overt" message at all. Except to those levels of the soul where true art goes. In Samarkand and Bukhara and Khiva we constantly encountered the same mix of authenticity and beauty with pretension and misdirection. Perhaps writing about the trip will help me sort out one from the other. I'll start with a bit of narrative.

We arrived in Dushanbe, the capital of Tajikistan, on the first day of spring. Our flight from Moscow brought us over the Aral Sea, still partly frozen, and long stretches of the KyZyl Kum, the red sand desert that makes up so much of Central Asia. Two days before we left we were told that we couldn't be received in Tashkent on the day that Geoffrey had asked for meetings and would we mind changing our plans? We would understand when we read the papers. Well, we were going to Dushanbe first anyway and didn't mind rerouting ourselves to go to Samarkand next, especially not Ron Halpin who was with us and who would have missed it otherwise. And of course, when we read that Mr. Brezhnev was going to Tashkent to present Uzbekistan with the Order of Lenin for its contributions to Soviet agriculture we had no trouble admitting that he took precedence over a Canadian ambassador! And the people in Tajikistan were extremely hospitable. Although a day of heavy rain had wiped out the street dances with which they traditionally celebrate the spring festival, a number of local people came to the hotel in the evening and danced with much energy to the orchestra in the dining room, many of whose pieces reminded us of Hindu film music. The Tajiks are a good-looking people, of Persian rather than Turkic stock like the other native peoples of Central Asia, and they speak a language very close to Farsi. For how many of them Islam is a religion rather than just a part of their cultural background it is impossible to know. But it is important and we sensed a good deal of pride and a certain amount of confidence among the people, who reminded me of the Georgians with their free and easy manners.

When we got up on the second day of spring, the sunshine had returned with some welcome warmth. We enjoyed the sight of the green willows and the early flowering almonds and then, when we turned the corner of the hotel, the sudden astonishing sight of the snow-covered mountains. Maybe the Tajiks are the way they are because they are a mountain people. And what mountains! Ninety-three percent of the territory of Tajikistan is mountainous and among those mountains, in the Pamirs, are some of the highest in the world. The highest is Mt. Lenin (of course) and the next is Mt. Communism (which used to be Mt. Stalin). We had some fun speculating about other towering ideologies but in fact the very high mountains are hundreds of kilometres from Dushanbe. Of course they would be wonderful to see but after a winter on the level plains of Moscow we found the foothills surrounding the city exciting enough. We took a lovely drive into them on the first afternoon of our stay, to visit the dam at Nurek, the highest earth-filled dam in the world, or so we were told. I'm not too keen about turbines and generators and millions of this and trillions of that, but I'm fascinated by the enthusiasm that building dams seems to create in those involved in the process, so that they go on from one to another as they are completed, and it looks as if the Soviet Union will be building dams for a while yet.

Before we went to Nurek we called on the President of the Council of Ministers and the Foreign Minister, and the next day we had a session with the Mayor of Dushanbe. These visits, together with a trip to the Exhibition of Economic Achievements (fifteen varieties of cotton plants and some new cotton-picking machines) and the local historical museum, gave us some feel for the past, present, and future of this republic. It has a very ancient past. The gap-toothed but knowledgeable guide at the museum rushed us from one dusty display window of stone-age implements to another. There are coins from the passage of Alexander and some Buddhist remains from the sixth century, but the Tadjik nation only began to emerge in the ninth century within the Persian empire of the Samanids. It was devastated by Genghis Khan and later by Tamerlane and subsequently became part of the Emirate of Bukhara until 1917. When the Bolsheviks inherited the Russian Empire all of what is now known as Central Asia was called Turkestan. When order was more or less restored after the Civil War the area was divided into five separate republics ostensibly on cultural and linguistic grounds. I haven't been able to find out why the borders were drawn the way they were—there are few natural boundaries between the different republics. Nor was there at the time of the Revolution a real state (like Georgia, for example) to which independence might have been given, so to speak, partly because the Emirates had spent most of the nineteenth century quarrelling among themselves while Tsarist Russia was gradually annexing their territory bit by bit and sending in large numbers of Russians to colonize.

Yet now Tajikistan seems quite a distinct entity in spite of the wholesale imposition of Russian institutions, from the kindergarten (the one we visited in Nurek had blonde Russian-made dolls sitting in exactly the same spot as I have found them in every other *detsky sad* I have visited from Moldavia to Siberia) to the state farm to the

Communist Party and the State Supreme Soviet. The Tadjik people continue to wear traditional dress and hang on to their grape arbours. The little girls have their dark hair braided in twelve different plaits and women are dressed in brilliant multicoloured silk. And the birth rate is rising and rising. Our Tadjik interpreter blushed when the Mayor spoke to us enthusiastically about the passionate nature of Tadjik men and women and she would only translate that the population was growing rapidly. In 1917 Dushanbe had forty or so mud huts and the Mayor showed us photographs of what it looked like then. Now it has 500,000 people and expects to have 800,000 by the turn of the century, and by then Uzbekistan will have thirty million, most of whom will be non-Slavs. I think it used to be called *la revanche du berceau* ... The afternoon we left we had lunch with the Foreign Minister, who was very expansive and quoted Omar Khayyám to us in Tadjik and presented Geoffrey with a coat of many colours, which he wore while he made his reply to the last and most important of the many toasts to everybody's health and children and real or hoped-for grandchildren and Canadian-Tadjik relations and international peace and a better future for all the world.

The flight from Dushanbe to Samarkand was extraordinary. Although the two cities are only 400 km apart they are separated by the Hissar Mountains and as we flew northwest over them I couldn't take my eyes off the snowy peaks fired by the setting sun fading slowly into the deep blue sky. So we arrived in Samarkand as if on a magic carpet. However, the enchantment didn't last long after we checked into the Intourist hotel, even though we found some high school students from Selkirk, Manitoba in the next room giddy on their first bottle of Russian champansky! I had very mixed feelings about Samarkand. It is hard not to be stirred by the very thought of this ancient city on the old silk route, which, as Macaranda, had already existed for centuries when Alexander captured it in 329 BC and married his Bactrian princess, Roxane. There are some remains from this period and some, too, from the succeeding centuries when Samarkand was ruled by Turks, then Arabs, then the Persian Samanids, and then the Turks again. But most of the city was destroyed under the first onslaught of the Mongols in 1220. In 1369, however, Tamerlane made Samarkand his capital and then its great period began, lasting until the death by assassination of his astronomer grandson, Ulug Beg, in 1449. Three centuries later the Jantar Mantar was built in New Delhi on the design Ulug Beg drew up to build his observatory in Samarkand; this was the first monument we saw when we started our sightseeing tour. Although only a part of the great sextant is left, the site is on a hill from which we could look back through the clear spring air to the city with its blue domes and the snow-covered mountains beyond.

So far it was all very romantic and our next stop was best of all, the Shakhi-Zinda, a group of tombs built on either side of a narrow cobbled cul-du-sac and reached by climbing a long flight of steps and passing through a stone arch. Most of the mausoleums were built by Tamerlane for members of his family and companions in arms but the place has sacred qualities because it contains the tomb of Kussam ibn Abbas, Mohammed's nephew, who is believed to have brought Islam to Samarkand. And we could feel that it is still a holy place. Our guide had to admit that many believers came here every day. We could see that for ourselves—old men in their turbans and their long blue-striped coats matching the incredible blues of dome and tile, and the women and children in their brilliant silk dresses loose over multicoloured trousers, heads partly covered in shawls tinselled with gold and silver thread. And they left coins at the tomb of Kassam and bowed low and went their way. There were many busloads of people, schoolchildren from Turkmenia and Tajiks from the South, and the colour was wonderful, crimson and yellow and orange against the blue, green, white, and garnet tiles, rich and satisfying. And then we went to the market, where I could have stayed for hours until everything was sold and the light faded out. Fruits and vegetables such as I haven't seen for months and all kinds of fancy breads and rows of turbaned old men sitting on the ground with little cotton sacks set out in front of them filled with all the spices of the Indies! This is where the commercial life of Samarkand really takes place and not in the dreary state shops, and I took comfort in the sight.

But after that we went to see the great Mosque of Bibi Khanym, which is in the process of total restoration and is losing its authenticity with each newly laid brick. I say this because the famous buildings of the Registan (the fifteenth- to seventeenth-century

Medressahs) surrounding Central Square have been restored to the letter and the spirit has completely fled. It's unnerving to stand in the middle of dead beauty. Luckily this has not happened to the Gur-Emir, which, although restored on the inside in 1969, still contains the tomb of Tamerlane and you *know* he is there. It has a lovely ribbed dome covered with blue tiles and when I went back to visit it in the evening the courtyard was full of children playing and there were old men drinking tea. In 1500 Samarkand fell to the Uzbeks, who beat off Babur in 1511, sending him southwards to establish the Mughul Empire in India, *faute de mieux*! But in the middle of the sixteenth century power shifted to Bukhara and the beautiful gardens of Tamerlane were abandoned and the buildings pillaged by nomadic tribes. The Russians under General Kaufman came in 1868 and a new town was built like an Indian cantonment, and then came the Revolution and industrialization. Samarkand is a big, important city now but I felt little reconciliation there between past and present.

Bukhara is different. Perhaps because it is smaller and because the life of the people is still taking place in and around the ancient monuments. Besides, many of those monuments were civil structures and the caravanserai and covered markets are still being used in one way or another, and even one of the Medressahs serves its original purpose as a Moslem religious school, the only one in the USSR. We arrived in Bukhara after a very early flight from Samarkand, so early that Geoffrey had no water for his shower and had to carry our suitcase down nine flights of stairs because the elevators hadn't been started up yet for the day. The weather was fine when we arrived although the wind blew and it was very dusty as we walked through the narrow streets of the old town between rows of adobe houses where grape arbours will soon provide shade from the burning sun and flowers will bloom on the flat roofs.

Bukhara is built in an oasis like Khiva to the north and these places in the middle of the deserts of Central Asia have almost certainly been inhabited since early times, though as a city Bukhara is probably not as old as Samarkand and did not enjoy any real power and prestige until it became the capital of the Persian Samanids in 892. From that period dates the most beautiful monument in the city, the mausoleum of Ismail Samani, the founder of the Samanid dynasty. Built in 907, this is the second-oldest surviving funerary monument in all of Islam and the prototype of those tombs we used to see scattered throughout New Delhi and elsewhere in Northern India. And it is in remarkable condition, saved from the ravages of Genghis Khan because it was, and remained for a long time, partly buried in sand. Cube-shaped, surmounted by a hemispherical dome, an arched entrance in each side, it is made of honey-coloured brick so skilfully laid that the light is in continual play on its various surfaces and it almost breathes with a spirit of harmony and grace. One other structure in the city was also spared by Genghis Khan, either because he had some aesthetic sense or more likely because he was too super-stitious to destroy such a remarkable tower. This is the Kalyan Minaret (1127), 47 metres high, a building of great harmony and sim-plicity built of the same warm baked brick as the Samanid Mausoleum. Alas, it became known later as the tower of death because nasty Emirs of decadent times regularly had people thrown off the top. And in 1843, one of the nastiest of them all had two British officers, who had come to him to offer British assistance against the Russians, thrown into a pit with snakes and scorpions to make them become Muslims. They refused and died, but an Anglican clergyman who rode alone to Bukhara on a pony over the desert to obtain news of them survived because the Emir burst into laughter at the sight of him arriving in his presence in full canonicals and a stove-pipe hat! Most of the rest of the interesting buildings in Bukhara date from the second period of its prosperity, in the sixteenth and seventeenth cen-turies under an Uzbek dynasty, the Shaibanids (not to be confused with Persian Samanids, if possible!).

We spent a happy day wandering in a Muslim world of blue domes and cupolas and minarets and great archways decorated with beautiful tiles, guided for part of the time by a young woman who was half-Korean, newly married, and who liked being teased by Geoffrey. It was 20 degrees centigrade as we walked through the mar-ket in the late afternoon but in the middle of the night we were woken up by the shrill voice of our floor-lady talking on the tele-phone outside our door and, finding my feet cold, I had to get up to cover myself with my coat before I could get back to sleep. And in the morning when we looked out the window the ground was covered with snow and it was blowing in all directions! Snow in Bukhara at the end of March is absolutely unheard of and tremendous concern was expressed to us later in Tashkent about the distressing effect of such weather on the bees, who were too groggy to go about their business of pollinating the early fruit trees. And indeed it was almost impossible on this day to tell the difference between the flowering apricot trees we had admired the day before and the "cherries hung with snow ... " In Tashkent we were also told that the fault lay in the stars—or rather in the unusual alignment of planets that had just taken place. Although we were further informed that the Institute in Moscow that looks after such matters was reassuring everyone that the effects of the alignment were not too serious and would pass away in a year or so. But in Bukhara we had a cold, damp morning. The airport was closed and we kept ourselves warm while waiting with some cheerful Norwegian colleagues and some Irish coffee.

The airport opened suddenly and we were flung into a bus with a Finnish tour on their way to Tashkent, thus confusing the Protocol people who were trying to keep track of us, because while they went to Tashkent we flew off over the desert to Urgench, 1,000 km from the capital. Urgench is a long way from everywhere except the cotton fields and Khiva, the last of the ancient cities on our route. Urgench has no particular distinction except a fascinating Sunday market, which we visited on our last day along with thousands of country people who had come there by foot or bus or donkey cart from who knows how far away or from what distant past, and the most comfortable, cheerful, unpretentious hotel we have stayed at anywhere in the Soviet Union. Khiva, about 30 km away, is not as ancient as Samarkand and Bukhara and in fact it enjoyed its greatest success in the nineteenth century as a centre of the slave trade. And its monuments have no singular beauty, being derivative in style from the older cities. Yet the whole ensemble has a peculiar charm and I wouldn't have missed it for the world. It has been made into a museum town and apparently an effort was made to move people outside the walls into nice new apartment blocks. We were told we would find it dead but it isn't. People have refused to move away and we could see them crossing back and forth across the cobbled streets carrying rings of bread and bags of oranges. Yet any building that was modern has been knocked down. We're back in the nineteenth century at the very latest. And the day we were there, there were many colourful visitors from other parts of Central Asia, including hundreds of children on school holiday, the boys looking just like all those little urchins in the Delhi streets with their dark hair and mischievous black eyes. The only reason they weren't asking for *Baksheesh* was because they were slightly better off and preferred bubble gum. We saw a camel in the courtyard of one of the mosques who looked so very much in place that we were disappointed to hear from our guide that he was the only one around. He was patiently getting down and up again with another load of children on his back to be photographed. Life is infinitely better for these children now than in the heyday of Khiva, of that there can't be the slightest doubt. But what of the future?

We looked at the future the next day when we *finally* arrived in Tashkent. We shared our hotel with delegates to the Uzbekistan Congress of Young Komsomol. They were all well-behaved and serious but few of them looked Slavic. The sight of the city of Tashkent, which is in fact a handsome, modern city, should convince them of the virtues of being one of the Soviet republics but as they grow older and more experienced and become aware of a wider world, which will happen someday because Tashkent is beginning to see itself as an international city with links to Southeast Asia, their nationalistic feelings may take on new dimensions. The word "Uzbek," so we are told, means "he who commands himself."

We didn't do much sightseeing because we were primarily there to make official calls. And the weather was not pleasant. It had snowed and was melting into mud and slush. There's not much of an old town. There never was anything of much distinction there. It only became a town of importance after the Russian conquest in 1865. Then settlers came into it from all over the Empire and the city grew up like colonial cities in India, with the native population on one side in narrow, crowded lanes and houses of beaten earth and the Russians on the other with the railway station, gardens, and wide avenues. At the time of the Revolution, which was essentially a Russian matter, Tashkent became first the capital of all Turkestan and eventually, in 1924, when Turkestan was divided up, the capital of the Uzbek Soviet

Socialist Republic. Then the old Uzbek town began to disappear and Tashkent became a twentieth-century city, a process completed by the earthquake of 1966, which destroyed many of the remaining old quarters. Now it is a city of nearly two million inhabitants full of modern apartment blocks, fine parks, and impressive new buildings, many of which are attractive and unusual, having been designed by local architects and given a slightly oriental flavour.

Our official visits were of considerable interest as they always are, although we had the feeling that everyone was still preoccupied by Mr. Brezhnev's visit, which had lasted a day longer than expected and had perhaps worn him out. Besides, with so much invested in agriculture, they were worried about the weather. So our reception, while extremely cordial, was cast in a lower key than it had been in Dushanbe. The Mayor had recently passed through Canada on his way to Seattle, Tashkent's twin city. The Deputy Foreign Minister who gave us lunch had known Mr. Pearson in the old days at the U.N. We have to admit there is not much content (beyond courtesy) to Canadian–Uzbek relations! The Chairman of the Council of Ministers was in Samarkand inspecting snow damage so we were received by one of the Vice-Chairmen, who talked to us about agriculture, irrigation, and financing. Everybody told us to come back in September when we could admire the cotton crop, the "white gold" of Uzbekistan, and watch their unique cotton-picking machines. The birthrate was not considered a problem by anyone. Although the Government officials we called on (Geoffrey does not consider it appropriate to call on the Party) were not young, they impressed me as being proud, long-time participants in a nation-building process.

(April 20)

It is nearly three weeks since I started to write this account and I have had time to reflect. During our travels in Central Asia many things upset me, not the least of which was the travelling itself. I've decided that I prefer to be coddled a little when I'm in the air and it certainly makes me cross to find myself in accommodation that in no way justifies the amount we have to pay for it! So many things I saw disappointed me, especially the restoration work, both visually and by implication. Also I have to say that some of the statements we heard and attitudes we encountered were really disturbing. However, after pondering it all I find, a little to my surprise, that I have acquired a kind of confidence about the future of Soviet Central Asia. The Soviet Union has certainly contributed a great deal to its recent development. It's just possible to imagine the state it would be in if the Emirates were still fighting among themselves. Economic development, the emancipation of women, universal literacy, and extensive education are goals toward which the Central Asian republics have been helped to make giant strides. But now I think the splendour of their ancient past may begin to have an unanticipated effect. You can't play games around the tomb of Tamerlane when you are a small Uzbek child and not begin to think about what Uzbek means. And when you live in a part of the world over which the winds of history have blown for thousands of years, bringing devastation and conquest, yes, but also periods of great power and civilization, you are bound to have certain expectations and surely you have the knowledge that time is on your side.

LETTER NUMBER 36

June 1, 1982

We have been back for two weeks, the same length of time we were in Canada. We have been extremely busy and the time has flown, faster than it did in Canada, because although we were very busy there it was a different kind of busyness, richer and more intense, and it filled the hours rather than annihilated them, making the time pass much more slowly. Here so much of my time is involved in the details of administering the Residence, planning and organizing lunches and dinners and receptions, running to the gastronome for more wine or more cream or what-have-you that the days vanish but they don't leave anything behind. However, my time at home was very restorative, we are able to look forward to our return in August, and in the meantime there are many interesting and delightful things happening to us, not the least of which is the presence of Patricia and Frances (who I keep introducing as a niece because it seems much easier than saying she is my husband's first cousin once removed, particularly in Russian). Having the young around is a great treat. They both seem to be enjoying themselves and are fresh for almost any adventure now that they have begun to learn their way around the Metro system. They are good company for each other and seem to share a fair number of interests, including the taste for reading late and sleeping till mid-morning. I'm sending them off to *The Seagull* tomorrow at the Moscow Arts Theatre confident that they will both appreciate what it is to see a fine production of Chekhov in his own language by the company who staged the play in the first place. These are the last days when the Moscow theatres are open before the summer break so we are trying to get as much in as possible.

Many people are complaining because it isn't warm enough for them but I find the cool, breezy weather refreshing. It's great for sight-seeing and it retarded the tulips so that they only came into full bloom after our return and have lasted a long while, including a lovely bowl of double yellow ones that are brightening up our green and yellow sitting room. The garden is one of my preoccupations at the moment. Elaine Mathys and I are going out tomorrow to the Central Market and the Botanical Gardens to buy annuals and perennials. We've pulled down much of the old vine and replanted the lawn and are ready to add colour to replace the tulips as they die off. The lilacs are in full bloom and the chestnut is just past its prime. UPDK has almost completed installation of a very handsome lattice fence to separate the garden from the parking area, which they promised us a year ago, and altogether the view from my bedroom window as I type this has improved immeasurably. We have finally taken the decision to hold a national day reception, the first this Embassy has held since 1967, and we are counting on the garden to be an attractive place for all the distinguished guests. But more of that later.

So what have we been doing since we came back? Our flight was long but uncomplicated and much smoother than on the way out. So we really had more trouble during the first few days with time change than with fatigue. But we didn't have enough time to relax and integrate all the experiences we had had at home. I regret that because I think it is important to ponder and reflect on significant events or simply to enjoy the pleasure, in retrospect, of having been able to spend time with people you really care about. However, we found the bathroom still incomplete, various other household problems, much for the Ambassador to attend to, and a stack of invitations. By Saturday we had houseguests in addition to the girls who were settling in. One of my colleagues from the Commission for the Year of the Child, Madeleine Dubuc, arrived with Lily Tasso, a journalist from *La Presse*, after attending an international conference of female journalists in Hungary. They stayed until Thursday. We went to the circus and the ballet, did the usual tourist sights, and took a tour of the Metro. But from my point of view the most interesting opportunity their visit offered me was the chance to visit the editorial offices of the magazine *Soviet Woman* and meet with some representatives of the Soviet Women's Committee. The editor of the English-language version of *Soviet Woman* had just returned from a visit to Canada where she spoke to a meeting of the Congress of Canadian Women, an organization of which I must confess I have never heard, and her comments were more interesting than she realized. The editor of the French-language version had been to Lily and Madeleine's conference as an observer and Lily, who has just been elected president and who is both lively and shrewd, is determined to procure some Soviet involvement in her organization but since the next meeting will take place in Israel she doesn't anticipate early success. Still, our meeting with these women and their colleagues in their rather shabby but busy offices was friendly and informal and we all enjoyed ourselves in an easy and natural (on the whole) manner.

However, our visit to the Women's Committee was another affair entirely. It was very formal and we were exposed to a long lecture on the history of the emancipation of women in the USSR since 1917 that had all of us jiggling on our chairs in impatience, including some of the Soviet women, I was relieved to observe. Talk about being co-opted by the Establishment! I managed to evoke some real discussion for a few minutes when I asked them what plans the Committee had to bring about some change to the totally masculine face the Soviet Union presents to the world; no woman's image to be found among the portraits of the Politburo members that line the important streets along which foreigners pass at various times of the year; no dress to be seen along with the sober-suits in all the photographs of power; no lady ambassadors since the notorious Mme Kollontai, whom Lenin sent off to Sweden with her wild ideas about free love and other improper thoughts. They had to agree that there was a problem but the dialogue soon became a monologue again about women in the unions and state-sponsored childcare. We were all given stacks of literature to read, which I will look at and then I'll try to return on a more casual basis for further contact. Because the Committee has unquestionably made a real contribution to the status of women in the USSR and is genuinely concerned with the situation of children and I'd like to know more about it.

Lily and Madeleine joined most of the Embassy on May 24 for a Victoria Day barbecue in the garden and so did Anita Cadieux and Gaby Léger, the widow of our former Governor General, Jules Léger, who had arrived in Moscow with Anita's son François that morning. They stayed at the National Hotel but we were able to see a certain amount of them during the rest of their stay. It was a pleasure to see both of them. There were many conversations about their husbands and about old times in the Department. We were particularly pleased to be able to spend some time with Mme Léger, who seemed in good form and with whom Geoffrey was able to talk for a long time. We had a lunch for them one day which I think they enjoyed but they turned down the dinner party we had last Friday because they were tired after all their sightseeing and not anxious to meet a lot of new people. Which was easy to understand. It turned out to be a very good party, though. One of the Pushkin students sang Canadian folk songs for us and since she has a lovely voice and a charming presence she was a great success among our ambassadorial colleagues, and then I solved protocol by having everyone draw lots as to where they would sit at the small tables I had set about and although I assured them there would be the same number of men and women at each table the element of chance adds a certain spice. And so did the young, of whom there were several present. Tomorrow we have a large cocktail party for some Canadians who are here for two-week sport-training sessions, and then next week Senator Hazen Argue comes. In the meantime we watch Mr. Brezhnev on TV greeting the President of Austria (whom we got to meet, too) and the First

Secretary of Vietnam and the President of Czechoslovakia. So he's kept busy with formal occasions too! As well as Plenums and food problems and arms talks ... and who knows what else?

LETTER NUMBER 37

June 16, 1982

The weather has been very strange lately. At the beginning of last week it turned very cold. None of the plants that Elaine and I and the girls had put in has shown any sign of growth although they still appear to be alive. There has been practically no sun and we are becoming increasingly anxious that the garden will look sad and dreary for our national day reception. However there are still two weeks to go and perhaps everything will change. It did warm up a bit yesterday but today it is very windy and the air is full of pollen from the poplar trees. The Rands, who are staying with us at the moment, have gone down with Frances to stand in line for Lenin's tomb, carrying umbrellas, and handkerchiefs in case they sneeze. Patricia and I decided to write letters since the bag will be closing this afternoon. This letter will be shorter than usual, not because I have little to recount, quite the contrary, but because we have been so busy during the last two weeks that I have hardly had time to think and I really need both time and a little space to collect my thoughts.

Before the weather turned cold we had one perfect June day. Luckily it was the day chosen by the Canadian Club and some of our departing staff to hold the annual Canadian boat trip. We missed it last year because we were in Canada but we won't again if we can help it. A river steamer was rented for the evening and we set off a little after five (a bit late because someone had forgotten the gin and a dash had to be made back to town to fetch it) from the docks off Leningradsky Prospect. Because it wasn't just one of the little tour boats that ply up and down the Moscow River through the centre of the city but a real passenger boat with cabins and a huge deck. All the staff were invited including the Soviets, who probably enjoyed themselves more than the rest of us. They certainly danced the most! We went through the combination of river and canal system upstream from Moscow an hour and a half to the Bay of Joys. On the way we drank and ate and once there had an hour or so to stroll and get our feet wet in the water. Patricia and Fran would have swum if they'd brought their bathing suits, it was that warm and pleasant. We came back a different route through lovely countryside with little villages and everywhere great clumps of lilacs. I have never seen such lilacs as those in and around Moscow. They are everywhere and along with the chestnut trees in bloom fill the air with a wonderful scent. For three weeks we were able to cut great bowls of them from our garden for the Residence and they have only now come to an end. All the way back we danced on the deck. Around 10 o'clock the light began to fade but there was a full moon (or two or three depending on one's state) and everyone drifted off the boat when it docked at 11:00 in a very relaxed and happy mood. Most of them came back to the Embassy and the dancing went on in the Club for a long time but we went to sleep because the next morning we went up to Zavidova for a brief overnight stay. The weather began to change that night but the girls had a chance to row on the river and to lie in the sun during the day and I was very glad that Frances was able to see the quintessential Russian landscape of the Volga region.

We came back to Moscow Monday morning to prepare for the visit of Senator Argue. The Senator and his wife arrived that evening, rather tired after that long flight, and were rather quiet during their first two days. However, they revived as the week went on and by week's end, in spite of the very heavy program their Soviet hosts had prepared for them, they were enjoying themselves thoroughly. Mrs. Argue is an extremely nice woman and I enjoyed sightseeing and shopping with her in Moscow. However, neither of us went to Kiev with them and only Geoffrey met them in Leningrad because our good friends Pat and Calvin Rand had just arrived. He visited the port with them and saw Petrodvoretz and had a long, liquid official lunch and a jolly dinner in the Astoria Hotel, where he left them dancing at midnight in order to get some sleep. The next day they went on to Helsinki and he came back to play a soggy game of tennis with Calvin. He says he prefers Leningrad in the wintertime instead of during the white nights. The girls leave for Leningrad this evening,

where they will join up with François Cadieux (who has been studying there since September) and his brother (who has just arrived) for
four days of sightseeing, and the Rands will go on Saturday night to
be there for the summer solstice.

We have had a good time with Calvin and Pat Rand, whom we
got to know during our sessions at the Niagara Institute in Niagara-
on-the-Lake. Calvin is now the president of the American Academy
in Rome although he is based in New York. They came here from
Italy after two weeks there, and we took hours at the airport because
the two Italians in the customs line ahead of them had brought in
stacks of brand new blue jeans, as well as some interesting magazines
that the young customs official gazed at for a long time ... In view of
their interest in the theatre (Calvin is one of the founders of the Shaw
Festival) we took them to Gogol's *The Inspector-General* at the Satire
Theatre, which was a marvellous production, *Don Quixote* at the
Kremlin Palace of Congresses, in which Maximova and Vasiliev were
dancing for the last time so it was a real occasion with dozens of curtain calls and masses of flowers as well as some superb dancing, and
last night we went to see Turgenev's *A Month in the Country*, which
was much less successful. Geoffrey and the girls left after the first act
to walk home and Pat would have gone with them except she didn't
have the right shoes so she had to stick it out patiently with Calvin
and me. Actually, I rather liked it. It *is* long and wordy but I think it's
a very good play, both funny and tragic. Tomorrow we will go to
Vladimir and Suzdal for the day and on Friday we have arranged a
tour of those old parts of the Kremlin that are not open to the public.
We will also go to a midsummer dance at the British Embassy, which
should be fun as we assume they will be in a mood for celebrating the
birth of a royal prince (or princess).

LETTER NUMBER 38

June 29, 1982

Out of my bedroom window I am watching Commander Makin,
the sergeants, and the *dvorniks* raising the yellow waterproof tents we

have rented from Helsinki for our national day reception. It is pouring and they are doing their best not to get soaked while they straighten the poles and tighten the guy wires. We are feeling very apprehensive because it has been dark and cold and gloomy and wet almost continuously since I last wrote to you. Only two petunias are in bloom and the few peonies that struggled into the light of day are woebegone and bedraggled. Nobody seems to be refusing our invitation and we are likely to have at least five hundred guests on Thursday. If it rains hard they will all have to be inside and I hate to think of the crush. Luckily most of the official guests will depart around 1:00 p.m. and the remaining Canadians and friends can relax and have a buffet lunch and get to meet Wayne Gretzky and his family and the film crew that has come to make a film about him visiting Moscow and practising hockey with Tretyak.

I hope the Rands will remember their trip with pleasure. Outside of Moscow the weather sometimes improves. By the time we reached Vladimir on our trip to the ancient Russian lands the sun appeared amid scudding clouds and we were able to fully appreciate the effect of the remarkable religious and mythological bas-reliefs on the twelfth-century white stone church of St. Demetrius. And inside the great Assumption Cathedral (also twelfth-century) the bright light from outside combined with the spotlights of workmen to give us an extraordinarily clear view of the frescoes of Andrei Rublyov, a vision of the Last Judgment from the early part of the fourteenth century of such beauty, at once so spiritual and so comforting, that we were dumbfounded. We drove on in silence to Suzdal and sat on a grassy bank and looked across the water meadows and the browsing cows at the fortifications of the old town, the blue domes and golden crosses and white-painted conical roofs of the *kremlin* and Suzdal's several monasteries. From inside Suzdal looks like a museum, which it is, but from where we sat the Soviet Union vanished and we were transported centuries back, before the founding of Moscow even, to the time of the princes and a world that was to be radically changed by the Tartars. When we visited the Great Kremlin Palace in Moscow next day we moved forward in time to the tsars. The fifteenth-century Palace of Facets, the sixteenth- and seventeenth-century Terem palace, and the nineteenth-century palace built for Nicholas I are all joined together and only the huge painting of Lenin addressing the Komsomol at the head of the long ceremonial flight of stairs and the Hammer and Sickle on the façade facing the river remind you that the great October Revolution has taken place and that we are living in a transformed society. And a formal dance at the British Embassy on the other side of the Moscow River that very evening, where we could stand out on the balcony and see the Great Palace and the golden domes lit up above us in the transparent night air, maintained the illusion of being in another time.

Of course, the morning news on the BBC and the televised football games from Spain bring you right back to 1982. The news is good and bad. A royal prince is born. Railway strikes start and stop. Israel invades Lebanon and doesn't stop. Nuclear arms talks start and, we hope, continue. Canada marks forty years of diplomatic relations with the USSR. It is inconceivable that they will not go on into the foreseeable future. This country has a long history. It is very powerful. Who knows what will happen in the years to come, but Canadians are bound to be affected, one way or another. Suppose the Soviet Union stopped buying all that wheat? Mind you, with the weather the way it has been it doesn't look as if the harvest will be all that good this year either. But I don't know. We hope to go out to Siberia for a few days in the middle of July but of course I don't know what I am looking at when it comes to endless fields. So I have to rely on what the Western journalists say about Soviet agriculture, just like everyone else!

The Rands went off to Leningrad on the longest day of the year and we had a fairly quiet week. Quite a lot of people for lunch but uneventful evenings, with Geoffrey watching the World Cup. Among the people we had for lunch were the Canadian contestants in the Tchaikovsky competition, the Olympics of the musical world, as one of them told me. We had four participants and a judge, Stephen Staryk, for the violin section. Two of them have done quite well. A pianist of Korean descent named Ik Chou Mun and a cellist named Desmond Hoebig. Desmond has made it through to the final round and we went to hear Ik Chou play last Thursday in the second round. We thought he was excellent, playing a very demanding seventy-five-minute program ending with an exciting interpretation of a

Prokofiev concerto (they all play a lot of Russian compositions). However, he won't know till tomorrow whether he has advanced to the final round. The Russians take the competition very seriously. It happens every four years. We all remember the astonishing triumph of the American pianist Van Cliburn in 1958. The concert halls are full of eager young people and there is a lot of coverage both on radio and TV. It's kind of fun to be part of it even as a spectator. We've also had some cardiologists, here for a huge conference of cardiology, including Dr. Wilbur Keon of Ottawa with his wife, who came around for a drink. The evening they were here we watched the live broadcast of the space launch in which the French cosmonaut went up with two Soviets. I must say I found it very exciting and the Frenchman, who is extremely good-looking, added considerable flair to the event.

A curious phenomenon takes place in Moscow in mid-June when the poplars scatter their fluff. The tall, thin poplars that most of us know are more discreet but these fat trees cover the whole city in down so that it looks almost like snow. We missed it last year when we were home and I have never seen anything quite like it. Some Soviet planner wasn't an allergy-sufferer when he ordered them planted in parks and squares all over the city. And they don't really bother me but I felt like I was trudging through cotton batting as I made my way up Kropotkinskaya the other day to see the fantastic Munch exhibition at the Academy of Fine Arts. What a wonderful and unexpected gift! There was very little publicity but our Norwegian friends told us about it because it came from the major museums of Norway. Two hundred and fifteen works, oils, lithographs, etchings, woodcuts, drawings, displayed in several long, high-ceilinged rooms, a feast. Powerful, fascinating, disturbing, I love the large paintings, the landscapes, the bathers, the girls on the bridge ... Everyone else there was as absorbed as I was in the intricacies of his technique and the pull of his symbols. You never know what treasures you are going to come upon next in this great city. Or what you are going to miss.

July 12, 1982

Now let me tell you about National Days and hockey heroes. And about the weather. Why do I go on so about the weather? Presumably there are so many national days on or around July 1 because revolutions thrive under the summer sun. Still, when every reception you attend is cold and clammy you find yourself getting a bit obsessed about the climate! It didn't rain on Luxembourg on June 30 and I felt hopeful but a cloudburst in the evening made a marsh of our back lawn and the tent just made it worse. So first thing next morning we decided to have our reception indoors. Nikolai gathered up his friends, the drivers, and they moved out all the furniture they could. For 21 roubles Abramova from the Botanical Gardens sent us armfuls of gorgeous flowers, peonies and roses, lupines and carnations, and great branches of decorative greenery. Elaine and I and Victoria and Elena and others from the local staff filled all the vases we could put our hands on upstairs and down because although the official part of the reception for our diplomatic colleagues and Soviet guests was upstairs, we all came downstairs after they had gone and had a Canadian party in the Red Room with a cold buffet and more beer and less champagne and a colourful Happy Birthday Canada! cake baked by Robin Metz. Tamara and Zhenya produced toasted mushroom canapés and tiny meatballs and sausages and pizza. Pierre, one of the Italians who cook for the American Embassy, sent up cold canapés from the kitchen in the basement of the Canadian Club. Eight waiters from the Praga Restaurant manned the bars and passed the champagne along with our *dvorniks*, and the girls from our char staff carried the trays of food and washed glasses endlessly. Even Vera Petrovna, who retired a couple of months ago after cleaning the Embassy for nineteen years, came back with a bunch of flowers in one hand and immediately pitched right in to help. Nikolai supervised all the logistics very well indeed and everybody had plenty to eat and drink. In this country that really is the essence of hospitality.

How many people came? We are not sure. Well over three hundred, we guess. On the stroke of twelve they started flooding up the stairs, past Geoffrey and me and the others in the receiving line, on into the reception rooms. At 12:15 the "important guest" arrived, a vice-president of the Soviet Union. Vice-presidents come from all the republics in the Union and a different one is on duty each month to attend national days. This July is the turn of Turkmenia. Once he had come he went off with Geoffrey and other important guests to the room that is usually Geoffrey's study and I continued to shake hands. After one o'clock the tide receded back downstairs and we were left with the solid-core Canadians, a few hangers-on, and the Gretzky group. I'll get around to the Gretzky group in a minute but first a last comment about our National Day reception. Is it worth doing? After all, it is an enormous amount of work as well as considerable expense and took up a lot of my time as well as that of some of the Embassy officers during the preceding weeks. Mr. Ford hadn't given one for many years. But it was missed. In a country where the ceremonial occasion is an important means of communication much appreciated by the Russians as well as by many of our colleagues, and where a country that does not mark its national day is perceived as a nation somewhat lacking in self-esteem, such a reception as the one we offered holds unusual symbolic value. The fact that people claim to have enjoyed themselves as well is almost beside the point! Geoffrey's three-minute appearance on the national news in the evening with a few carefully chosen words completed the *Acte du Presence*, though one has to wonder how many viewers paid attention. Patricia remarked that they had forgotten to put makeup on his eyelids but otherwise he looked very distinguished.

And as for the Gretzky group, well, of course Wayne's presence along with Tretyak and another Russian player added a lot to the success of the party, for the Russians as well as for the Canadians. As Geoffrey said in his television comments, hockey is one of the things we have in common. Soon after the Gretzky group arrived in Moscow Geoffrey and I went out to the arena of the Soviet Army Team and watched the filming of Gretzky's three younger brothers playing hockey with a group of Soviet youngsters and under their helmets they were indistinguishable from one another except for the sweaters. Wayne's father, who is a really nice man, was teaching them all a few techniques. Wayne and Tretyak were also on the ice and Tretyak allowed the ten-year-old Gretzky to score against him without seeming to make it too easy. Cheers from the bystanders, who consisted of Wayne's mother and grandmother as well as his sister and his girlfriend and her mother. Add the producers and the filmmakers and some friends and the whole group added up to twenty-five! By the time we had them to lunch this past Monday, just before they left, they had dwindled to fifteen but they had managed to do and see a lot in spite of the continuing poor weather and I expect that the film, when it appears, will be very interesting about Moscow and the Soviets as well as the Great Gretzky and his clan. We liked him. He was easy and responsive and didn't seem to mind signing all those endless cards. I hadn't realized how blond he is and he looked very good at our reception in his white suit. Still, for those who prefer mature men, Tretyak is really something!

And the National Days continued. On July 2 in the pouring rain we went to Rwanda, who share July 1 with us but had postponed for a day on our behalf. And then of course there was the glorious fourth, which was held on the fifth, along with the Venezuelan National Day, in weather that was slightly improved. Last Friday we all crowded into the Mongolian Embassy but we will have to forgo the wines and cheeses with which the French embellish Bastille Day, as we will be in Siberia. The American reception was a real treat because we had hamburgers and ice cream cones in the garden and then all went inside Spaso House to hear Chick Corea and Gary Burton, who gave a superb jazz concert. They apparently had had a fantastic jam session with Soviet musicians a couple of days previously during a private concert at the House of Composers. Guests this time of the Ambassador and his wife, they want to come back. Let's hope they will.

PHOTO ESSAY

At the front door of the Embassy 23 Starokonyushenny Pereulok, Moscow, May 1981

The ambassador and his wife in the Embassy garden for Canada's National Day, July 1, 1982

Our children, Patricia, Anne, Michael and Katharine at Zavidova come, to visit, Christmas 1981

Hilary and my niece Annabel Mackenzie with me at Peter's Palace near Leningrad, May 1981

Katharine on the
Georgian Military
Highway
September, 1982

Anne in the pine
woods at Zavidova

Geoffrey in Red Square with Lenin and the "forefathers," Karl Marx and Friedrich Engels, May Day 1983

The last resting place of Nikita Khrushchev in Novodevichy cemetery, the black and white of post Stalin politics

The Bassein, the heated swimming pool where Geoffrey swam.
It was built on the foundation of a vast church destroyed by Stalin and
rebuilt in the 1990s

Geoffrey and Annabel at the grave of my hero,
the writer Anton Chekhov in Novodevichy cemetery, 1981

Tamara and Zhenya making a gingerbread house for our annual Christmas party

Part of our living room

*My sister-in-law
Dorothy Mackenzie,
Ilya our driver and
Victoria Ivanova, my
friend, interpreter and
social secretary on the
road to Leningrad,
September 1983*

*Ed and Nina Ryan on
the Lenin Hills after
their wedding,
September 9, 1982*

*Monique's daughter
Caroline in Leningrad
overlooking the Neva
Rivers and Battleship
Aurora,
August 1983*

*My closest friends
Monique Lussier and
our Katharine at
Zagorsk,
September 1982*

Ann and Dibby Robinson at Zavidova, March 1983

*Sam, John and Jane Legg with Patricia contemplating the grave of
Boris Pasternak, Peredelkino, July 1982*

Meeting between Mikhail Gorbachev and Canadian Parliamentarians,
Geoffrey, Minister of State for Economic and Regional Development
Donald Johnson, two MPs, Speaker of the House of Commons Jeanne
Sauvé, and Mikhail Gorbachev, August 1983

Justin Trudeau, Prime Minister Pierre E. Trudeau, Senator Hazen Argue,
Geoffrey and me, paying respects to the body of Leonid Brezhnev,
November 1982

Companion of Mme Gromyko, Inger Steenberger, wife of Danish Ambasssador, Margaret Keble, wife of UK Ambassador, Mme Andrey Gromyko, me, Cristina Angelides, wife of Cypriot Ambassador International Women's Day, March 1981

Prime Minister Pierre E. Trudeau with Justin Trudeau and Embassy children, November 1982

Newly accredited Ambassador to Mongolia accompanied by the chief of protocol, May 1981

My brother Michael Mackenzie at the foot of Peter the Great in Leningrad, March 1983

*Wayne Gretsky, Vladimir Tretyak with Geoffrey and me at the
Soviet Army Hockey Rink, June 1982*

*Canadian Minister of Agriculture Eugene Whelan tells a funny story with
the interpreter behind him and Mme Mesyats, the wife of the Soviet
Minister of Agriculture beside him, September 1981*

Rostov Velikhy

The Gur Emir in Samarkand, The Tomb of Tamurlane

Young children at the end of their 30 km pony race on Mongolia's National Day, July 1983

The Red Army comes to Mongolia

Big brother helps Mongolia modernize (with a view of Ulan Bator)

Michael, their grandson, in front of St. Basil's in Red Square, 1982

Lester B. and Maryon Pearson in the Kremlin in front of the Tsar's Bell in 1954. (He was the first NATO foreign minister to visit the Soviet Union after the fall of the Soviet Union.)

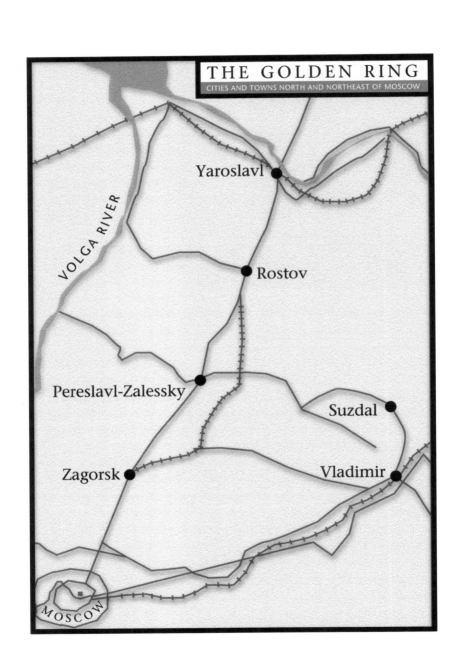

THE GOLDEN RING
CITIES AND TOWNS NORTH AND NORTHEAST OF MOSCOW

VOLGA RIVER

Yaroslavl

Rostov

Pereslavl-Zalessky

Suzdal

Zagorsk

Vladimir

MOSCOW

PART III

LETTER NUMBER 40

September 14, 1982

Today we have no one to lunch. Katharine and Monique have gone to Kiev for two days and our parliamentary visitors have departed the country with their companions. I *should* be able to sit down at the typewriter for as long as it takes me to write you. I don't expect any interruptions but then one never knows. What a busy time we have had since our return! After such a good home leave I must confess that we left Canada again with reluctance. And alas, the weather has been chilly here ever since we came back, although no leaves have fallen and the garden really looks quite nice. But summer does not linger long around Moscow. In fact, those of our acquaintances who stayed in town said it wasn't much of a summer at the best of times. So people left. Nikolai bundled his family into his Moskvich and drove south. The first time he stopped to get gas he met some Muscovites with dark faces and took their advice to go to the Sea of Azov, where he had a wonderful time. That's where Zhenya went as well, with her sister. She swam every day and acquired that lovely golden tan that you only get by the salt sea. Tamara and Ilya stayed in the Moscow region and relaxed at their dachas. At least Tamara did. Ilya, who now sports a handsome moustache, must have had to work very hard if he was able to accomplish all the improvements he has been telling me about. He wanted to know all about the construction of our "dacha" in Canada and emitted little sighs of envy when I described some of the material we have used at Burnett, although he *has* been able to obtain some double-glazed Finnish glass for his living-room windows. Sometimes I'm amazed that we manage to discuss so many technical questions as we drive back and forth from the gastronome, given my limited Russian and his non-existent English, but after a while one does learn to communicate pretty well. In the Residence now we are having long conversations about the mice in the kitchen, who seem to have made themselves at home during our absence. UPDK has promised to send us their exterminating lady but meanwhile Tamara has become quite an expert and we have trapped seven at the latest count.

Anyway, Ilya is now driving the car down to Georgia where he will meet Geoffrey, Katharine, and me on Thursday at the unpronounceable town of Ordzhonikidze. Then we will drive the full length of the Georgian Military Highway, 211 km through the greater Caucasus Mountains to Tbilisi. Geoffrey is not too sure about this venture but the glorious descriptions of this route by Pushkin and Lermontov and, later, Tolstoy as a young cavalry officer have convinced me that we must travel it if we are going to understand the relationship of Russia to the lands of the Caucasus. We will be gone for six days, three in Georgia and three in Armenia. Then we'll fly back from Yerevan leaving Ilya to come back up along the Black Sea coast to Rostov-on-Don and thence north again to Moscow, loaded with fruit and vegetables and wine. The car, that is, not Ilya! Soviet regulations are so strict about driving and drinking that none of the Embassy drivers will take even so much as a sip of wine when they are driving us about the country.

Now let me tell you about what has been happening since we got back. We launched straight into dinners and lunches and national days and the formal farewell to the British Ambassador. There were the new people who had arrived at the Embassy during August to greet, as well as some Canadian visitors. Dr. Frank Sommers (who is chairman of the Canadian group of "Physicians for Social Responsibility" and an intelligent and sensible man) and Bill Epstein came on to Moscow after the Pugwash Conference in Warsaw with interesting things to tell us. And of course we have had our parliamentarians (of whom more later), as well as Monique Lussier, one of our dearest and oldest friends, who arrived September 7 to our great pleasure and enjoyment. And we have had a bridegroom!

The bridegroom was Ed Ryan, a lawyer who now works with Imperial Oil in Toronto and who married a Russian girl here last Thursday. He met her last year on the steps of the Bolshoi when he

was here for the ballet competition as a member of the Board of the
National Ballet School. We had them for lunch on the day before the
wedding along with Ellie Tesher, who is a good friend of Ed's and
was able to persuade *The Toronto Star* to send her to cover the wedding. Some of you may have read her account last Saturday but I do
have my own version. We liked Ed's fiancée, Nina, very much
indeed. She is both natural and determined, qualities she will need in
the months to come because her situation is not an easy one. She
loves this country and has very strong ties to it through her family
and friends. And she feels passionately about Russian language and
culture, although she speaks excellent English. She had a good job
and was a member of the Communist Party until she had to resign
from both in order to marry a foreigner. Now she has applied for an
exit visa. She is thinking of leaving simply because she fell in love
and wants to live with her husband, not because she wants to desert
her country. She wants to be able to come back to visit. Of course.
Why not? Well why not, indeed. It is clear she will require all the
resources of her strength of character, her intelligence, and her grace
to surmount the obstacles in front of her.

The wedding itself was moving. She is so much in love with him
and he is so besotted with her that everything was transformed and
I felt privileged in my romantic soul to be part of it. Geoffrey was
busy with the parliamentarians so I went with Jacques Drapeau (our
consular officer) who acted as Ed's witness. We picked up Ellie and
met the photographer she had engaged outside the wedding palace
near Prospect Mira where, on Thursdays, foreigners are married. It is
a nineteenth-century mansion, pastel green and decorated with a
frieze of white stucco. Ed and Nina soon arrived in an undecorated
Volga. Ellie wanted all the new wedding traditions but Nina is a
woman of taste and there are limits ... She was wearing a Maple Leaf
tartan kilt and white flannel blazer that Ed had brought her. It was
not what I had expected but she had been married before and, with
her armful of roses, she really looked lovely. Inside the "palace" we
mounted a fine staircase with an art deco wooden balustrade and
were greeted by a pretty girl in a white shawl who, full of smiles and
best wishes, directed Ed and Nina to the room where their documents had to be shown and innumerable papers signed. The fact that

their file could not be found for a few minutes created a slight tension, which increased slowly as we waited in the parlour (I can think of no other word) for the actual wedding to begin. Two of Nina's friends had come and with Ellie and myself and Jacques and the bride and groom that was all the bridal party.

At long last the pretty girl came and lined us up in proper order. She wished Ed and Nina much happiness and then flung open the doors of the marriage hall, which we all entered to the strains of the Wedding March from *Lohengrin* played by a string quartet augmented by a harp placed in one corner of a large, handsome room with fine proportions and a large window overlooking a formal garden. In front of the window behind a long desk stood the city magistrate who was to marry them, a slender young woman wearing a long brown dress, a simple woollen knit with long sleeves. Her dark hair was held back by a clip at the nape of her neck and she wore an impressive chain of office. Only Lenin watched from the walls. She spoke to them very seriously about the nature of marriage, about mutual love and mutual sacrifice, and about children. She asked them separately if each had made the decision to marry the other fully and freely and without coercion. When they had answered *"da"* they went forward to her desk to sign the register, which she indicated with a carved ivory (plastic?) wand, and while their signatures were being witnessed the musicians performed a "romance" the like of which I hadn't heard since I had tea at the Empress Hotel in Victoria, B.C. Then the magistrate came out from behind her desk with a silver dish in which the rings had been placed and she asked them to put them on each other's fingers. That done she stood before them and said very solemnly that on that day, September 9, 1982, in the Hero City of Moscow, had been registered the marriage of Citizen Edward Ryan of Toronto, Canada and Citizen Nina Sibiryakova of Moscow, USSR and she wished them happiness and good health. It was all so serious and touching that I cried. A few more notes from the musicians and it was all over. In the evening Geoffrey and I went to the wedding supper with the bridal party, a few additional friends, and Nina's brother, in the Green Room of the National Hotel. We had caviar and champagne and quite a lot else as well. We toasted their union and we wished them, perhaps a little uncertainly, a long and happy life together ...

As for the Canadian Members of Parliament and their companions, it was a rather tense visit about which you may now have read something in the papers. I won't say more here except that, in fact, we enjoyed seeing them. In addition to our formal lunch for them, Flora MacDonald was also able to have supper with us. David Smith told us funny stories down in the Club about off-track betting and we had a good talk with Ian Deans whom we liked and respected. Their visit was serious. It can only be hoped that in the name of humanity and of common sense it will prove to have been helpful.

In between times Katharine and Monique and I have been sightseeing. They have been to the Bolshoi and the Palace of Congresses and the three of us even went to the U.S. Embassy to see ET! And we talk—and talk—and talk—and I think about you all.

LETTER NUMBER 41

September 26, 1982

The day is grey and dreary and Katharine has just left on her long journey home. How we will miss her! We have had a wonderful month and feel greatly privileged to have had her here for so long. By good fortune the Embassy dacha at Zavidova suddenly became available on the weekend and we were able to spend the last day of summer up there with her. The Russians call the golden days at the end of September *babye leto*, or "woman's summer." As we drove along the highway we could understand why. In front of the high fences of their gardens in every village along the way we saw the old women sitting together on benches enjoying the warm air and watching the traffic go by. Those that weren't actually at the roadside, that is, with their pails of apples and potatoes for sale. Or holding out bunches of flowers hoping for a few roubles to save up against the winter shortages. Already their houses were looking cozy as well as attractive. Birch logs were piled high against the side wall covering this year's fresh coat of blue or green or brown paint. The geraniums had been taken in but were still blooming in front windows set off by the white fretwork decoration that renders every wooden cottage in

Northern Russia just a little different from every other. Most of the fruit from the private plots had been picked but the shaggy front gardens were still full of asters and dahlias and golden-balled chrysanthemums. I suppose these little houses do not have the conveniences of the modern blocks of flats that rise in serried ranks in the *sputnik* towns that encircle Moscow, but they have so much more character.

After the marvellous excesses of Georgia and Armenia a day on the Volga rowing along the yellowing shore and among the rattling weeds was both peaceful and invigorating. We also walked through the stubbled fields and played a little tennis and rode bicycles (or at least Katharine and I did) to the bridge over the Shosha. All that exercise and country air calmed our livers and gave us time to sort out and store our impressions. I thought I would easily be able to complete this letter for this week's bag after we returned to Moscow. But I have been reluctant to give up time that I could share with Katharine. Now she has gone but instead of a clear day ahead until the bag closes this afternoon I find that the Soviet Ambassador to Canada, Alexander Yakovlev, and his wife Nina are coming to lunch. Naturally we are anxious to see them before they return to Canada on Monday. So I will finish my letter next week.

LETTER NUMBER 42

October 4, 1982

Now for Georgia and Armenia. What generous and hospitable people live there! We had a fascinating visit without any untoward incident whatever. We were only frustrated that we did not have more time. Early on the morning of September 16 a smooth Aeroflot flight brought us in two hours to the city of Ordzhonikidze where Ilya, who had taken three days to get there, met us with the car. Coming down we had a marvellous view of the mass of the snow-capped Caucasus but then we descended through cloud and never saw the snow mountains again. However, the drive along the Georgian Military Highway was all the more romantic for the mist that swirled around the craggy peaks. This road through the wild gorges and up over the mountains has been in continual use since caravans from Persia passed along it in ancient times. At the beginning of the last century it took a month to cross from the Sarmatian Gates to Tbilisi. But then it became more important for military reasons and the route was constantly improved. It took us less than five hours. This is the very best season. Later the narrowest parts will sometimes be choked with sheep coming down off the high meadows. In the winter there are snowfalls and avalanches. Rock slides come down in the spring. No doubt it will be all fixed up one day with tunnels and proper grading but at the moment it is still wild and dramatic and it may be dangerous and I loved every inch! When we reached the Pass of the Cross the clouds stayed on the Northern side and we descended to Tbilisi in sunshine watching the bright green sheep-studded slopes give way gradually to arid hillside and dusty village and smoggy town. All the way from Ordzhonikidze we had been preceded by a series of noisy *militsia* cars and 80 km or so before Tbilisi we were met by the chief of protocol, an engaging man, who greeted us warmly and became very much a part of our lives for the next three days, speaking excellent English and knowing, as far as we could tell, everyone in town! With the plane trees fully leaved and the grape arbours covered, Tbilisi is more attractive than it was in January and we were lucky enough to have fine, warm weather.

We had a splendid view from our corner suite in the Hotel Iveria and could watch the play of light on the river and the hills during the few minutes of the day when we were actually in our room. Our program was *very* crowded. Official calls on the First Deputy Chairman of the Council of Ministers and on the Mayor, and the standard visit to the Park of Economic Achievements left our heads aching from the effort to absorb statistics and five-year plans. Visits to the glorious exhibition of gold from the legendary times of Jason and Medea and to the treasure of silver icons and rare cloisonné enamel work from the early Christian centuries as well as to ancient churches and monasteries and the open air museum of Georgian architecture left our eyes dazzled and our feet sore. Wine-tasting in the old city followed by a visit to an underground café where we drank thick sweet coffee brewed for us in little pots stuck in hot sand, followed in rapid succession by a stop at the wedding palace, half an hour at a sophis-

ticated and amusing marionette show very much for adults, a walk
through a children's art museum featuring the posthumous show of
a recently deceased highly talented seventeen-year-old (through
which we were conducted by his dramatically grieving aunt), and
terminating in a tea-room with a feast of *khachapuri* (a Georgian bread
and cheese dish) accompanied by unusual-tasting cream soda drinks,
left us as exhausted as I am sure this sentence has left you. And I still
haven't told you about the wonderful male choir or the one act of the
ridiculous opera that we sat through or the trip to the agricultural
institute to inspect the grapes (and taste some more wine) or the visit
to the studio of a Georgian painter much influenced by Modigliani
where we looked at endless imagined nudes and ate ripe figs.

I think Katharine would agree that, in some ways, the highlight of
our visit was the dinner on St. David's Mountain with the First
Deputy Minister, two of his colleagues, and our friends from the
Georgian Foreign Ministry. It was memorable not for the Georgian
food (we had a superb lunch of national dishes on the day we left that
remedied that) but for the particularly Georgian flavour of the whole
evening. Our host was not one of the men who usually entertain official foreign guests so he was determined to demonstrate to us the
very best of Georgian hospitality: Georgian wines and Georgian
toasts, which go together, of course. Toasting in Georgia is a very serious business and the host or toastmaster as he calls himself spends
most of his time standing up, wine glass in hand, touching on every
topic that might possibly be of interest to his guests. Dinner lasted for
three hours. He was on his feet for at least half that time. Our poor
friend the chief of protocol, who was translating, would just be lifting
his fork to his mouth when our host was up again. Geoffrey says he
made fourteen speeches. I can't imagine how he kept track! And
Geoffrey managed some very good toasts too, especially as the
evening wore on, but in no way could he match the measured sonor-
ity of the Georgian language as our host dwelt on the importance of
"first love" (I think he drank to that several times) or "the friends
who have passed on" or "to that *very* moment in the future wherever we might find ourselves when we would remember *this* moment
when we were together in Georgia." He was so genuine and so
human and so eloquent that we were all moved. Katharine was called

upon to toast her parents and the rest of us willingly toasted our children and the man next to me, who had said very little all evening, finally burst out that he had a son at Moscow University and how long was Katharine planning to remain in the Soviet Union? At the end of the evening we embraced one another very warmly (Katharine was embraced several times over!) and next morning some bottles of excellent Georgian wine appeared in our room so that we could start remembering right away! And what good wine it is! The Georgians have been making wine for seven thousand years and they really know what they are doing. Unfortunately it is difficult to obtain the best vintage wines even in Moscow let alone Canada. I expect they save them for themselves and for evenings like these!

Last January when I went to Georgia and Armenia with the international ladies I recounted a certain amount of local history in my letter to you because I was so fascinated by it. I'll try not to repeat myself although the Armenians are informed by their history in ways that few other nationalities are except, perhaps, the Israelis. The Georgians are very proud, their customs and traditions are quite distinct, and they are passionately attached to their beautiful and fruitful land. But they ride lightly on their history. The Armenians, on the other hand, are obsessed by it. Of course they have lived through an almost unprecedented number of national disasters and those who remain in this rather dry corner of their ancient territory view the Russians as protectors as much as anything else. Because every day (weather permitting—and it usually does) the citizens of Yerevan and the religious city of Etchmiadzin see *their* Mount Ararat in all its beauty just across the border in Turkey.

Armenia is different from Georgia in almost every way—although they also make delicious wine (and better cognac). From Tbilisi we drove with our Georgian companions south across the plain, over a twenty-kilometre stretch of Azerbaijan, where a tongue of Islam reaches into the Christian lands, the people suddenly change appearance, and there are Moslem cemeteries along the road. When we reached the border with Armenia we said goodbye to our friend the chief of protocol and his two colleagues. They handed us over to two young men from the Armenian Foreign Office who had come to meet us with a Chaika. What with a screaming *militsia* car, our own LTD, and the

Chaika, we were an intimidating procession as we climbed the curves of the Lesser Caucasus, rising into the clouds and coming out at last into the brilliant sunshine with Lake Sevan spread before us. What a beautiful lake! It was sapphire blue in the late afternoon light, flecked with whitecaps and surrounded by bare mountains. Nearly 2,000 metres above sea level, it is one of the highest large lakes in the world. We climbed up to two ninth-century churches on what was once an island before the water level sank, and breathed in the fresh clear air with delight. Lake Sevan irrigates all of the Ararat valley but it should sink no more because they now, they told us, have it properly controlled. The double highway down to Yerevan was excellent and the massive construction all around the city gave the impression of relative prosperity, an impression confirmed throughout our visit.

Geoffrey had to get back to Moscow for a fisheries delegation so our time in Armenia was even shorter than in Georgia, but very rich nonetheless. Katharine was a little taken aback by being offered Armenian brandy at 10:00 in the morning by the Foreign Minister and at 11:00 by the Prime Minister and at 12:00 by the Mayor, but she enjoyed the gorgeous fruit. When we called on the Catolicos of the Armenian Church at Etchmiadzin the next day he shared with us the most beautiful bowl of fruit I have ever seen, all gathered in the Cathedral gardens and lovingly assembled on a great platter adorned with fresh vine leaves. It made sense of the decorative elements we saw everywhere on the old churches we visited. The Catolicos is a serene and beautiful old man who spoke excellent French and thanked Canada, through her representative, for her generosity to the Armenians of the Diaspora who have settled in our country. Obviously Armenia has more contact with her far-flung population than most other Republics of the Soviet Union and this adds sophistication and a certain intellectual openness to conversation. Officials hastened to condemn the terrorist attacks on Turks in our country but they feel their own historical pain most acutely. Even some of the pictures in the remarkable Gallery of Contemporary Art were permeated with this pain, but, in addition to all that is dark, there is wonderful colour in Armenia and most of the paintings were brilliant as well as being highly individualistic. The streets were full of life and the fountains played under coloured lights in the central square until close to midnight. So, unfortunately, did the music over the loud-speaker outside our hotel room ... The quietest and most serene spot in the city was the ancient site of Erebumi, built by Argishti I, king of Urartu, in 783 BC on a hill in the southern outskirts. Katharine and I went there at the end of a strenuous day when the sun lay aslant the rosy brick of ruined temples and palaces. No one else was there and we felt ourselves caught by the distant past and by the remarkable powers of survival of this remarkable people.

LETTER NUMBER 43

October 19, 1982

From my window I am watching the snow dancing over the garden, blown this way and that by the first storm of the season. The wind rose during the night and stripped the big chestnut beside the Domik house, but the two linden trees that kept the grass from growing all summer are still densely leaved and still green. The fur hats have all come out and people are shaking their heads and exclaiming to one another. But the mood is adventurous. Nobody really expects the snow to last. How could it? Two days ago, on Sunday, it was balmy. We drove the Gibsons to the airport in a fog caused by the warm air. Gordon travelled in his shirt sleeves and the customs officer only looked slightly surprised. When we came back to the Embassy the fog had lifted and sun was shining. Geoffrey raked leaves and I cut back the peonies. Then we went for a long walk in the Lenin Hills, in the wilder part of the park, away from the ski jump and the brides having their photographs taken, and closer to Gorky Park. We had never been that side before and found it beautiful in the sunlight, although the paths were slippery under the fallen leaves and our shoes were soaked by the time we climbed back to the car. Because it had been raining a lot. The weather was not kind to the Gibsons while they were in Moscow but they didn't mind a bit. Gordon said that grey was how he had always imagined it to be and that the hour of brilliant sunshine when they visited the Kremlin made up for all the rest.

Gordon and Pam were wonderful company, so interested in everything that it was a pleasure to see Russia through their eyes. As of October 10 we are into our third year here and, while I would hardly say that I have become jaded, I am no longer surprised by what is positive and, on the whole, my mood is sadder. So it is refreshing to be able to show all the good things about this city to enthusiastic and responsive guests who didn't really expect to find things the way they are. In addition to all the sightseeing they managed a fair sampling of the public entertainment: the Bolshoi for ballet, the Moscow Arts Theatre for *The Seagull,* Moldavian folk dancing at the Kremlin Palace of Congresses, *Don Juan* at the puppet theatre, and an evening at the New Circus where I gave Geoffrey's ticket to a large and excited lady with seven gold teeth, who clutched her ample bosom at every dramatic moment (of which there were many) and who was a perfect example of why the Circus is so popular in this country. She was transported for an evening into a world where human beings can defy physical laws and get away with it. Of course the clowns and the animal acts engaged her attention too, but it seemed to me that it was the performers overcoming the constraints that keep us normal mortals earthbound, with grace and flair, who touched the deepest emotions in her substantial being. She was totally absorbed. And so were her fellow-citizens all around her. Every city in the Soviet Union has at least one permanent circus and I can't imagine that there is ever an empty seat!

On Tuesday morning I greeted the Gibsons returning from Leningrad with a handful of old photographs that I had discovered during my weekend. There were some particularly good ones of Geoffrey and Gordon on the Peace River. The two of them have known each other now for fully forty years and the night before the Gibsons left a considerable amount of vodka was consumed to celebrate that! We loved having them here. I hope what I have said about their visit will confirm those of you who have not yet been here, but who are planning to come, in your intentions. It's a very special experience.

Life in Moscow for the foreign community is now beginning to settle into its autumn routine. All the new arrivals at the Embassy have been greeted and are beginning to find their way. There are many more families with young children than there were last year. We now have twenty-one of them under fifteen! The mothers are eager to contribute to community activities so I expect there will be a lot of events all year long, starting with the Hallowe'en party. Elaine is contributing to the health of the Embassy by offering a Jane Fonda workout program in the Club twice a week after work. And since I have started my gymnastics again on a regular basis I should be in good shape to confront the temptations of the Christmas season! The International Women's Club has had its first meeting at Spaso House and I have begun the group that I will lead this year on Twentieth-Century Russian Literature. Preparing for it has already been full of discoveries for me, especially Maxim Gorky's reminiscences of Tolstoy and Chekhov and the stories of Ivan Bunin. And the dinner parties have started, as well as the occasional cultural delight such as yesterday's concert at the Chinese Embassy by an enchanting group of young artists, singing, dancing, and playing the unusual (to us) Chinese instruments. Time will pass quickly and, on the whole, pleasantly but I will always feel regretful about our institutionalized isolation from the real world around us. I make what sorties I can but it will never be very satisfying. My Russian is now improving quite rapidly and I will continue to take four lessons a week, one of which will be a visit with Natasha to one of the many small museums around and about, or to a special exhibition, or, next week, to the new fashion house on Prospect Mira. I will pursue my visits to children's institutions with Victoria. But I will never be left alone with a small group of children to make friends with them, nor will I ever be invited to spend a long evening around someone's kitchen table. That makes me sad.

LETTER NUMBER 44

November 3, 1982

The snow that was coming down the last time I wrote didn't stop for three days. And after that it was cold for a week and one had the feeling, as one often does, that in Moscow it is always winter! But of

course that is not true. Now the snow has all vanished but so has all
the colour. Except for the rowanberries, which are exceptionally thick
and red this year, a presage, the folk say, of extreme cold. Maybe it
will snow again on the National Day. It often does. But then there will
be banners and lights and fireworks to set against such a reminder of
the long, confining months ahead. Once again we'll be watching
most of these activities on our television screen while the journalists
scan the stands to see who is there. Everything conspires to make any
participation in the public life of this country difficult! However, for
the observers that we are compelled to be there are nevertheless lots
of goodies, and the last two weeks have been full of them, always
remembering that being a foreigner in this country has a very selective effect on what one observes. The longer I'm here the more conscious I become of the multiplicity of layers in this complex society,
to most of which I can never possibly have access. So all these gener-
alizations I can't resist making are to be regarded with due caution!

There is one area of course that may, ironically, be more open to
resident foreigners than it is to the average Soviet citizen. Because it
is relatively easy for us to obtain tickets through our efficient Helen
we can go to the theatres and to concerts as often as we can find the
time and energy. And to museums and exhibitions without having to
wait in line, although I did persuade Geoffrey to stand for ten or fifteen minutes outside the Pushkin Gallery the other day while we
watched *others* going in with special passes! Anyway, our access to
officially sanctioned cultural events is limited only by our language
ability where language is terribly important, and it isn't always, and
certainly not in the greatest works of art. Last week, for example, we
went to a concert of Stravinsky's works at the Chamber Music
Theatre on Leningradsky Prospect. This is a small theatre in a basement room where the performers and the audience find themselves
in close and intimate contact. It was a wonderful evening, with
young performers full of talent and energy. The most exciting piece
was *The Soldier's Tale*, which some of you may have heard, but never,
I'm sure, with the Russian narration where the musical sound of the
language becomes part of the musicality of the whole composition.
So I don't really mean that language isn't important to a great work
of art but rather that total fluency is not essential to full appreciation

when the work transcends national boundaries. We went to see an excellent modern play last week, too. We had read the English translation so we could follow the sense of what was being said and that was really enough because the quality of the play didn't reside in precisely what was being said but rather in the marvellous characterization, so much of which was non-verbal. The play was called *Duck Hunting* by a young playwright named Vampilov, who, most unfortunately, drowned a few years ago. It's a funny and moving study of an engaging and feckless man who can't quite get it together and only discovers too late that he really loves the wife whom he has provoked into leaving him. The central character was brilliantly acted by the actor of the Moscow Arts Theatre whom some of you have seen as the young man in *The Seagull*. He is really middle-aged and balding. Or maybe he isn't? Anyway, the play was completely non-political and quite universal. It is very popular. Language in the movie we saw on Sunday was even less important. *Mexico in Flames* is the first half of Bondarchuk's version of the story of John Reed. We understand that the Mexicans are not so sure this version of their revolution makes any sense to them, but there are some glorious scenes of uprising with masses of peasants in their sombreros streaming this way and that and the old hacienda crumbling under attack. The audience wasn't too convinced either, although they really enjoyed the display of Ursula Andress, nude on a silk coverlet, as Mabel Dodge in her villa in Italy. They only laughed when John Reed started to *talk* to her! And finally language was totally irrelevant to Andrei Gavrilov's rendering of Mozart and Chopin, which we listened to, spellbound, at the Conservatory a couple of nights ago.

And more cultural events. Last week Geoffrey and I took part in the opening of an exhibition of photographs by Cavouk at the "House of Friendship" on Kalinin. He and his wife had arrived in Armenia from Toronto the day after we had left and he had had a very successful show there, having taken the portraits of many Armenian personalities with love and care. We liked those photos and many of his Canadian ones, although not all. His work is a little too formal for some of his subjects, but the study of Governor General and Mrs. Schreyer, which he has presented to the Embassy, is very effective. We had him and his wife to lunch with some of his

Armenian acquaintances, including a larger-than-life sculptor who brought along his "beauty," a Georgian girl, and who has invited us to his studio for an Armenian feast. We will be able to see some of his work at an exhibition of art from all the Republics of the Soviet Union that will open on Friday at the Manège. They are really working up to the big celebration of the formation of the Soviet Union sixty years ago, which will be formally held at the end of December. Every week there is another television program on Intervision all about yet another Soviet Republic, although I don't know how large the European audience is for all that folk dancing and all those rolling tractors! Ten days ago we went to the studio of another sculptor whose work will *not* appear at the Manège Exhibition Hall although he is actually a member of the Artists' Union and has two fine abstract sculptures on the lawns of two of Moscow's multitudinous institutions. He is a very fine sculptor, a remarkable graphic artist, and a joyous and wonderfully erotic painter. Our prolonged visit to his studio was a delight. We went with a knowledgeable friend and, together with the sculptor and his wife, had many cups of steaming tea and a long discussion about his work and about the state of art in the Soviet Union. His continuing creation of very original work in spite of a variety of difficulties is very good news indeed.

Perhaps the highlight of our last two weeks was the Whitman evening at Spaso House. The Russians are great admirers of Walt Whitman. I guess that's not too surprising. The latest edition of his poems in translation is just off the presses here, handsomely illustrated too. The evening was a culmination of a Whitman symposium that had been held here between American and Soviet scholars, under the auspices of some special exchange program. The various participants got up and recited the poems of their choice in their own languages in front of an audience made up of the élite of the Moscow literary and theatrical world, a certain number of resident Americans, the Ambassador of Luxembourg, the Ambassador of Kuwait, and us. It was a treat. One of the American participants, Helen Vendler, a most distinguished critic, read one of Whitman's unpublished homosexual poems, a very moving one. The ravishing poet, Bella Akhmadulina, read her own free translation of a favourite poem so beautifully that this time we really did regret our inadequate Russian. She was followed by her ex-husband, Yevgeny Yevtushenko, who is a great showman, and who had something to say to her that we couldn't catch, though his expansive reading of Whitman was everything that one could wish. Donna Hartman read part of Whitman's *Letter to Russia*. She has promised me a copy. It is so relevant! These two giants so continually obsessed by each other, so often employing the same global rhetoric! Only the names are changed! The Whitman evening was an emotionally powerful but benign encounter between them—would that there could be more of them ...

LETTER NUMBER 45

November 23, 1982

After the aeroplane carrying Mr. Trudeau and his companions roared off last Tuesday into a whirl of snow, I thought I would be able to return to the Embassy and write to you immediately, for last week's bag, all about the momentous events that had just taken place. But I couldn't. As soon as I sat at my typewriter I realized that I would need some time to get a "fix" of my own on what had happened. After all, you will already have read almost all you ever wanted to know about Brezhnev's death and you will have been exposed to endless speculation about the changes at the top, to biographies of Andropov, to reflections about what's in store for the Soviet Union now, to queries about new directions in US–USSR relations. So I'll give you no more of that; just some very personal impressions of everything that I was able to witness.

For me, the sequence of events began on the 7th of November. The weather was cold and windy and I, at least, was quite happy to watch the parade yet again on television. However, by the time we arrived at the Kremlin Palace of Congresses for the official reception the clouds had cleared away and the golden domes were brilliant against the deep blue sky and the snow sparkled in a light layer on the grass. The old men looked ruddy from standing so long in the cold. Mr. Brezhnev read his brief speech firmly although I thought (I was standing with some of the other diplomatic wives directly facing the men) that Mr. Tikhonov was looking at him rather anxiously. Brezhnev and the other Politburo members shook our hands with surprising vigour and attention, considering how many of us went through the line, and then they fell to the buffet with gusto. So I really was surprised on Wednesday night when the American Ambassador was called away twice to the phone in the middle of the delicious dinner we were eating at the Greek Embassy and came back with a worried look. And later, when we were dancing, we wondered whether we should be. But there had been rumours before. It was only next morning when I drove back from gymnastics and a trip to the gastronome and saw that our flag was at halfmast that I realized it was true. So, being of a practical nature, I immediately rushed back to the gastronome to stock up. For the rest of that day life in the streets proceeded much as usual but on Friday the official mourning began; all the red flags sprouted black organdy ribbons, the centre of the city, within the garden boulevards, was sealed off, there were soldiers everywhere, and the weather turned grey and dreary and wet. We got the news that Mr. Trudeau would be coming on from Germany with quite a large group including a number of journalists.

The Embassy rallied in force during the next couple of days preparing both for the known and for the unpredictable. The Canadians were terrific, but so were the locals, particularly, from my point of view, Nikolai and Tamara and Zhenya. At 3:00 on Sunday we set off for Sheremetyevo 1, where we shared the VIP waiting room with several other Embassy groups each waiting for *their* delegation. Such a flurry of diplomatic activity, you can well imagine!

"Kanada," called out a plump, blue-uniformed Aeroflot lady, and she led us all onto a bus that drove us standing and swaying out onto the tarmac to the Canadian Armed Forces plane that had just taxied to a stop. The bright oblong of the door, the red-carpeted stairs, the official greeting by the Deputy Prime Minister, handshakes all around, photographs, and into the waiting Zil. Then a rapid ride into the city along deserted streets, Mr. Trudeau leaning over occasionally to explain something to Justin in the jump seat, who was staring intently out of the window. After settling into the

Rossiya Hotel and putting on suitable clothes (I reversed my padded coat from white to black) we went to the Dom Soyuzov, the House of Trade Unions, to pay our last respects to Mr. Brezhnev lying in state in the Hall of Columns, his body a little dwarfed by the banked wreaths and the display of his medals, each one on a separate piece of red satin six inches square. The Dom Soyuzov is a fine eighteenth-century building near the Bolshoi Theatre on Prospect Marxa. It used to serve the noble classes for social assemblies. With its handsome proportions and its great chandeliers swathed in black net it looked properly solemn and impressive for such an occasion. The orchestra was playing the sixth symphony of Tchaikovsky as we stood there silently and I was moved by the sight of the folded white hand that had shaken mine so briskly just seven days before. Justin was very quiet. I'm sure he was relieved to be able to run as we returned on foot to the hotel across the vast, unpeopled expanse of Red Square, so haunting and mysterious in the dim yellow light.

We had an excellent dinner on the top floor of the Rossiya with its view down on St. Basil's and over the Kremlin walls. I sat with Geoffrey at a "working" table beside Mr. Trudeau and across from Michael Pitfield, the clerk of the Privy Council. Senator Argue was on the other side of Geoffrey as were Bob Fowler and Ted Johnson. The conversation was about the major issues raised by Brezhnev's death and the change in leadership as well as about the gamut of bilateral concerns, but all the while Mr. Trudeau kept a weather eye out for Justin at a nearby table and occasionally got up to find out how he was getting along. When we had finished eating and talking he got up from the table and carried Justin piggyback out of the restaurant. The waiters were delighted! Pavel (still an Embassy driver) recalls with unfeigned admiration how Mr. Trudeau climbed onto one of the motorcycles belonging to his police escort when he was in Moscow ten years ago and roared off around Red Square!

Next morning Geoffrey went off to join Mr. Trudeau and the three or four others who were able to attend the funeral, and I settled myself in front of the television set. Victoria and Elena joined us to translate the commentary and the speeches. Soon after it started George Hazen sent up Lorna (aged eleven) to watch it with us and

François brought Justin, who had decided that he would rather watch it in the Residence than at the hotel. Both of the kids were very patient. Justin buried himself in *Star Trek* during the funeral speeches and Lorna vanished into the bathroom as soon as the coffin was opened in front of Lenin's tomb and did not reappear until it had been closed after the final kisses of his family and safely lowered into the ground out of sight, and all the factory whistles had begun their three-minute salute. But otherwise they were quiet and attentive. There was very little commentary during the transmission so one's whole attention was focused visually. One of the cameramen obviously had an eye for composition and I was much struck by the formal beauty of the aligned and balanced forms and colours; the red of the Kremlin wall, the red and black of the Lenin Mausoleum, the grey of pavement, of military squares marching in awesome synchrony, and the clear yellow of the eighteenth-century palaces beyond the Kremlin wall. But the most vivid image I retain of the funeral is the sight of the massed wreaths, two or three hundred of them, carried up the slope alongside the blood-red brick wall of the towered and turreted historical museum, evoking, somehow, strange echoes of Birnam Wood ...

After the funeral Geoffrey and the Prime Minister and the Senator went to St. George's Hall to meet Andropov, Tikhonov, Kuznetsov, and Gromyko and then back to the hotel for a late lunch. I joined them about 4:00 for a little sightseeing. We went up to the Lenin Hills in the rapidly fading daylight and the Soviet security officer assigned to Mr. Trudeau (a Lieutenant Colonel at the very least) practically had a fit when Justin slipped over the red marble balustrade and somersaulted backwards down the slope! Then we went to Novodevichy and were able to make a quick visit to the rich golden interior of the Cathedral of the Virgin of Smolensk (1513), which was opened and lit up for us. Then we drove through the Kremlin gates to deposit Mr. Trudeau and Geoffrey at Mr. Tikhonov's office. Justin and I went back to the Embassy but at least he had had a chance to glimpse the churches of the Kremlin lit against the night sky. He disappeared immediately to the Domik where he joined Antoine (who is exactly his age) and Benoit at the Mathys' newly acquired pool table. I did not see him again for quite a long time!

At 6:30 the Embassy families began to drift upstairs with their children and the group arrived from the hotel, and Geoffrey arrived with Mr. Trudeau not long after. I think everyone managed to meet him, at least I did my best. He talked easily and pleasantly with everyone, particularly the older children, and had himself photographed with all kinds of combinations of young and old. He and his companions stayed on for dinner with the Embassy officers and their wives (except for the younger military, who were entertaining the plane crew down in the Club). This is when I was especially pleased with Nikolai and Tamara et al. because a cocktail party for a hundred, plus kids, followed by dinner for forty is really quite an undertaking and they did it very well. If we had had more time to plan it might have been less spontaneous and therefore less successful. As soon as he had finished dessert, Mr. Trudeau slipped off to the Domik with Elaine and had a couple of games of pool with Justin and the other boys and then brought him back to say goodnight. Some of his group stayed on after he left so we were able to have a good talk about events in Canada as well as in the Soviet Union.

By next morning at 9:00 a real blizzard was blowing and the ride out to the airport was decidedly unnerving. Geoffrey and Mr. Trudeau were talking and didn't pay much attention but Justin was wide-eyed and I was hanging on tightly to the back of his seat! I'm sure I will never ride in a Zil again so the drive would have been memorable even if we hadn't driven so fast. However, it was rather a relief, after we heard the aeroplane take off (we couldn't see it through the snow), to ride back sedately to the city with Ilya. The snow stopped as we came down Gorky Street and by noon it had all melted. The weather has been unusually mild ever since but somehow all those extraordinary effects of light and weather that marked the days of the funeral and the hours of Mr. Trudeau's visit were totally appropriate. Events have taken place whose effect on both our public and our private lives will be profound even though it is still very difficult to guess what those effects will turn out to be ...

LETTER NUMBER 46

December 8, 1982

The weather has been growing steadily colder and there is now a light sprinkling of snow on the ground. Last week we pruned the rose bushes I planted in the spring and covered them up with some pine branches that were brought down from Zavidova. On Saturday the parking area behind the Embassy was cleared of cars and the air resonated with the sound of rubber balls hitting the garage doors, shouted instructions, calls, and laughter as both the men's and the women's teams had their first broomball practice of the season. There is talk of flooding the back garden for a small rink if the lawn can stand it. However, on Sunday there was silence. Early Sunday morning, driving back in a convoy along the Ring Road from a party of charades, one of our young staff members skidded on the ice in front of the American Embassy, struck the concrete wall where the road dips to go under Kalinin Prospect, and killed himself instantaneously on impact. I didn't know him very well and I don't think any of you had met him because he only arrived in August but he was a nice young man and everybody liked him. His wife and young son had left only two days before to return to Canada for the Christmas holidays and he was to join them at the end of this week. In a small community like ours the shock of such an event is very powerful, particularly so for those in the other cars that witnessed it. So I am afraid that this darkest part of the year has been darkened even more by the weekend's tragedy and we feel our isolation here ever more acutely. We'll do what we can over the Christmas season to lighten the sense of loss and of vulnerability but we will grieve for his wife and child and for the waste of his young life.

Otherwise life has returned to normal after the dramatic change of leadership. I'm not sure what the journalists are finding to write about. One can always speculate about changes in policy and all that but there aren't too many signs to go on yet. Watching Mr. Andropov meet dignitaries on television is a change, of course, because he is much more animated than his predecessor, but we still have no idea what they are talking about! So at the Embassy we have been concentrating on our own official visitors, from government, from business, and the delightful ice skaters who came to take part in the Izvestia Figure Skating Competition. They were not very experienced and they placed respectably but not brilliantly. However, the programs at the Sports Palace were fun to watch (we went twice) and there was usually a small contingent there from the Embassy with flags and cheers. And we had a reception for them here that gave us a chance to talk with them and to meet some of the remarkable Soviet skaters-turned-trainers, like Irina Rodnina and her husband Zaitsev. Canadians who come here are awed by the resources that the Soviet government pours into its sports training programs but I think we do pretty well, considering, and there is a point where the price of such state support may result in the destruction of spontaneity. The Russian skaters are fantastic though, and they now inject a lot of humour into their exhibition performances, at least some of them do. And those same ones are now wearing some unusually attractive costumes. Watching the competition on television, I saw the camera focus briefly on another Zaitsev, the fashion designer. I don't know whether he is any relation to the skater I met with Rodnina but, for sure, he is responsible for the best-looking outfits. How do I know? Well, let me tell you about his show.

You may remember that I mentioned the possibility of attending a Soviet fashion show in an earlier letter. Well, three times Natasha and I organized an expedition for the women of the Embassy and three times we were put off for one reason or another, the last time because of the unexpected demise of Mr. Brezhnev. However, we finally made it the week following the funeral, twenty-five of us, and we all applauded with enthusiasm. I never thought I'd be tempted to return to Canada with a Soviet-designed dress, but I've changed my mind. I had heard about Zaitsev, "the Red Dior," ever since I arrived, but he only opened his own fashion house on Prospect Mira five months ago so I had not actually seen any of his designs. He has been to Paris many times, so I have been told, but his ideas are unmistakably Russian. There were echoes of the twenties, of the Constructivist designs of the painters Popova and Rodchenko. There were colourful clothes inspired by peasant motifs so authentic yet so far from the repetitive and banal costumes that appear on the smiling young girls

194

LANDON PEARSON

and the muscular young men of the endless folk dance troupes that you feel like shouting "hooray!" The Soviet Union produces lovely crèpe de chine and there were beautifully draped dresses made of it in red and black and off-white, shown off to us by his model of an "elegant age" who looked a bit like Ingrid Bergman and had had the veins of her legs stripped. I could tell. And there were the most gorgeous evening coats I've ever seen, embroidered in big traditional designs, black on black or silver on black. If I don't buy one of the elegant dresses maybe I'll buy an heirloom! And there were just as many clothes designed for and modelled by young men as there were for women. The male models were athletes or actors or students and they looked surprisingly at ease. I tried to imagine the men of the Central Committee sitting around in these rich autumnal colours and what Zaitsev described as his "Renaissance" styles. I failed.

By coincidence, the following week we went to the International Trade Centre to see the autumn collection of Nina Ricci accompanied by French wines and cheeses. *Le Tout* of international Moscow was there and, of course, a French Collection is a display of great beauty and art. We were told, in a hushed whisper, that the wedding dress that completed the show was worth $60,000. The swirling shot silk evening dresses and the ebony mink coats couldn't have been much less. But Geoffrey, who has never seen a fashion show before (and is unlikely to see one again), wondered where the young women had acquired that peculiar gait and I was too awed to be tempted by anything. Being puzzled as to why Nina Ricci and Air France would put on such a big splash (because I didn't meet anyone there who had actually paid for the ticket), I was told that there is a fantastic market in the Soviet Union for French perfume. At 50 roubles an ounce, each shipment sells out practically overnight!

In addition to household management and the organization of lunches and receptions, my own life is very busy these days. I have three personal projects going. One is the group that I lead for the International Women's Club on twentieth-century Russian literature. None of us is very knowledgeable so each week brings a new discovery: the autobiographical books of Maxim Gorky, Zamyatin's *We*, a brilliant anti-Utopian novel written in 1920 full of uncanny predictions of the totalitarian state, the life and poetry of Sergei Esenin, the extraordinary vigour of Mayakovsky. It means a lot of reading but, thanks to Mr. Ford, the Embassy library is well stocked and we borrow back and forth. Unni Kroyer, the wife of the Icelandic Ambassador, who has taken responsibility for the Anna Akhmatova and Marina Tsvetaeva, is going to organize an evening of readings (with someone to translate) and other members are being equally inventive. It's a very stimulating group. My second project does not require so much homework. It is going with Natasha (in lieu of a grammar lesson) to a museum or exhibition once a week where I can practise my listening comprehension and learn something new about the country. Because I always do. And my third project, with the help of Victoria, is visiting schools, children's clinics, libraries, sports facilities, pioneer palaces, and other institutions concerned with children in the Soviet Union, as well as meeting knowledgeable people in many different areas: a couple of female lawyers last week, experts in family law; a well-known writer of fiction for young people the week before; a visit to the institute for studies in preschool education as soon as I get permission; and a meeting with Sergei Obraztsov at the Puppet Theatre next week for sure. The red tape is cumbersome but once we get through it the people I meet with are extraordinarily cooperative and interesting. I could not have done this during the first two years we were here because neither my Russian nor my knowledge of the country were sufficient. Even now I feel inadequate but what I am learning is impressive and the people who work for and with children seem to be the most energetic and positive as well as the most open, on the whole, of those I have met here.

LETTER NUMBER 47

January 12, 1983

When Katharine phoned from Vancouver on January 2 to announce her engagement to Doug I knew that 1983 was going to be a good year. Already Zhenya had told Hilary, with me translating, that everybody knew 1983 was to be a particularly lucky year for weddings, though unfortunately Zhenya speaks so quickly now that she is convinced I can understand her that I miss the most interesting parts of what she has to say. By what magic calendar do the Russians actually operate? Tonight they celebrate what is known as the old New Year. Last week, the day after my Twelfth Night party, they celebrated Christmas. I don't know how they celebrated it but I do know they were all well aware of the date. And under that there is probably an even more ancient calendar tied to the seasons and rhythms of nature. I'm sure that's the one they consider propitious this coming year for ceremonies of commitment and renewal, because another Russian friend (yes, I actually do have some Russian friends now) told me that babies born this spring will be exceptionally fortunate in their lives. I only hope that the unseasonably warm weather we are having this winter will not sap the strength of the good spirits abroad or undermine the success of the winter crops!

Because the weather really is odd. Some of you will have heard from Hilary and Patricia how we spent Christmas in the fog at Zavidova, cozy in our dacha with turkey and trimmings but frustrated in our desire to skate or explore the fields and woods on skis. The day Hilary left it suddenly turned very cold and our ears froze as we walked back to the Residence after greeting the New Year in a festive Spaso House to the tunes of a lively jazz group from New Orleans, and in the company of our diplomatic colleagues and their visiting young. But two days later when Patricia left the weather turned mild again.

It was lovely for us to have Hilary and Patricia here for Christmas in spite of the weather. I can only too easily imagine how bleak it would be to spend Christmas alone here without family and I rejoice that next year we will be back in Ottawa not only with all our own, I hope, but with the additional members! In the meantime we will do our best to make the most of our remaining months in the Soviet Union.

So we started the year with an official trip to Leningrad. We took the midnight train on the day of Patricia's departure and found ourselves once again amid the bronze bears in the Astoria Hotel. We had two very busy days with meetings and visits stretching out on either side of the brief daylight hours. Visiting Leningrad officially is, of course, a very different experience from being there as a tourist as I had been two other times but any type of visit is infused by the extraordinary quality of the city itself. Every venture onto the streets is an aesthetic experience. There was a light layer of fresh snow everywhere. The Neva was frozen in chunks with ribbons of dark water opening up behind the little icebreakers and closing again after the last small boats escaped from the final freeze-up. The sky was not leaden like Moscow's but opalescent, sometimes faintly rose and sometimes tinged with that yellow glow so special to the northern winter sky. When we went to Smolny the sun actually came out and Rastrelli's passion for the eyes of the Empress Elizabeth stirred once more as her convent church stood out blue-green against the drifting cloud. Moscow closes in, Leningrad opens up. The Neva, the canals, the long, low, elegant buildings, the noble proportions of street and square, the wide bridges, the graceful spires of the Admiralty and of the royal church of SS Peter and Paul carry the eye up and out. I don't know what the city is like to live in but after several months encased in Moscow I found myself wondering why I don't visit Leningrad more often.

The first important item on our first day there was to be a hockey match between the Canadian Junior Team and the Norwegians in the context of the World Junior Hockey Championship. But we had an hour free first and immediately took advantage of our special status to go and see the gold collection at the Hermitage, with a marvellous guide who could tell us everything we could have possibly wanted to know about the treasures of Scythian design that overflow the cases, and the pieces of finely crafted jewellery and precious *objets d'art* proclaiming the wealth and generosity if not always the taste of the Tsars that fill another room. Watching the hockey game, in a sports stadium near the University, was fun, although the game itself was very uneven. The young Norwegians, being very inexperienced and coached in English by a despairing young Canadian, were defeated by our team 13-0. However, we enjoyed meeting the team members and the others involved in the championships, both the Canadians and the Soviets, who treated us to various rounds of brandy and toasts to more competitions between our two countries. They still think we are their only true opponents in hockey although we must wonder sometimes! Slightly reeling on brandy and cheers we returned to the hotel for a late but welcome lunch. Then we went to the University to meet the Rector and discuss the relationship between Leningrad State University and Carleton University, which has existed for some years, as well as the new one we have just established between Leningrad and Dalhousie. Eight students will be arriving in February to participate in a program similar to the one offered in Moscow by the Pushkin Institute. So we will have fewer students in Moscow this year but we do look forward to the time they spend here because they add a new, fresh dimension to our community life. In the evening we found ourselves (by choice, because I knew Geoffrey would not want to go to the Kirov for *Lohengrin!*) at a most remarkable play called *The Story of a Horse*, based on a short story by Tolstoy. It was a *tour de force*. The central character is a horse, played with astonishing talent by an actor named Lebedev who must have spent hours in stables and at racecourses. He did not dress up as a horse but he was a horse and I cried when he died!

Our second day was even more charged than the first. In the morning we went to the Smolny Convent where we were given a reverential tour of the office from which Lenin conducted the course of the October Revolution and its immediate aftermath, and the little apartment where he and his wife, Krupskaya, spent a short time and which displayed, along with other memorabilia (and historical revisions), a little mirror left behind by one of the girl students moved out of Smolny, marked "Souvenir of Niagara Falls, Canada." Then Geoffrey went off to meet Mr. Romanov, the Politburo member from Leningrad, and the Mayor. I was not allowed to come, even to take notes, because it was not "customary," so I went back to the University and had a very interesting talk with two professors of sociology, discussing the attitudes of young adolescents. Then I joined Geoffrey for lunch with the French consul and his wife, from whom we learned a great deal more about the life of foreigners in Leningrad than we did from the American, who was nevertheless hospitable and gave us dinner on our last evening.

After lunch we visited the Institute of the Arctic and the Antarctic for discussions with the director and some of his staff on questions of mutual interest. As we sat in the large office of the director (the Institute is housed in a beautiful eighteenth-century palace on the Fontanka) and stared at the huge map of the Arctic on the wall across the table from us, a map that showed the landmasses of Canada and the Soviet Union circling the North Pole, it was brought home to us very forcibly that we are indeed "neighbours across the Arctic." Our last visit was to the deputy director of the Vavilov Institute of plant genetics from which the horrid ghost of the lamentable Lysenko is still being energetically exorcised. Both of these visits were basically courtesy ones, because our joint knowledge of the subjects these institutes study is, well, minimal. However, for Canada as a whole the contacts are important and we would be short-sighted indeed not to maintain good connections. Then, dinner with the Americans and home by the midnight train.

LETTER NUMBER 48

Easter Sunday, 1983

Spring has come a whole month early. The buds on the chestnut tree beside the Domik in the courtyard are like small balled fists and the tulips are up in the garden, the Canadian ones that I planted two years ago and the Russian ones that went in last fall. The birch branches we brought back last weekend from Zavidova have sprouted on the window ledge in the pantry setting off the grey velvet pussywillows with their delicate pale green leaves. When I walked to the Easter service this morning the lawn at Spaso House was painted with crocuses. The sun has been shining since the beginning of the week and today Moscow is apparently the warmest capital in Europe! All the *shapkas* (fur hats) and heavy winter coats have come off; people can hardly believe their luck! Of course, no one has yet got around to sweeping up the winter debris. That will clutter up streets and apartment doorways until Lenin's birthday in mid-April and the annual "volunteer" clean-up day. But today people are strolling or chatting on park benches or playing dominoes and chess. And the children are digging in the sand piles or riding their bright new bicycles up and down the boulevard. Even after a mild winter the Northern spring lifts the heart and brings one out into the streets with a lighter step.

Exactly four weeks ago, when I returned from the wedding, it was still full winter. The weather was so cold that when brother Michael arrived from Zurich on March 10 we were able to go skating on the paths in Gorky Park and skiing on fresh and sparkling snow at Peredelkino. Within a week the winter was gone and when our old friend Diana Kirkwood left her ballet tour to spend the weekend with us the rain was slowly dissolving the great heaps of dirty snow. There was not much left when Dibby and Ann arrived although when we went up to Zavidova for the first weekend of their stay the fishermen were still hunched on the frozen Volga and we were able to tramp through the spring fields in our boots because enough ice remained in the muddy furrows to bear our weight. The river ice broke when we were in Pskov on Good Friday and we could watch great chunks of it swirling past the ancient *kremlin* wall. And yesterday, on Pushkin's estate, we drove through a river in spate.

So, one month later, the remarkably fine weather we enjoyed in Toronto during the week following the wedding has come to Moscow. I'm sorry that most of you have not heard from me in all that time. I'm sure you are able to understand why. I was worn out when I got back, really spent. The last couple of times that I have flown back and forth between here and Canada I have felt as though I was being literally catapulted from one place to the other. Now that I have energy invested in both environments the tension between the two is getting stronger and stronger. On that side of the Atlantic are almost all the people who really matter to me, but on this side is the home I live in and my day-to-day responsibilities and here, for the time being, my mind and my sensibilities are engaged. When we move back to Ottawa for good in September I will gather up my *lares* and *penates* and bring them back with me leaving few regrets behind, but now I find the transitions between Canada and Moscow wrenching, particularly after such a rich event as Hilary and Michael-John's wedding. So it has taken me quite a long time to get my bearings again. Then Michael was here, and Diana on her tour, and now my long-time friend Dibby Robinson and her daughter, my goddaughter Ann.

We have had a very good time with all our visitors. Every pair of eyes sees something different and adds to our own perception of the

Soviet Union. With brother Michael I got plenty of exercise keeping up with his energetic stride. I particularly enjoyed travelling to Leningrad with him where we spent hours exploring the city on foot, and talking. We saw beautiful live tigers at the Circus and the same shabby old stuffed one being hauled across the stage of the Kirov Theatre that we had seen two years ago when, with Anne and son Michael, we attended our first performance of *La Bayadère*. Michael greatly enhanced my appreciation of the Italian painting at the Hermitage as well as many other things and on our return to Moscow Geoffrey was somewhat bemused to have two Mackenzies in residence with him instead of just one.

Diana and her group arrived on Friday and Michael set off for Casablanca on Sunday but in between the four of us had a very good dinner at the National Hotel, with Michael as host, and walked back to the Embassy through the damp, dimly lit streets, full of good cheer. On Sunday evening Diana found herself with us unexpectedly watching a Canadian mime group, Theatre Beyond Words, playing to a packed and enthusiastic house at the Rossiya music hall. The Canadian impresario, whom she had known in Ottawa, was astounded to see her when we went backstage and we were amazed to hear of the extraordinary success they had met during their short tour of the USSR. But then, even on a large stage, they were remarkably touching and funny and the young Soviets loved them.

On Tuesday Dibby and Ann arrived slightly frazzled from having had to argue their way onto an overbooked Aeroflot flight and get through passport control with a visa that the Soviet Embassy in Ottawa had forgotten to stamp. Those difficulties over they immediately settled in to enjoy themselves and have continued to do so ever since. Ann gets such a kick out of the whole spectrum of human experience she would be disappointed if she did not have at least one *contretemps* to recount. On Wednesday evening they will go to see *The Seagull*. I can see her now acting Nina but I anticipate with relish the day she absorbs all her Russian experience and gets to play Arkadina.

So far our theatrical choices have been quite successful. We try to give our visitors a taste of what is best in Moscow and see something new ourselves. By a happy chance we took Michael to see a classic performance of Gogol's *Government Inspector* at the Maly Theatre not knowing that the one and only role he had ever acted on the stage was that of young Khlestakov when he (Michael) was a tutor at Pickering College. With Victoria, Ann and Dibby and I went to see *Ten Days that Shook the World* at the Taganka Theatre, a production that is still brilliant and innovative after ten years in the repertory. We thought we knew the story, but we didn't, at least not that version. Still, we were fascinated by it.

The two of them are very companionable and, armed with a street map and a diagram of the metro, they have happily visited the city on their own. I've been very busy with representational work plus a series of interviews with doctors and nutritionists about babies and young children. Since they have been here we have given two receptions, two formal lunches, and a dinner and film showing to which we invited a number of Soviets from the cultural world and screened *Gala*, the NFB film about Canadian dance. In the midst of all that Tamara phoned in one morning in agony from a kidney stone but the emergency service arrived rapidly, she was given an injection, and on Monday morning she reappeared quite cheerfully and fully recovered, bringing her little stone in a paper packet. The next couple of weeks look relatively peaceful but you never know. Life in Russia is full of surprises.

Our trip to Pskov for part of the Easter weekend was one of them. Pskov is a small town in the northwest of the Russian Republic, 700 km north from Moscow and 240 west from Leningrad. It is very old. It is first mentioned in the chronicles in 903 but somewhat earlier, on his way down to found the Kievan state, the legendary Rurik was rowed across the river at Pskov by his future wife, Olga, who probably wouldn't let him off the ferry until he agreed to marry her. Ten centuries later the hapless Nicholas signed his abdication papers in the Pskov station thus bringing Tsarist history to a close. Some of our Moscow friends had been for a visit and described it as a charming place. So we decided to take Ann and Dibby there and then send them on to Leningrad while we returned home. On the advice of our Danish colleagues we thought to make a courtesy call on the Mayor before getting on with our sightseeing and sent a message to that effect. Little did we anticipate the delegation that met us at the station early Friday morning! What appeared to be half the city council was there along with the Intourist guide, who looked almost as surprised as we felt. But I hardly had time to reflect on my unkempt appearance before I was handed a bunch of tulips in which I could bury my face and marshal my Russian small talk and my morning smile. We dashed off to the hotel in a cavalcade of cars catching tantalizing glimpses of ancient whitewashed churches and of the walled *kremlin* above the flooding spring river. Then everybody crowded into our room and discussed the program for the next two days, which was already typed out. Was it all right? Well, of course. And did our *sputniki* (our satellites) wish to be included? Dibby and Ann were not too sure about that description of themselves but, except for the formal and rather lengthy visit to the Mayor's office, which they sensibly avoided, they joined us in all the activities and were made to feel most welcome. And my goodness what a welcome! I don't think we have ever experienced such hospitality in all our travels in the Soviet Union. Ann counted fourteen times that her wine glass was topped up during the official dinner on Friday evening and the next day we had had two glasses of white wine and one of champagne before we got to elevenses. Every meal was a feast and every course had to be accompanied by two or three toasts. Sometimes we had to stretch a bit to find the common interests between Pskov and Canada once we had done the bit about peace and friendship and hockey and all that, but we managed. We still don't really understand why we were accorded such treatment and thoughts of Gogol did pass through our minds but as has been said in other circumstances, the best thing to do is relax and enjoy it. So we did.

We visited the *kremlin* and the old churches and the city museum. Geoffrey deposited a great basket of tulips at the memorial to the Unknown Soldier. We saw the room where Lenin spent three months in 1900 on his way from exile in Siberia to his years of preparation abroad. On Saturday we drove off in seven cars preceded by the *militsia*, 120 km in less than ninety minutes, to Mikhailovskoye, the beautiful country estate where Pushkin spent two years of his exile. We met with the director, Semen Gaichenko, a marvellous one-armed man of eighty, comfortably ensconced amid his collection of 364 samovars and full of anecdotes and tales. For the last forty years the Pushkin Estate has been his passion and he has recreated, amid the woods and hills and lakes of this lovely place, the atmosphere of the early nineteenth century and an authentic feeling of Pushkin's genius. It was driving to another part of the estate that we met the spring flood and drove in our cavalcade along 100 metres of submerged road without even pausing! Only the cows and a few villagers looked at us in astonishment. When we went through the gate into the sixteenth-century monastery where Pushkin's body was brought secretly for burial after his pointless death duelling with his wife's admirer, we were handed fresh roses of a haunting fragrance to lay on his tomb. I did so with some emotion. It is partly to read Pushkin that I will continue to study Russian because his vigorous and racy style, which I am just beginning to appreciate as I work away with Natasha, does not translate well into English.

So our visitors have brought us much pleasure and we look forward to the others who will come before we leave. But I could only wish that the promise of this early spring in Moscow could be matched by some improvement in the relations between East and West and a lessening in the tension that affects us all. But, alas, winter hangs on in the Halls of Power and casts a chill on the warmth of the people. The Russian folk tales that Pushkin loved are full of snow and ice but somehow Ivan the Simpleton and Vasilissa the Beautiful manage to win through in the end, Baba Yaga vanishes in a puff of smoke, and everyone sits down to a fine feast! But those are only fairy tales ...

LETTER NUMBER 49

April 19, 1983

When Ann and Dibby flew off on April 8 they took the spring away with them and it hasn't returned yet. Last week was cold and dreary and the whole Embassy was depressed even more by the fact that the courier arrived empty-handed. Our personal mail was forgotten back in some corner of External Affairs' Mail Room. Nothing could reinforce more our long-standing sense of being neglected by Ottawa! However, this week there will be twice as much as usual and on Saturday Geoffrey and I will go south in search of spring, to Volgograd (Stalingrad) first and then to Baku on the Caspian Sea. We will be gone for six days and when we come back the garden will (surely) be full of daffodils.

Our life has been rather uneventful since I last wrote. The continuing ritual of diplomatic life—a couple of lunches, a dinner, a reception last night at the British Embassy for the London Symphony Choir (whom we will hear perform Elgar's *Dream of Gerontius* on Friday evening), a national day or two, and the farewell to the Belgians—has not kept us as busy as it might appear. A chat with the Chinese Ambassador about Norman Bethune and a pleasant but brief encounter with the writer Fitzroy MacLean, who is preparing to turn his life-long interest in Russia into a television series, are hardly earth-shattering events and small compensation for those extra pounds that are creeping onto my hips ounce by ounce! And the translation of new recipes into Russian for Tamara, the purchase of frozen salmon from the wife of the Belgian Ambassador, Rosa Taelemans, as she cleaned out her freezer, the counting of whisky bottles in the pantry to see whether we have enough for the Canadian journalists who are coming tomorrow night, and the regular trips to the understocked gastronome are hardly the stuff of dreams, or of nightmares either for that matter. Going to the Central Market is more rewarding. Lettuce is back in the stalls along with new radishes and a variety of green herbs from the south. Today I bought some wild daffodils from a little round ball of a woman who counted them over and over again to make sure she hadn't cheated me and who told me she had picked them early this morning in a sheltered part of her garden. And yesterday the Georgian who last week was selling tomatoes at 1 rouble 60 kopecks each had lowered his price and placed a glass jar of lilac blooms amid the garlic and onions in front of him, not for sale, just for pleasure.

And going to Valentin, who tries, not very successfully, to sculpt my hair into an elegance appropriate to the diplomatic sorties of his imagination, is always worthwhile. Sighing, as he wipes the twenty-year-old (he told me that himself) yellow plastic roller on his white jacket, and placing his other hand on his heart, he tells me his woes. Every week he goes for a cardiogram and last week it was even more irregular than usual. His condition is deteriorating due to the frustration of doing all these diplomatic heads in such disorderly surroundings! Mr. Pearson (whose hair he also cuts from time to time) really should complain to Mr. Andropov about the extraordinary inefficiency of the work brigades who are supposed to be *remont*ing the hairdressing salon. You may remember when I first mentioned the *remont* over a year ago! At this rate it will be at least five years before they finish. And what a thing, Valentin says, for his foreign clientèle to be witnessing week after week. Particularly since, in the last few months, we have watched through his window an entire building being modernized by workers brought in from Yugoslavia. The building belongs to the Ministry of Defence.

So much for the minutiae of my diplomatic days. Most of the rest of my time (when I'm not writing home, though even then to a certain extent) is spent trying to come to terms with this country. And from that point of view the last little while has been quite fruitful. What's on at the movies in Moscow can tell you a lot about what is going on in Soviet life. So can the theatre, because people can at least choose what they would like to see from among the available offerings even if they can't always get tickets. In the absence of advertisements or hoopla or even reliable criticism the message about what is worth seeing usually gets around by word of mouth, and so what is popular has a special significance that it doesn't have at home. During the last couple of weeks we have been to two movies, a ballet, a play, a musical, and a couple of art exhibitions, all of which have been extremely popular and received with enthusiasm.

The most popular movie in town, which I went to see the other day with Natasha, is *Railway Station for Two*, a black comedy extremely well acted and directed, which is built around an unlikely and rather sentimental story but draws in the crowds because it is full of sardonic vignettes about the shadier side of contemporary Soviet life. Furthermore, it actually shows scenes from a Siberian prison camp, which in this country is quite daring. Although none of the writers I discuss below would recognize the prison director ... A couple of days later Geoffrey and I went to see one of the hits of this year's theatrical season, Tennessee Williams's *Rose Tattoo*, upstairs on the experimental stage of the Moscow Arts Theatre. I read it during the afternoon and enjoyed remembered visions of Anna Magnani and Marlon Brando. Somehow I found myself with Slavs on the Baltic instead of among Italian immigrants on the Texas coast but the acting was so good that the illusion of torrid sex and raw emotion really worked! During the last few years there have been two or three plays by Tennessee Williams on stage in Moscow at any one time. I think it has something to do with sublimation. The ballet we saw was done by an innovative and very much admired group from Leningrad under a young director called Eifmann. In the first half (among other short pieces) they danced a speculation about how Claudius seduced Gertrude before the opening of *Hamlet*, which was fascinating (and much sexier than *Rose Tattoo!*) The main work, after the intermission, was a passionate and moving transformation of two masterworks, Tchaikovsky's Sixth Symphony and Dostoevsky's *The Idiot*, into a third medium, dance, where each was shown up in a new way. I thought it was terrific. Geoffrey, as usual, was more reserved. But Elaine agreed with me. Outside the Lenin Komsomol Theatre, the young people crowded for spare tickets. There we saw a rock musical based on poems by Pablo Neruda called *The Stars and Death of Joaquin Murietta*. It has been in the repertory for five years but still has a great following. Chileans in the California Gold Rush. Star-crossed lovers, a big bar scene (best in the show! more sexy dancers!). Shoot-outs. Lots of loud music. Geoffrey felt too old to be there but we really enjoyed it!

Of all the things we have seen, *Andrei Rublyov* will stay with me longest. It has been running in Moscow off and on for ten years. In black and white and with extraordinary attention to detail, the director, Andrei Tarkovsky, has recreated the life and times of the great icon painter who died at the Andronikov Monastery in Moscow in 1430, at an advanced age. Scenes of mediaeval craftsmanship alternate with scenes of man's inhumanity to man culminating in a powerful portrayal of the sack of Vladimir by the Tartars, a horror that Rublyov is assumed to have witnessed. Toward the end of the film, and the end of the painter's life, the black and white landscape of fifteenth-century Russia is slowly transfused with colour. Then the camera lovingly reveals one after another of Rublyov's surviving works, coming at last to the great icon of the Old Testament Trinity, which is now in the Tretyakov Gallery. Out of the brutality that surrounded him, the bitter experience of his own life, and all the suffering that he saw, a gifted monk was able to create glorious paintings full of compassion and tenderness. And Tarkovsky has echoed his achievement over five hundred years later. As have many of his contemporaries (particularly the women), whose remarkable writings I have been reading in connection with a discussion that I led last Monday for my Soviet Literature group on works associated with life in the prisons. Three women: Galina von Meck, a direct descendent of Davydov, one of the Decembrists exiled to Siberia in 1826 (and a granddaughter of Tchaikovsky's patroness), who was imprisoned as a class enemy in the twenties and for who knows what reason in the thirties; Olga Ivinskaya, Pasternak's late love, his model for Lara in *Dr. Zhivago*, who was imprisoned on his behalf twice, both before and after he died; and Eugenia Ginsburg, a young Communist and wife of a member of the Central Committee, whose brilliant book *Into the Whirlwind* describes the beginnings of her eighteen years "out there" in the late thirties on trumped-up charges that made no sense whatsoever. And three men: Solzhenitzen, of course, *A Day in the Life of Ivan Denisovich*; Varlam Shalamov's bleak but superbly crafted *Kolyma Tales*; and Georgy Vladimov's spare and telling novella about what happens to a noble but specially trained dog when the prisoners he has always had to guard are released after Stalin's death. It is called *Faithful Ruslan*. To comment about the implications of these works and their impact on me would extend this letter by many pages so I won't, but read them if you can.

From all this it may seem that my life here is rich and full of interest and to a certain extent that is true. But there are barren patches. Friendships with Soviet citizens are successfully inhibited, I do not have my children with me to introduce me to the wide variety of supportive friends I found in India, and the foreign community, including our own Embassy, is too transient and too defined by the roles people play to allow for real intimacy, particularly at the level at which we find ourselves. So I long to be home where I can pick up the phone and reach any one of you. But then I'll stop writing letters!

May 10, 1983

Yesterday was Victory Day in the Soviet Union. In every town and city old men and women laden with medals and ribbons gathered to remember the German surrender and recount their war experience. In Moscow the veterans traditionally congregate either in front of the Bolshoi Theatre or on the paths of Gorky Park. It was to the park that Anne and Michael and I went after lunch and saw them sitting in twos and threes on freshly-painted white benches along the river bank, holding up hand-painted signs for identification, collecting their comrades. Young people brought them flowers, tulips and narcissus mostly, and stopped to listen to their stories. Someone produced an accordion. A pair of old soldiers started to sing army ballads. Their gold-toothed comrades-in-arms began to dance in the middle of a small circle of well-wishers; it swelled rapidly as the curious arrived from all sides. A quartet of veterans spread out a campaign map on a rickety table and traced advances and retreats for any interested passerby. The whole park was jammed. Red tulips shone in the sunlight. The green grass glistened. The leaves were full out. Some young soldiers were there, too, with their girls. But mostly it was the usual motley crowd of Muscovites and visitors, only multiplied ten times. People were lined up everywhere, to ride the ferris wheel, to row about on the ponds, to buy "Eskimos" (ice-cream bars covered in chocolate) or bottles of Fanta or, if they were both patient and lucky, as many bagels as they could hold, scooped up from baskets on the ground in front of white-coated babushkas who were seated here and there on camp stools among the bushes. A good-humoured crowd having a good time, out in the park to enjoy the peace that those veterans had so painfully won for them. And when they have all gone, when there is no one left who remembers what it was really like during those bitter years, will we be better off or worse? It seems to me that living memories produce a better antidote to war than any number of heroic monuments, so I think it fortunate that those old warriors find a willing audience once a year on a sunny afternoon in May.

As for heroic monuments, well, *now* let me tell you about our last official trip. We started with a day in Volgograd. Memories of the Battle of Stalingrad pointed us in that direction. As the Germans knew too well, Volgograd is on the way to Baku. We flew there from Moscow in time for dinner on April 23. A thousand kilometres southeast of the capital, we found that spring had fully arrived. In the hotel dining room there was lily-of-the-valley on our table along with a Canadian flag. We ate some Volga sturgeon and drank to the birthdays of LBP and wished there had been more of them. The next day was Sunday so we made no official calls. Instead we entrusted ourselves to our engaging Intourist guide, Galina, who was much too young to possess any memories of the days when her town was named after the Man of Steel. Before she entered school the city was re-named for the great river along whose banks it now stretches for more than sixty miles. And yet the Volga, so rich in meaning for the whole of European Russia, does not contain the soul of this city. That is to be found up on a hill called Mamayev Kurgan, in the gigantic figure of the motherland, brandishing a sword over the city with her right hand while her left is flung back toward Berlin. Perhaps for most of its one million inhabitants Volgograd is a normal industrial centre, specializing in the production of tractors, of rolling stock and hydro-electric power, and providing all the usual amenities of a Soviet city including x-number of schools, medical centres, palaces of culture, sports complexes (any one of you who has been here can recite the rest of the list). Further, it offers river trips and a handsome embankment and lots of parks that are extremely well lit at night, as we discovered when we went for a stroll after dinner. Perhaps most of those people walking up and down the sidewalk pay little attention any more to past events. But for the tourist, Volgograd is one vast monument. The first stop on our city tour was the new diorama, which places one right on top of Mamayev Hill during one of the coldest days of that endless winter battle. What we saw brought back vividly the terrible devastation of Stalingrad that we used to hear about day after day on the radio, or see on the newsreel when we had occasion to go to the movies. I turned twelve when that battle was being fought, and Mr. Suslov, who looks after Canada in the Ministry of Foreign Affairs as head of the Second European Division, was one of those young gunners on the canvas in front of me. He was eighteen.

Near the diorama only one building has been preserved as it was when the last shot was fired on February 2, 1943. The rest of the shattered city was levelled and then rebuilt by armies of volunteers as well as by the German prisoners of war who were kept around until the mid-fifties. However, the buildings they erected were designed in such a ponderous style that they remind one more of the past than of the future. And the huge memorial on Mamayev Hill is essentially a frozen battle. One can almost hear the guns and mortar as one walks through it. Visually it is much more interesting than I had expected from the photographs I had seen. Mounting the steps from the riverside toward the fierce figure in her blowing draperies, her heroic proportions are balanced by the monumental sculptures of struggle and death that rise up on either side. But emotionally the complex is numbing. There is no presentation of the battle as a personal experience, nor any hint of individual tragedy, and somehow one feels it would be impious to speculate independently on the implications of what one sees. Most of the war memorials we have visited in the Soviet Union are built around common graves or the "flame of the (generalized) fallen." Even when separate names are inscribed on a wall they blend indistinguishably into a symbolic pattern. I have never seen anything here that has moved me in the same way as the simple rows of white crosses in the military cemeteries of France. Perhaps the Soviet losses during the last war were so massive as to almost defy individualization, and yet the lively presence of those veterans in Gorky Park yesterday did more to make me think about what war actually means, and to convince me of the real desire of ordinary Soviet men and women for peace, than could any number of heroic and expensive war memorials.

We spent two nights in Volgograd. Very early on April 25, while it was still dark in fact, we took off for Baku. We flew east over the wide delta and as day came up we swung out over the Caspian Sea, turning south to fly past the snow-covered Caucasus glowing in the early morning sun. Almost before we'd swallowed our cold chicken breakfast we came in to land among the oil derricks that cover the land on either side of the airport. The Chief of Protocol greeted us cordially,

accompanied by a young graduate student of English with extraordinarily wide-set eyes who was to practise on us for the next two
days. He thrust a lovely bouquet of cellophane-wrapped carnations
into my arms; we retrieved our bag from the aircraft and piled into
the waiting Chaika. Driving into the city (for once we weren't preceded by an officious *militsia* car, thank goodness!) we had a brief
glimpse of mosque and minaret among apartment complexes, smoke
stacks, and oil storage tanks. And we climbed the hill to our hotel
through European streets lined with plane trees and nineteenth-century mansions, relics of the Nobels and the Rothschilds, the oil mag-
nates from the west who controlled the flow of Caspian oil that (at the
turn of the century) was supplying a major percentage of the world's
needs. From our hotel suite we had a magnificent view of the city and
its bay and the derricks marching out through the blue sea to the far
horizon. We unpacked quickly, had a cup of coffee with Paul and
Judy Meyer (Paul is a political officer at the Embassy), who had flown
in from Moscow the previous evening to join us for the Baku part of
the trip, and then set off with our companions to learn all about
Azerbaijan, past, present, and future.

Azerbaijan's past seems harder to catch hold of than the past of its
Trans-Caucasian neighbours and its history does not appear to have
forged the distinct national identity that is so marked in Georgia and
Armenia. Still, fire has always been its element. That's what "Azer"
means, apparently, and among the earlier inhabitants of the territory
there were Zoroastrians who tended altars of eternal flames. On his
way east (or west), Marco Polo saw "unextinguishable fires" near
Baku, probably oil burning in the marshes. And the oil has gone on
burning down through the centuries. However, the land was always
being overrun and bloodied, first by a number of tribes, then by
Persians, Arabs, Turks, Mongols, Persians and Turks again, and finally imperial Russia. Arabs brought Islam in the eighth century, and the
Turkish language took hold in the ninth. The present population is a
middle-eastern mixture, plus Armenians and Russians. Azerbaijan
continues to be Islamic, perhaps more by custom than belief, but still
this is enough to set it apart from Georgia and Armenia, which were
so dramatically shaped by their Christian traditions, and it helps to
account for the failure of an independent Transcaucasian Federation

to stay outside the Union of Soviet Socialist Republics in 1923. Besides, conditions for the oil workers were pretty bad at the beginning of the century, giving rise to lots of local revolutionary activity. We were shown a whole room in the local history museum devoted to the famous twenty-six Commissars of the people of Baku who were transported across the Caspian Sea by the British authorities and allegedly executed by them in the Karakum desert on a hot September day in 1918. While Fitzroy MacLean writes in his book *The Back of Beyond* that the British have been unfairly blamed (they were really done in by Russian Social Revolutionaries), they became the sort of martyrs that strengthened Soviet power, and Soviet Azerbaijan has since gone from strength to strength, being fortunately preserved from the Nazis by the battle of Stalingrad.

Our first call was on the Foreign Minister, who turned out to be a woman of considerable experience, deceptively red-haired, pleasant and hospitable. She told us a bit about her long career, discussed our program, and sent us off to the Mayor. He was rather fun. After giving us the usual number of statistics concerning the city—which I promptly forgot—he began to discuss the demographic situation. Like his colleagues whom we met last year in Central Asia, the Mayor of Baku was delighted with the birth rate. Why, he had an uncle, he said, who after thirteen sons finally produced a daughter! He was a big man, the Mayor went on, weighing over 100 kilos, and his wife weighed less than 50 ... Now those are the kind of figures that for some reason I never forget!

From the elegant nineteenth-century mansion in which the Mayor's office was located, we drove up the hill and back into the centuries to visit the old town within its ancient walls. From the fifteenth-century palace of the Khans on the summit, the houses tumble down on all sides separated by narrow curving lanes, each one more picturesque than the next. On top of the hill we were enchanted by the mediaeval craftsmanship revealed by the light fluted arches and delicate stone tracery of the Diwan Khan; at the bottom we admired the incredible workmanship that had gone into designing, weaving, and knotting the beautiful carpets on display in the Azerbaijan carpet museum. Some are contemporary; some date from the last century; all of them are fine. Well, almost all of them. I prefer my designs abstract or traditional. Political iconography does not belong on the loom. Inside the walls of the old city the sun was hot on crumbling stone and small boys played with sticks and pebbles. Once through the gate we re-entered the Soviet Union. We returned to our hotel for lunch and a chat with our waiter about the latest Canada–USSR match. The World Hockey Championship took place during our trip, and everywhere we went we encountered the most tremendous interest! Few people in Azerbaijan have ever seen an actual hockey game, but most of them know all about the Montreal Canadiens! You can imagine how popular our little maple leaf pins were!

But our first day in Baku was only half over. In the afternoon we were taken to the historical museum where dusty artifacts lurked in unlit cases and the twenty-six Commissars were executed five times over. Then a rapid passage through the library of old manuscripts and miniatures where I would willingly have lingered over the lively and expressive work of a sixteenth-century painter named Sadiq bek Afshar, except that the Lenin oil refinery was next on our itinerary. There, glasses of hot tea and some delicious *barfi* and an engaging "hero-labourer" who actually blushed when his boss praised his competence in handling the Swiss-made American-designed master control panel compensated for the forgettable statistics and the familiar rhetoric to which the Director treated us.

In the evening the Foreign Minister was hostess to a good dinner featuring lots of lamb, local wine and tea, plus toasts and conversation in Azerbaijani, Russian, English, French, and Arabic. Standing on our balcony for a few minutes before sinking gratefully into our beds, we gazed at the full moon reflected in the waters of the Caspian Sea, and it was almost possible to believe that, with its wide, sweeping curve, and with much of the city disguised by night—except for the twinkling lights stretching over the surrounding hills—the Bay of Baku is one of the most beautiful in the world.

The second day of our visit was not quite so hectic. The four of us started out together with the ritual visit to the Park of Economic Achievements where bits of loose carpeting always trip up the unwary admirer of pale blue machine tools. Then we separated. The day before I had expressed to our Azerbaijani hosts an interest in visiting an institution connected with children, a hospital perhaps, or a school. In not untypical Soviet fashion, while Geoffrey and Paul Meyer were calling on Mr. Bagirev, the First Secretary of the Communist Party of Azerbaijan, Judy and I found ourselves at an Institute of Cardiology that, of course, had practically nothing to do with children. However, it turned out to be a remarkable visit that I would have hated to miss. We were provided with an Intourist interpreter and a young man from the Ministry of Foreign Affairs to keep an eye on us, but the star of the occasion turned out to be the Director of the Institute himself, an attractive, intelligent, and sophisticated man who rapidly understood that there was a mismatch between my interests and his specialty, but who nevertheless did his best to find us relevant information where possible and to ask us all kinds of questions about Canada and about our physical lifestyle. Then we had fun with his machines—he had lots of them—most from Western Europe and the USA, except for the computer-programmed diagnostic machine that now contains some invented fragments of my medical history! The Institute has a hundred beds and altogether was in much better condition than any other such place I have visited in the Soviet Union. Even the patients in Intensive Care looked cheerful! He and his assistants couldn't have been kinder or more attentive. We left with an armful of roses and a strong pulse. One never knows what to expect next!

Well, *next* we met Geoffrey and Paul for lunch at a reconstructed caravanserai just outside the old walls where, alas, our status as important visitors isolated us in a damp cave with too much to eat. *Our* idea of being "special" would have been to sit in the sun with tea-drinking locals, but unfortunately that did not coincide with what our hosts had in mind. Never mind, we had a long, unaccompanied walk in the afternoon and at 6:30 boarded the Moscow train to chug up the coast to Derbent.

A disadvantage to travelling "soft" class in the Soviet Union is that although one may get flowers in one's compartment, one's car is inevitably attached to the very end of the train, so when we arrived in Derbent five hours later we had a long way to climb down onto the track. A small crowd leaped to catch us before we fell, consisting of the tall skinny young Mayor, his short round deputy, and various other hangers-on, all of whom were most cordial and welcoming. We

were taken to a comfortable guest house where a great bouquet of
fresh lilacs scented the night air while we sat around drinking the
local cognac and talking about what we might do. Without an interpreter the discussion did not last long, but there was lots of goodwill
and we found ourselves looking forward to an interesting day.

We weren't mistaken. Our short stay in Derbent really was the
highlight of this particular trip. Derbent is not Intourist territory. Last
year the British Ambassador had come and the year before that the
French, but otherwise foreign visitors have been few and far
between. Yet it is one of the most interesting towns we have seen in
this country. Derbent is in Daghestan, an autonomous republic within the Russian Federation. The border with Azerbaijan lies just south
of it. It has been inhabited for a very long time—2,700 years we were
told. Strategically placed at the point where a spur of the Caucasus
reaches to within three kilometres of the Caspian Sea, it has for centuries been a gateway to the East. In the fifth century a citadel was
built halfway up the slope of the mountain, and from it two walls led
down to the sea. The town was contained within them. No one could
pass north or south without paying a toll. There was no lack of travellers. To the west the mountains of the greater Caucasus stretch
unbroken for hundreds of miles; to the east is the wide expanse of the
inland sea. Today the sea has drawn away from the land, but the
citadel is still there and remnants of its walls. Within them are old
houses and communal baths and a fascinating mosque built in stages
from the eighth to the fourteenth century. The interior space is low
and wide and every inch of the floor is covered with carpets. Islam is
much more than custom in Derbent. The full length of each beautifully chiselled silver handle on the main doors is tied with knotted
strips of faded cloth, each one a special petition. And the stunted
trees overhanging the seventh-century tombs of the forty martyrs
who brought Islam to Derbent are dripping with the prayers of the
faithful. The cemeteries of Derbent are unlike any I have seen elsewhere. From every viewpoint in the modern town that has spread
out beyond the old walls and along the coast, you can see the forests
of tall, narrow gravestones leaning seaward. Beautifully carved with
sinuous arabesques and passages from the Koran, each stone carries
a symbol, a bird for a woman, a horse for a man, to indicate the sex

of the bones beneath the ground. They have been accumulating on the slopes for centuries, more numerous, one is sure, than the living inhabitants of the town.

But I don't want to give the impression that this is a town more dead than alive—quite the contrary. We visited a carpet factory that was a real treat. Fifty women sat at looms in a large and airy room, full of sunlight and green plants, and knotted coloured skeins of wool into many intricate designs. An equal number of women work at home. The finished carpets, which are displayed in an open shed in the courtyard, are very beautiful (although, alas, when I went with Anne to buy carpets last week in Moscow, none of the Derbent carpets was half so attractive, so I bought you a Turkmenian one instead, Katharine, for your wedding present). One of the senior workers at the factory, a tidy, competent woman, is a deputy to the Supreme Soviet of the USSR and she and a co-worker, both excellent cooks, prepared shortbread and delicious honey cakes which we enjoyed with our morning tea. Then, for lunch, we went to the cognac factory, where we tasted all the products of the Derbent vineyards and sat for a long time over our meal. A teacher of English from the local high school had been found to interpret for us and communication became more substantial. Still, conversation was a little stilted. We lingered at table more because the Mayor was uncertain (we were his first "important" visitors) how to bring the meal to an end than because we had much to say. It was a little awkward, but in the evening, after more sightseeing and a visit to the brick-coloured seashore, we were all more relaxed when we ate and we climbed quite regretfully back onto the train that had deposited us in Derbent twenty-four hours earlier, feeling that we had been much closer to the life of a small Soviet town than is usually possible for foreigners. On the whole we were impressed. The energy and ability are there for the future—and so are a number of young sons. When our hosts sat with them in front of their television sets the next evening to watch Canada being defeated by Czechoslovakia, we hope they were all wearing our maple leaf pins and remembering us with some pleasure.

The train journey to Rostov-on-Don was rather long. Planning the trip, I thought we would be able to see the Caucasus in the early morning. But we overslept and the snow mountains were out of sight when we woke up with a jerk. We were stopped at the neo-classical train station of Mineralnye Vody, the spa where intellectuals and aristocrats came to flush out their livers in the nineteenth century, and where now organized groups of factory workers from the big industrial towns clear out the toxins from their systems. Then all day we clacked and clattered north across the steppe. The weather was still beautiful and everything was fresh and green, but alas, we seldom had an uninterrupted view of open plain because the track was bordered everywhere with thick copses. Rather disappointing. I sat and read Fitzroy MacLean's *The Back of Beyond* instead, and Bulgakov's *The Master and Margarita*.

In the late afternoon, after waiting a long time, we crossed the railway bridge over the Don and drew into the station at Rostov. Train travel is a mixed experience in the USSR. What one sees is not always that interesting and there isn't enough track for all the trains so there are often tiresome delays. Still, it's worth it from time to time to be able to observe people living and moving about without being watched ourselves!

I'll take you quickly through Rostov. This letter is already much too long. Actually, it's a pity to rush because Rostov is really a charming city, much more attractive than Volgograd. It, too, suffered greatly during the war, being occupied by the Germans for many months. But it was better designed in the first place with wide boulevards and spacious avenues, and parks full of shade trees absolutely essential in the hot, dry summer. And while there was much war damage, many buildings survived and a number of streets are lined with the attractive, two-storey houses typical of the Armenian storekeepers who used to live above their places of business. So many of them were settled in Rostov by Catherine the Great that the population is now almost one-third Armenian. The city is built up on the steep right bank of the quiet Don and overlooks the open steppe that stretches south and east, to Caucasus and Caspian. It is not hard to imagine the Don Cossacks riding across its endless distances. Having ended our journey there, it is altogether appropriate that last night, after our encounter with the veterans in Gorky Park, we should have ended our Victory Day listening to the Don Cossack chorus singing their haunting song *Meadowlands*. It was my favourite song when I was in the London South Collegiate Glee Club, and now, at long last, I understand why!

Such a long letter! I hope you haven't given up! No more travelling for a while, but *lots* of visitors, official and other. Thankfully some of them are our own children.

LETTER NUMBER 51

Zavidova, May 29, 1983

It is ten in the evening and I have just come off the porch. I was stretched out there on the camp bed reading the remarkable forty years' correspondence between Boris Pasternak and his cousin Olga Friedenburg. Daylight is finally fading and there is, of course, no electrical outlet there. Geoffrey is sitting in the living room under the only portable lamp standard anyway. He is reading the briefs prepared for the upcoming visit of the Trade Minister, Gerald Regan, various officials, and assorted businessmen who will be participating in a meeting of the "mixed economic commission" with their Soviet "counterparts" (I guess *that* is a rather misleading term). Anne is straining her eyes a bit at the dining-room table under a 25-watt bulb finishing a philosophy paper that she hopes to send back in Wednesday's bag. I've finished my book, which reads almost like a novel, so interesting are the personalities of the two correspondents, their complex relationship, and the terrible and tragic times they lived through (she spent all nine hundred days in Leningrad during the siege) to which they are only able to refer obliquely. The letters, however, are accompanied by extracts from her diary, which are much more explicit and which make narrative sense of what they say to each other. Now, before it is full night, I'll get started on my letter to you hoping that I'll be able to complete it before the delegation arrives.

We have had two lovely days at Zavidova. The dacha became available because the Canadian Club had a "Fifties" party last night and those who were supposed to come here this weekend decided to grease their hair and wear bobby socks instead. Given the fact that our bedroom is only two storeys above the Club dance floor we welcomed the opportunity to escape! Besides, the weather has been beautiful. This morning we rowed across the Volga to enjoy the pine woods on the far shore. We would have felt happy and at peace there crunching last year's dry cones under our feet on the deserted paths if we hadn't been pursued by huge insects out of Monty Python, a cross between wasp and deerfly, and by the sounds of Soviet pop music coming at full volume from a barge advancing slowly upstream. It was hard to say which was the more disturbing! Back on our side of the river we sat on the dock for a long time with John Burns (the *New York Times* correspondent) and various other agreeable people who had come up for the day. Geoffrey and Anne swam, John sailed, some of the others water-skied. Later, Anne and I had a sauna and then I was glad to get into the river, wrapped in a white sheet! Toward evening we drifted off toward our dacha but, as we turned back to say goodbye to the others picking up on the dock, we saw beyond them in the Shosha a swimming horse being pulled slowly across the river into the sunset by a small motorboat. You really never know what you are going to see next in this country!

Never has there been such a month of May in Moscow. At least not that anyone can remember. Day after day the weather has been sunny and warm, sometimes unseasonably so, sometimes just fresh and clear. Of course the tulips and the lilacs and the chestnut blooms came and went so fast that they could hardly be appreciated and already the poplar fluff is drifting through the streets, coming in through the open windows, making a mess of the red carpets downstairs. From time to time there has been a little rain, just enough to keep everything green and growing. They are even predicting a good harvest for the first time in many years. UPDK delivered a load of topsoil to the backyard and it has been spread on the lawn, which has now been rolled and freshly seeded. But whether we will get new grass or baby poplar trees is anyone's guess. One of the *dvorniks* has taken on the garden part-time and I have willingly abandoned my efforts to him. Next spring someone else will be watching the tulips push up and will be rejoicing in the thick new grass. I'll be starting my rock garden at Burnett!

For Michael the fine weather provided an entirely new experience of the Soviet Union. He and his friend, Gordon Robertson, went off to Kiev for a couple of days and swam in the Dnieper. Before that we drove westward through rolling countryside to the battlefield of Borodino, coming back to Zvenigorod for a late lunch with Victoria and her family at their dacha on the Moscow River. Michael played chess on a bench in the garden with Victoria's husband Gennady. On another beautiful day we went to Vladimir and Suzdal, stopping near Vladimir and walking a kilometre or so across the water meadows sprinkled with daisies and buttercups to look at the enchanting little twelfth-century Church of the Intercession on the Nerl. Multiple power lines stretching between metal towers destroyed any illusion of mediaeval peace and yet the proportions of the little church, standing quite alone above the River Nerl, are so perfect as to transcend all time. Michael was also able to talk to a number of people here about Soviet foreign policy so I think that all in all he had a memorable and agreeable visit.

After Michael and Gordon left, Anne got down to work on her paper and I started to prepare for the onslaught of June's official visitors. We both took a break last Friday, driving out to Zagorsk to visit the Toy Institute there. Zagorsk has long been famous for its toys. In the old days, when the monastery was functioning, people wanted to take away something as a souvenir of their pilgrimage and little toy figurines were the cheapest thing to produce and offer to the mass of pilgrims, who were very poor. The monks carved and painted wood and made some other things of clay. Toward the end of the nineteenth century "toy" production for pilgrims declined but Russian artists took up the cause of locally-produced crafts and toy-making left the monastery to become the local industry of the town. The famous *matrioshka* dolls were invented there at the beginning of this century and fifty years ago the All-Union Toy Institute in Zagorsk was formed to make toy policy for the whole country! No toys can be mass-produced anywhere unless they have the stamp of approval of the Institute. In fact most new toys are designed there anyway and much research is done to make sure they are properly educational! Working with toys seems to turn people on and they were the jolliest group we have met yet. I only wish I saw more of their toys in the shops! We had a discussion about war toys and different toys for girls and boys and were told about "patriotism" and "equality." They confessed that they are now designing video games as well because the demand is so great but they don't really approve! Then we went to the Toy Museum where some wonderful toys were on display from earlier times, full of imagination and humour. It was an entertaining morning and we stopped for a while on the way back at a nineteenth-century estate some kilometres off the main road and strolled about amid the woods and wildflowers.

What else to tell you? The Kirov is in town for a few weeks and so far we've been to a lovely production of *Eugene Onegin* as well as an exciting performance, more a musical than an opera, with lots of action and terrific sets, of a work by a contemporary composer on the life of Peter the Great. We've walked in the Botanical Gardens and taken a boat ride along the river enjoying the sunbathers and wondering at the swimmers. There are big crowds everywhere, even during the week. For a whole month I don't think Muscovites have worried about anything much except being able to get away from work and enjoy their unusual luck. We feel pretty sorry for you all back in cold and clammy North America!

LETTER NUMBER 52

June 12, 1983

Last night we went up the Moscow River on the annual Embassy boat trip. Alas, the fine weather of May has not followed us into June. It is generally much cooler and there has been a fair amount of rain. Of course the rain has been welcome to the Ministry of Agriculture to say nothing of the *dachniki* who so carefully cultivate the garden plots surrounding their little summer houses, if not to the tourists, and anyway, it has not been coming down steadily day after day as it did *last* June. In fact last night was quite pleasant if rather chilly and we had no trouble keeping warm by dancing on the deck and playing "frisbee" at the Bay of Joys during the two hours we stopped there.

This year one of the senior officials from UPDK came along as a guest with his wife and so did Victor and Inga Sukhodrev. Their presence contributed greatly to the success of the evening. Victor showed off his double career as high-level interpreter and as Foreign Ministry official in charge of Canada by wearing both his Camp David windbreaker and a red and white Canadian sporting cap. I don't know where his jeans came from. Most of the local staff came along and the drivers danced with their usual flair and bounce. We floated cheerfully into port at 11:00 p.m. and then down Leningradsky Prospect and into the Canadian Club. Geoffrey and I came upstairs to bed but I eventually had to send a message down to lower the sound. Enough is enough ... !

We have had a couple of other invitations to riverboat parties this month, at least one of which we will accept along with some of our journalist friends. They are fun, even if they do tend to go on too long! June is turning out to be a very busy month altogether. Tamara's kitchen calendar is marked with Xs—at least three events a week culminating in the National Day celebration on July 1. And many of the evenings when we are not entertaining here we'll be out, for dinner, or a reception, or another National Day, as well as attending concerts and theatre. One is tempted to say that June is the "season" in Moscow if such a term didn't sound a little odd in the Soviet context.

The visit of Gerald Regan, his wife, and the various officials from Ottawa who participated with him and Soviet counterparts in the meetings of the Mixed Economic Commission appears to have been successful, at least according to the practical criteria by which *I* measure these things. I know that George Hazen's brow got more and more furrowed as he tried to organize all the comings and goings of the fifteen or so businessmen who accompanied the group, as well as set up meetings with the Ministries of Forestry and Mines and Gas and Oil, etc. for some of the officials. However, nobody got left at the airport or missed his appointment or lost his luggage. Whether deals were negotiated and contracts signed is another matter. Mr. Regan seems to have been satisfied with the level of meetings that were arranged for him, including one with Mr. Gorbachev. Everyone made lots of positive speeches. Mrs. Regan and I were the only women present at the formal lunch I organized for the group at the Residence. Yury, the Embassy carpenter, made two new tables for me out of heavy packing cases so that I could seat all forty-five of us comfortably in the dining room. The spread looked attractive and tasted good although the salmon was just a trifle underdone and there was no whipped cream for the frozen lemon soufflé because it had turned sour in the storm overnight. We had to get everybody in and out in a little under two hours, which included waiting for one important guest who never arrived and listening to two substantial speeches. So no one could have seconds and if they didn't serve themselves enough the first time, too bad for them! Mr. Suslov, the Deputy Minister of Foreign Trade and Mr. Regan's co-chairman on the Commission (the Minister, Mr. Patolichev, is very elderly and infirm), is a man of presence and humour and for the first time in my entire experience here a guest of honour made a special effort to compliment the hostess and thank her for organizing the event. I really appreciated that and passed on the compliments to the staff who had had to work hard all week and not only for that lunch.

The official program for the whole group included *Swan Lake* at the Kremlin Palace of Congresses. If possible, of course, *Swan Lake* is featured on *every* official program! Mr. Gromyko is reported to have seen it eighty-two times. This performance, however, given by the Kirov Ballet before a rapturous audience, was quite exceptional. The Prince was a true *danseur noble* and Odette-Odile was danced by Mezentseva. As the white swan she was elegant and lyrical; as the black, provocative and dynamic. In both roles her control was total. Within traditional boundaries the sets and costumes were fresh and imaginative. And the orchestra was superb! In that huge, impersonal auditorium there was true theatrical magic. Mr. Regan talked about it for the rest of the week. The businessmen were starry-eyed!

During the middle of that busy time Geoffrey received a phone call that Averell Harriman, the distinguished American diplomat, was in town and would like us to join him for dinner. We regretted that we couldn't but we did have a drink with him in the Mezhdunarodnaya Hotel, where he occupied the penthouse suite that is usually reserved, we have been told, for Armand Hammer, the American oil magnate and the Soviet government's favourite capitalist! What a fine old gentleman Mr. Harriman is! A little deaf, he is ninety-one after all, but fully alert, fondly remembering LBP and recounting a number of Stalin stories from the war years when he was US Ambassador to the USSR. He was to see Andropov the next day, so many years his junior! We tore ourselves away reluctantly and went downstairs to have dinner in the "Japanese" restaurant where a tall blonde in a kimono silently served us large cubes of "Kobe" beef and cabbage salad in a little room where we had to take off our shoes. We drank vodka from little china cups and pondered the inevitable "regression toward the mean" that takes place in any restaurant in the Soviet Union once the imported chef leaves. The first thing our blonde did was to check off on the menu all the items that were no longer available! Never mind, the company that evening was very jolly and the thick pieces of meat were actually delicious.

The Regan visit took place during the first week of June. Last week, between a reception for a sports group from Concordia University and a buffet luncheon for departing Canadians and their Soviet colleagues, Anne and Patricia and I went to Estonia. Everyone told us that Tallinn was the most attractive city on the Baltic Coast and that, once there, we would hardly know that we were in the Soviet Union! If you only have two days to visit the Baltic States, they said, that's the place to go. So we did. The charm of the city and its surroundings is very real and it is not Russian but like every place I have visited within the borders of the USSR it is undeniably Soviet. Not totally. We arrived by plane on a sunny morning and took a taxi into town to a comfortable modern hotel *and* there were stoppers in the washbasin! The whole day we wandered around. It was lovely to be unprogrammed and unorganized. The old part of town is delightful. Many buildings date from the thirteenth century and the period of the Teutonic Knights. Others show the prosperity that Revel (the old name of Tallinn) enjoyed through the commercial activity of the Hanseatic League in the fifteenth century. The streets are steep, narrow, and cobbled, the churches are Gothic, the walls of the citadel are rough, grey stone, the burghers' houses are northern European, tall and thin with sharply angled tiled roofs and square windows. There were flowers for sale on every corner and the lilacs were in bloom. The winters must be long and damp by the Baltic Sea but we were fortunate to encounter sunny patches and must have seen the city at its best. And we had lots of daylight to see it by. Tallinn is not quite as far north as Leningrad but Patricia, who stayed awake reading, said it was still light at one in the morning.

On our second day we took a city bus along the coastal road a few kilometres to the Olympic Yacht basin where we watched a hundred beautiful boats slip out into the Gulf of Finland to race on the blue water. And then we sat and sunned ourselves on the long, sandy beach, looking back across the Bay to the spires of St. Olaf and the Domkirk. We returned to Moscow by the night train, fourteen hours, much of it through forest and agricultural land. Given its history it is surprising that Estonia has such a strong national identity. But it did have a few lucky patches. Ivan the Terrible drove the Estonians under the protection of Sweden, which turned out not to be such a bad thing for the peasants. And, although progress stopped when Peter defeated Charles XII and the Baltic lands came under his control, real reforms were offered by Alexander I and a process of nationalization began that grew in such strength during the early part of the twentieth century that Lenin signed a peace treaty with Estonia in February 1922 recognizing her independence "in perpetuity." Of course it was a very difficult period in which to be independent, particularly as her two neighbours grew ever more powerful during the thirties. The history of the war years was terrible. Now there is relative prosperity but even on such a short visit we were made quite aware of the surviving national spirit. One cannot help but wonder what changes another century will bring to the peoples of Estonia and the other Baltic States. I'm glad I was able to go to Tallinn and get to see it for myself.

LETTER NUMBER 53

Sunday, July 2, 1983

Today is a perfect July day, bright and breezy and hot. The Arbat is deserted because those Muscovites who are not at dachas or rest houses or sanatoria or Pioneer camps are out sunning themselves along the Moscow River or beside the ponds and pools, swarming with small boys, of all the city parks. We are dreaming of northern lakes and summer docks but you needn't feel too sorry for us because we have just spent a couple of hours in the peaceful back garden of the Danish Embassy eating fresh marinated salmon and sipping cold champagne with Poul and Inger. We were drinking to the pleasures of knowing them here, to their imminent departure from the Soviet Union, and to our next encounter in Ottawa or New York, where they will be attending the UN General Assembly this autumn. What a time this is for departures! Many of our favourite colleagues have already left for holidays or on to new postings. The Embassy itself is emptying out for the summer. Elaine Mathys left yesterday morning with her children and I will miss her greatly. They have been posted to Brussels so I expect it will be some time before I see her again. Anne left in the afternoon and with her gone, after having said good-bye to Patricia last week, we feel quite bereft.

Yesterday was our National Day, of course. For those of us standing for two hours in the receiving line it's hard to tell whether or not a successful party is taking place in the rest of the Residence, but we were assured by departing guests that everything was just fine. Certainly there were no problems. It was easier to organize than last year's because we had that experience behind us. We knew that Elena was the best person to bring in beautiful flowers from the Botanical Gardens. And that we could get all the ice we needed for a couple of bottles of Canadian whisky! Nikolai is getting very good at organizing his troops and everyone was still smiling when it was all over! The enormous crash we heard at the end turned out to be a case of empty tonic bottles, and other damage was minimal (except for a couple of burns in the carpet). I still believe that it is extremely important to mark our national day in such a traditional and ceremonial way. The "main" guest this year was the vice-president from Armenia, who was large and a little warm in the muggy weather. He stayed the usual twenty-five minutes but most of our numerous other Soviet guests lingered for a long time. The Canadians tended to come a little later and helped us to relax toward the end. Then we could feel that is really was our day and celebrate! Still, it is a relief to have it over. It takes so much planning and organizing. And the endless trips to the gastronome!

During all those trips I have made during the last month, I saw a miracle happen. The gastronome and the little farmers' market where I usually buy my expensive winter greens are located in an area of the city named for the Georgians who have settled there, perhaps on the profits of bringing vitamins and fresh flowers to snowbound Muscovites. Anyway, in front of that market in a small triangular park, I have just witnessed the erection, in *three* weeks, start to finish, of one of the most extraordinary structures I have yet seen in this country of monumental art: a 43-metre obelisk of granite and copper and bronze that commemorates the two-hundredth anniversary of the "union" of Georgia with Russia by interlacing Russian and Georgian letters saying "Peace-Work-Unity-Brotherhood-Friendship." These letters mount the obelisk in welded copper, the whole being surmounted by an incredibly ornate wreath of wheat and grapevines. Apparently Voznesensky, who originally trained as an architect, was involved in the design. He'd be best to stick to poetry. The construction of this monster caused many traffic jams and much confusion, but miraculously it was completed.

On my way back from the gastronome I am still being held up by roadwork taking place on the street that runs perpendicular to Starokonyushenny from my hairdressing salon at Gogol's Boulevard to the foreign ministry. During several weeks the sidewalks were taken up and replaced and then the road was repaved. For a couple of days we drove smoothly and then last week it was all dug up again, this time to lay new pipes for the Generals' apartment building. Driving back from taking Anne to the airport yesterday we saw that a huge crane had fallen over in front of the block, crushing the blue spruce I had admired all year, and being spied upon by gleeful spectators. "No wonder we have no unemployment," is one comment I've heard. And "So much for central planning!" to say nothing of "Who cares? It's all government money anyway." I wonder if it will be finished by the time we get back from Mongolia.

In among trips to market and gastronome and innumerable social events we managed to make a couple of interesting excursions to Peredelkino in the last two weeks. The first time we visited the house of Kornei Chukovsky, best known as a children's writer, whose delightful cautionary tales in verse would fit happily with those of

Edward Lear and Hilaire Belloc. Once his work was banned as being entirely too fanciful for the new Soviet child but luckily that was only for a short period in the thirties. He himself managed to survive those terrible years, writing and doing what he could for his fellow writers who had more difficulties, such as his Peredelkino neighbour, Boris Pasternak. He died in 1969 and his dacha, through which we were shown by his enthusiastic granddaughter, was made into a "literary museum" thus coming under the direct responsibility of the Ministry of Culture, a much more reliable "landlord" than the Writer's Union, as we discovered when we went later to visit Pasternak's house. Chukovsky was obviously a man of considerable breadth and widely read in various languages. Patricia was struck by the fact that the libraries of both houses contained copies of the *Alexandria Quartet* because she wants to read it. I was curious about Chukovsky's copy of *The Arts in Canada* and wondered how he came by it. We sat for tea and pound cake in the comfortable dark blue living room and felt that the memory of Chukovsky was being safely preserved by his relatives, as it quite deserves to be, with some substantial assistance from the Ministry of Culture.

Pasternak, on the other hand, is still in limbo. The Chukovsky granddaughter gave us the telephone number of Pasternak's son, Evgeny, and we made arrangements through him to visit the house a week later. We were met there by his wife, a couple of granddaughters, and the young husband of one of them, as well as assorted dogs and cats. House and garden are in poor repair. There is obviously little money around. The house still belongs to the Writer's Union, who have made a number of moves to repossess it and split it up although it's not all that large. Various interventions have prevented that but until the state can make up its mind to recognize the full genius of Pasternak there is not much likelihood of the dacha being made into a museum, although he lived here for over twenty years and wrote much (including *Dr. Zhivago*) on the desk in the upstairs room overlooking the field and the village up the hill and those three trees in the cemetery under which he is now buried. In the meantime the family does what it can. They live in a small cottage on the property and maintain the big house to the best of their ability, with some of Pasternak's books and personal possessions and some wonderful drawings and pastels by his father. We sat surrounded by these works of art in the family room downstairs and drank tea with our kind hostess out of cracked cups, and talked a little with the young people. I gave my copy of the correspondence of Pasternak and his cousin Olga to the granddaughter of the beautiful Zinaida. The other family already had one. We felt an intense melancholy.

Among the groups that we entertained during the latter part of June were several members of the Canadian branch of the Physicians for Social Responsibility who had come on from an international meeting in Amsterdam to meet with some of their Soviet colleagues on their own home ground. Among them were the Altons, the parents of Melanie, the Pushkin student from Toronto whom we all got to know quite well this year; Dr. Frank Sommers, the psychiatrist and sexologist who is the Canadian president; a very articulate and energetic physiotherapist from Montreal named Dorothy Goldin Rosenberg, whom I had met last year at Couchiching; and a delightful young female doctor from Saltspring Island who brought along her husband and two small children.

With Dorothy and some of the other women in the group I went to the Soviet Women's Committee to screen *If You Love This Planet*, Helen Caldicott's chilling vision of nuclear war, for them. The film was sent to them as a gift from the National Film Board's Studio D, along with one about Paraskeva Clark called *Portrait of the Artist as an Old Lady* and *Greatgrandmothers*, about the settling of the Canadian west from the point of view of the women who took part in it. I don't know what they'll make of those two but this one they watched with intense interest. And it is a good film. I was seeing it for the first time. The discussion afterwards had its frustrations. As I have been made aware before, executive members of the Women's Committee profess no interest at all in what we would call feminist issues, but the younger women present, while they didn't speak up, followed Dorothy's arguments with complete attention and, one felt, a certain understanding. The discussion was prolonged and occasionally heated, a provocative, albeit minor, ideological skirmish with unknowable consequences. I tried to keep quiet. Altogether it was quite a day because in the evening I went to the American Embassy with Anne to see *Sophie's Choice*. The diplomats in the front rows watched in absorbed silence, while the Soviets, who tend to sit toward the back of the room, busily translated for one another. Alan Pakula was there as a guest of the Hartmans and said a few words before the film began. Afterwards there doesn't seem to be much to say, at least not for a little while. I thought it was very involving and very well made. Donna Hartman woke up in the middle of the night, crying.

Since I last wrote, the Pope has visited Poland and Andropov has become President, and since I started this letter, the blue skies have clouded over and we have had one of those sudden sharp thunderstorms that occasionally occur here and remind me to ask Hilary to check about the lightning rods for Burnett.

LETTER NUMBER 54

July 25, 1983

Our eleven days in Siberia and Mongolia were so eventful and interesting that I can't possibly do justice to them in a single letter. So I'll split my account into two parts, and it would be less complicated if I do it by geography rather than chronology. This week I'll write about our days in Siberia and next week about our visit to Mongolia, which took place in the middle of our trip.

We left Moscow around noon on July 5 and flew, uneventfully, to Omsk. On the second leg of our journey we were just approaching our destination after listening to the stewardess's short spiel about the hero city of Irkutsk, how the exiled Decembrists had settled there, and how many hospitals and factories had been built since the Revolution, when I noticed that the setting sun had suddenly appeared on my left and that we had turned north. The stewardess returned to the PA system with her little book and proceeded to read out to us all we never wanted to know about the city of *Bratsk*. Anyone who has travelled on Aeroflot is well aware that while one gets information aplenty, one never gets explanations. It was only because we were near the front and overheard the captain talking about the fog in Irkutsk and the poor visibility that we understood why he had sensibly diverted the plane to Bratsk. Unfortunately many other pilots had made the same decision and the small airport was jammed. Hundreds of passengers occupied every available bench and the bathroom on the ground floor was unspeakable. Looking for a usable one on the second floor I found the Deputatsky Zal (VIP room) tucked away in a corner and we made our way in. The couple already ensconced there turned out to be the Second Secretary of the Irkutsk Oblast and his very pleasant wife, who were returning home on our flight from the Supreme Soviet meeting in Moscow and a holiday in Czechoslovakia. We soon learned that he had been in Canada to visit Alcan, and, while he tried to raise someone on the telephone, we broke out our bottle of scotch. We never travel without one! By the time it became clear that our flight would be delayed overnight it was 2:00 a.m. local time, but he still managed to arrange for the four of us to be picked up and driven to a guest house not far away. It was very clean and comfortable and we climbed into bed gratefully.

In the morning we discovered we were in a charming wooden lodge overlooking the Bratsk Sea and that the Irkutsk airport was still closed. Since it was sunny in Bratsk with the wind blowing softly in the pines, sand crunching underfoot, and lilacs blooming, we didn't much care. About 10:00 a.m. we were swept off by a dynamic, good-looking, boyish man to visit the giant hydroelectric station and tour the surrounding settlement. The guest house belonged to his enterprise, Bratskgesstroi, and he was the Chief Executive Officer. What a fellow! Bratskgesstroi is the enterprise that was responsible for constructing the power plant (one of the largest in the world), which was completed in 1967, and it has now diversified with activities all over eastern Siberia. Our host rushed us here and there in his minibus, holding frequent conversations on his "executive" telephone while he pointed out the sights. He took photographs wherever we stopped and they were sent on to us in Irkutsk where we received them a week later from our Intourist guide, Vladimir, on our return from Mongolia—much to our astonishment and pleasure, because he is an excellent photographer. A man of many interests, he has lived there since construction on the dam began late in 1954. He has every intention of staying because, he told us, he loves downhill skiing and the area is being developed for winter sports. I learned later that he has ambitions to attract the Winter Olympics to Bratsk before he is finished.

The sense of freshness and enthusiasm one encounters in Siberia is a contrast to Moscow, where the officials often seem rather tired. Twenty-five years ago Bratsk was only a small settlement on the Angara River in the middle of the Taiga. Now there are 280,000 people and a whole variety of undertakings, pulp and paper, aluminum, as well as power. The city is not well planned. It straggles 70 km along the river. Yet most people have summer cottages and lots to do summer and winter. Life is not at all bad. While we were at the dam looking at the gigantic turbines inside the huge and spotlessly clean powerhouse, the message came that our plane was ready to take off, so we bounced back to the airport and made our way in some embarrassment past all the waiting passengers to our seats in the front. It's the first time a plane has ever been held for us, but it was really worth it!

We flew the 600 km south to Irkutsk in just fifty minutes, enjoying a splendid view of the Angara. What is called the Bratsk Sea is, of course, the Angara above the dam, and it is now extensive because the Angara is a fast-flowing river, deep and wide, the only outflow from Lake Baikal, immensely powerful and beautifully green. Creating electricity as it passes across several dams, not only Bratsk, it flows north to join the Yenisei and thence into the Arctic Ocean.

By the time we landed in Irkutsk it was clear and hot and the poplar fluff was blowing in all directions. We only had time to drive into town for a late lunch and a walk along the embankment before returning to the airport for another spectacular flight, this time in a low-flying propeller aircraft, across Lake Baikal and up the Selenga River to Ulan Ude, capital of the Buryat Autonomous Republic. Our stop there was planned and we were extremely well looked after. I was fascinated by what I discovered during our short visit. The Buryats are closely related to the Mongolians and, like them, used to be a nomadic people living in yurts, herding sheep and cattle, and practising a form of Lamaism somewhat mixed with the Shamanism that has been the dominant religious mode of the native peoples of the Baikal area for many centuries. Now the Buryats are settled and secular and Soviet, but doing quite nicely, on the whole, thank you. There are quite a lot of Russians among the population. A migration came from Byelorussia in Peter's time and Catherine sent out a group of Old Believers who were exemplary farmers. At the time of the Revolution the Red Army came and went and came again, and then went down into Mongolia to help Sukhe Bator defeat the Mad Baron and "liberate" Urga (Ulan Bator) on July 11, 1921. So one way or another the Buryat population is being overtaken. Nevertheless certain traditions are maintained and the language survives. There is a good deal of national pride but not all that much resentment, at least not that we could detect. Most of the officials we met were distinctively Buryat, although we spoke Russian together because that was our only common language! The only time we had a translator was when we called on the Mayor. A soft-spoken scholar had been summoned to interpret for us, a specialist in ancient Chinese philosophy who happened to speak English as well as Chinese, and who looked so much like the Buddhist monks I have seen in Mongolian hangings that as I looked at him his sports shirt and trousers were transformed into saffron-coloured robes!

The most interesting thing we did in Ulan Ude, at least as far as I was concerned, was to visit the outdoor ethnographical museum. There I was struck by the section devoted to the Evenks and other native tribes from around Lake Baikal—the "Indians" of central Siberia. The clothing and household objects, the hunting weapons, the traps, the birchbark and skin wigwams, transported me back to Canada. There is, perhaps, a greater use of soft furs than in North America and surely there are many other differences as well that someone knowledgeable would recognize. However, the museum director reminded us that scholars have generally agreed that the native peoples of North America actually originated around Lake Baikal and made their way many thousands of years ago across the land bridge to Alaska. The director and his colleagues knew about the Frobisher Bay Conference of Arctic Peoples that is taking place this summer and were disappointed to learn from us that the USSR has decided not to send any representation.

It is hard to learn much about the native peoples in this country, as opposed to the nationalities such as Armenians, for example, or, indeed, Buryats. I came back to Moscow and read what I could find in our library and asked around among Soviet acquaintances. Certainly native peoples do not play anything like the same role in the Russian national mythology that they do in our country. They are very far from the consciousness of the average European Russian when she thinks about Siberia. She is more likely to think (romantically) of nineteenth-century exiles or (grimly) of twentieth-century victims. Of course now, the Soviet government is trying to surround Siberia with an aura of adventure and high endeavour in order to attract the workers needed to exploit its enormous resources, but native peoples play no part in that "message" either. I have read that government policy toward the indigenous peoples has been generally benign in intent, if not in practice, both during the Russian centuries of fur trade, exploration, and settlement, and the Soviet period of resource development. While there were skirmishes during the push eastward there was nothing similar to the French and Indian wars, and no real history of treaties made and broken. Nor did the church send out active missionaries. So how do they live now? Most of the comments I hear are about impressive successes in the dominant culture. We gave a book on Eskimo sculpture to the director of the ethnological museum—all pieces created *since* 1975. His eyes (he is a Buryat) widened in admiration. We know they are still herding reindeer and contributing to the food supplies of other Siberians through traditional methods but it is not generally known what else is happening to them. They are not vocal.

A jolly glass of vodka with the station-mistress of Ulan Ude and some of her comrades launched us on to the Moscow–Peking train. We chugged up the line along the Selenga River valley through pleasant fields spoiled by the occasional belch of smoke, the tell-tale sign of industrial development among the rolling hills. We decided to try out the Russian dining car before it was turned back at the border and were much entertained by our decision. Our stubble-bearded, blue-eyed waiter was breezy and cheery as he flicked off the remains of the previous four diners at our table and urged us to order the only dish that remained on the menu. Luckily there was still some caviar to render the rest of it edible, and while we ate, our enterprising waiter sold off several cartons of juicy oranges to Soviet passengers. After paying our bill we gave him a maple leaf pin and he went off gleefully to talk hockey with the rest of the grubby dining car crew while we went back to our compartment to await the border guards.

Five days later, after the Mongolian experience that I'll describe next week, we returned to Irkutsk by air, only fifty minutes from one world to another. We were driven directly from the airport to Lake Baikal along 60 km of northern Ontario road. But Baikal itself is unlike any other lake I've seen. Our hotel was perched on a hill high above the lake and was decidedly—well, rustic, in spite of its magnificent view. The trouble with Soviet hotels is that they are designed to look smart when they are well kept. When they are not, which is almost inevitably the case, their pretensions make them look even shabbier. Never mind, for two days we enjoyed perfect July weather and were constantly surrounded by the delicate fragrance of the most astonishing quantity and quality of wild flowers I have ever encountered. We climbed up and down the hills, walked quite alone through forest paths and along the shore road. We read *The Brothers Karamazov*, which had fortunately fallen apart so I could read the first part while Geoffrey was reading the second! It was a good break from official activities and I would willingly have stayed longer if it had been possible. I was especially enchanted by the flowers. About the lake I wasn't so sure.

Lake Baikal is a phenomenon, that's for sure. And it is beautiful, particularly in the evening when the changing sky is softly reflected in the waters below. But it is cold and unapproachable. In summer the water temperature rarely rises above 12° C, which makes it unswimmable and basically unboatable. The only tourist trip available to foreigners is an hour in an enclosed hydrofoil, which somehow seems appropriate. Of course, if one could travel the many hundreds of miles of its shoreline, it would no doubt reveal all sorts of wonders, and in the fall, apparently, when the larch on the mountains turns gold, it is a haunting sight. Surely the native peoples who lived around its shores had extraordinary legends to account for its cold fruitfulness (for the lake does teem with fish) but such tales are not passed on to such as us. Instead we are told all about its characteristics as a rare natural phenomenon, its tectonic formation, its record depths, the crystalline quality of its water, the abundant flora and fauna, the successful battle to preserve its purity. But I would have given a lot for a good swim and a paddle. I think I'll make up my own legend about Baikal but I'm not ready yet. I'll have to wait until I have been back in Canada for a while.

Our last twenty-four hours in Siberia were spent in Irkutsk. We came up the Angara by hydrofoil and spent our last evening on the eighth floor of the Intourist Hotel watching a thunderstorm breaking over the river below us and a rainbow forming in the east near Baikal out of scattered showers and the last rays of the setting sun. On the morning of our departure we walked through freshly washed streets and met with various members of the Irkutsk branch of the Academy of Sciences, particularly the Energy Institute. The return flight to Moscow seemed unusually tiresome and the streets looked gritty as we drove through them to the Embassy. I recall different feelings returning from Mongolia and Siberia two years ago. Somehow the bloom is off or perhaps we are just tired.

LETTER NUMBER 55

August 5, 1983

And now for MONGOLIA! In my last letter I brought you right up to the frontier. Once there, it took us over four hours to make the crossing. Considering the close relations between the two countries it is surprising that it should be so difficult. When we pulled into the station on the Soviet side about 11:00 p.m., an absolute flood of baby-faced border guards, wearing capes against the drizzle and carrying shabby briefcases, poured out of the station house and spread across the platform and into every entrance to the train. Half an hour later the guards retreated again, briefcases bulging, in order to register each passport laboriously under a 10-watt bulb assisted by a flashlight, while passengers jogged up and down along the track in their electric blue suits. All this we could see from our compartment window. Footsteps above us signalled a roof search. There were repeated bangings on the undercarriage. Two hours later we chugged along to the first town in Mongolia, where the whole process was repeated. It was a disturbing night and as we approached the outskirts of Ulan Bator next morning we were held up again. When we eventually arrived at the bustling station and made our way through the streets to our hotel, the reason for the delays became clear. Crowds of Mongolian

workers, obviously delighted with their break from "building communism," were streaming away from the central avenue, rolling up
their flags. They had been lined up there to greet their State Guest for
the National Day celebrations, their President's fraternal ally, Babrak
Kamal! Needless to say the Mongolian Embassy in Moscow had not
warned us of his impending visit and his presence during the festivities provoked much discussion among the Ambassadors resident in
Ulan Bator from Great Britain, France, Japan, and China, and including Geoffrey, as to how to participate in all the official activities to
which we had been invited without either acknowledging the presence of the State Guest or insulting our hosts. In the event it all
worked out. The Mongolians were not unaware of the problem and
no one was placed in an impossible position. And observing the
Afghan delegation (from a safe distance) participate in the archery
competition, we were led to reflect on the real differences between the
two countries in their "relationship" with their northern neighbour.
Babrak Kamal could scarcely pull back the bowstring, while President
Tsedenbal shot his arrow quite a respectable distance.

When we returned to Moscow from Ulan Bator in the middle of
July, I re-read the letter I had written you all two years ago after our
first trip there, when I accompanied Geoffrey for the presentation of
his credentials. Then the country was completely new to me and I
was fascinated by its ancient history as well as by its cultural and
ethnic connections with other parts of inner Asia; in fact everything
about it that made it different from the Soviet Union. This time I
could not help but be struck by the structural similarities between the
two countries and by the fact that every institution, whether political
or social or economic, has such *very* close ties with its counterpart in
the other country, thus reinforcing the State-to-State relationship.
And yet I was delighted to see that certain folk traditions have managed to survive with exceptional vigour. During the National Day
celebrations these two facets of Mongolian life were quite clearly
demonstrated. The parade, the ceremonial concert, the speeches, the
formal reception, even the fireworks, all reflected the Soviet model
with the shimmer of the true satellite. One could even speculate
about how long it had taken the light to arrive because the speeches
and slogans echoed the rhetoric of the fifties rather than what we

now hear in Moscow. One the other hand, the most popular event of the three days of celebration was the Naadam, the Festival of the Three Manly Sports, which has taken place regularly for more than two thousand years! It is appropriate, I think, that the Mongolian national flag, which is partly red and partly a lovely shade of blue, features an ideogram composed of ancient symbolic elements, including the yin-yang principle of opposites!

July is a good month for a national holiday (much better than November!) and the Mongolians really go all out. All energies are focused on the festivities. This meant that Geoffrey had difficulty doing any business, although he did manage to see the Foreign Minister and the Minister of Trade. Not, of course, that there is much business to be done. The Mongolians, for the time being, have quite sensibly decided to do most of their business with the Soviet bloc (and I must add here that, up to now, the USSR has poured far more into Mongolia than it has taken out; of course there have been strategic reasons for that ... still ...). However, there does exist a Canadian proposal involving knitting needles (there are lots of sheep in Mongolia and cashmere sweaters are both warm and cheap) and we do have this ongoing interest in dinosaurs! If we really want to explore the Mongolian market then we will have to send out a small trade mission as the Finns are planning to do this fall, but somehow I don't see this happening in the near future.

So, having disposed of what official business it was possible to do, we decided to enjoy ourselves, and we did. The weather was helpful. The first two days were very hot and sunny but then there was just enough cloud to shade us as we stood in the central square to watch the parade and to protect us from sunstroke in the stadium later. The wife of the British Ambassador had lent me an elegant black straw creation and had also furnished head coverings for Geoffrey and our colleague from Finland in case of need. There was no need, but I wore mine anyway because it was so smart!

The official events started off on July 10 with a wreath-laying ceremony at Lenin's feet (which Geoffrey forwent) followed by a respectful march through the Mausoleum of Sukhe Bator, the revolutionary leader who died in the same year that Lenin did, and Choibalsan, the Stalin-like figure who succeeded him, consolidating and holding power until his death in 1952. The mausoleum is a small replica of Lenin's tomb but inside, Geoffrey said (I wasn't allowed), in the place of the preserved body there were two rather ghostly statues, busts from the waist up! Then the procession drove off to the War Monument on the hill across town where it is not exactly clear which war is being commemorated but where it is firmly indicated that Soviet and Mongolian forces were always fighting side by side. Some of you may remember the photographs of the yurt settlement that I took from that site two years ago. The yurts have now vanished, to be replaced by the concrete apartment blocks one sees all over the Soviet Union. While I'm sure it is very welcome to have indoor plumbing I'm still not convinced that these blocks represent a real improvement in the *quality* of life!

In the afternoon we all attended the ceremonial concert, preceded by an hour of speeches that, unfortunately, we could understand only too well. The Japanese gadgets on our ears transmitted to us an instantaneous English translation. After a break for a glass of lemonade in the lobby, we returned to listen to patriotic songs interspersed with scenes from *Spartacus* and the occasional gaudy folk dance. The whole was completed by a rousing performance of the first movement of Tchaikovsky's concerto for piano and orchestra such as would have shaken the rafters of London South Collegiate Institute! I wouldn't be so critical if I hadn't been so impressed by the authentic Mongolian singing and dancing I had seen on TV the night before.

Our hotel was near the huge central square and next morning, from the windows of our suite (all visiting ambassadors are put up in suites that are actually very comfortable and not as expensive as a simple Intourist room!—I won't speak about the hotel food …), we could see the crowds beginning to line up. So many of the inhabitants of Ulan Bator took part in the parade that there were relatively few left to watch and we were able to have an excellent view from our diplomatic tribune. The centre of the main square was filled with young pioneers in white, holding flags and squares of coloured cloth which they waved rhythmically as the various groups marched past the assorted dignitaries standing on top of the mausoleum just as they do in Red Square. First of all the Mongolian Army passed us, saluting smartly. That didn't take long. Then came the squads of young workers carrying the obligatory portraits of Sukhe Bator, Choibalsan, Lenin, Marx, Engels, and all, followed by posters of the present-day members of the Mongolian Politburo and of Mr. Andropov. The latter was a little hard to recognize. Perhaps the local artists are not quite certain of the iconography yet! The rest of the parade consisted of groups pushing or walking alongside floats that portrayed all the areas of Soviet-Mongolian cooperation as well as standard appeals to world peace, with anti-American slogans and leaden doves. Since the floats seemed to be totally lacking in Mongolian inspiration we concentrated with relief on the people. There were some marvellous old men in national costume, the all-purpose knee-length dun-coloured brilliantly-belted wrap-around called the *del*. Bowlegged (from riding or rickets, who knows) and booted, they wore pointed felt hats on their dark, weather-beaten, grinning faces. And there were many extremely pretty young girls who were also wearing *dels*, but theirs were made of richly coloured silk and they skipped around the square laughing and chatting all the way. And some of them even carried bunches of wildflowers instead of the Soviet-style crêpe paper carnations of their companions. A child lost her shoe and dropped out of line to be absorbed by a friendly group in the platoon behind her. It seemed to me that the young people were glad to march in the parade along with the veterans. They are proud of their country and for the moment they are more taken with the advantages of their improving material standards than with asking questions about what might have been.

July 11 commemorates the foundation of the Mongolian People's Republic in 1921, after the "liberation" of Urga (as Ulan Bator used to be called) by Sukhe Bator and his Mongolian forces (700 strong) ably assisted by 10,000 Red Army troops. You may remember that I wrote about the Mad Baron von Ungern-Sternberg in my first Mongolian letter. A renegade officer from the Russian imperial army, he took advantage of the fact that once the Manchurian overlords had been eliminated by the 1911 Revolution in China, the traditional Mongolian leaders proved themselves to be rather inept. So he marauded around the country for two or three years while revolution and civil war were occupying the Russians to the north and the Mongolian nobility were becoming increasingly indebted to Chinese moneylenders. In February 1921 the Mad Baron took Urga, massacred 10,000 Chinese there (among others) and proclaimed himself the Mongolian ruler. All this time there had been a spreading revolutionary movement in the country. Life was not very promising for a young Mongolian in those days. In fact it was most likely to be "nasty, brutish and short." Neither the religious nor civil leaders of Mongolia (and the two were often the same) were reform-minded and they were quite unable to deal with the problems besetting the population. There was considerable wariness of the Chinese for a number of historical reasons. So, seeking support, the revolutionaries looked north of the border, where, of course, they were warmly welcomed by the Bolsheviks, who were quite aware of the strategic value of the existence of a fraternal state between themselves and China. Sukhe Bator, who was a gunner in the Mongolian forces, and Choibalsan, who had been a boy runaway from a Buddhist monastery subsequently educated in Russia, were the chosen leaders of the Mongolian Communist Party, and they brought down the Red Army from Siberia to topple the Mad Baron and establish Communist power.

While Geoffrey was meeting with the Minister of Trade on the day we arrived, I set off in search of the art museum and found myself, instead, in the museum of revolutionary history. There I saw the early history of the Mongolian People's Republic presented as they would like to have it remembered, with a series of reverent images of Sukhe Bator's one and only meeting with Lenin in Moscow on November 5, 1921. At that meeting Lenin apparently made Sukhe Bator and his comrades feel how very important Mongolia was and would continue to be as a friend of the Soviet Union and he suggested that it would be all right to bypass capitalism and form "islands of socialism" in the economy. Not being a Marxist, I find it hard to imagine how any other development could have taken place once the friendly bonds had been established. Anyway, from then on the direction was set. Sukhe Bator died in 1924, Choibalsan then took power and held it until his death in 1952, and he in turn was succeeded by Tsedenbal, who is still President, and the history of the fraternal cooperation has been unbroken for sixty-two years.

After the parade we walked back to the hotel for lunch, and then the best part of the festivities began. First we went to the stadium for the opening of the Nadaam where some horses raced around the field, little children did gymnastics, and the wrestlers made their ritual entry. This particular "manly" sport was prominent during the religious festivals of former times. The contestants still wear a colourful tight-fitting traditional costume consisting of a long-sleeved jacket with no front, held on by strings across the belly, a jockstrap, and soft leather boots. They prance around simulating the flight of the mythical Garuda bird by leaping slowly and rhythmically from foot to foot while they lift their shoulders and flap their crooked elbows. It is an open contest (only the boys get to wrestle separately) and they come in all shapes and sizes. Many of them have competed for years and have acquired the titles Titan, Lion, Elephant, or Falcon that enable them to choose their opponent. They lean toward each other, grabbing at the shoulder and trying to trip up the other by hooking a leg just as I remember doing (and failing) when my brother and I used to wrestle as children so many years ago! The winner of each contest is crowned by his trainer with a special fur-trimmed cap and then performs a swooping victory dance around a pole in front of the presidential box, while the loser retires dejectedly from the field. The competition goes on until there is only one man left. Needless to say, we didn't stay. It takes two days.

From the stadium we drove to another part of the sports complex to watch the second manly sport, archery. Actually some women of various ages were also participating in this, as well as some quite young children. Teams of four, wearing maroon *dels* and pointed hats, line up with crossbows and soft-tipped arrows to shoot at a triple-tiered construction of small wooden bricks. On each side of the target stand two men (or women, if the archers are women) who are also traditionally dressed and who hold both arms upright in the air indicating the score with their fingers once the arrow has knocked down some bricks. The entire activity is accompanied by a kind of moaning, which rises to a crescendo as the arrow is loosed. One erect old woman was a particularly fine shot and the chanting of her scores sounded triumphant!

The last of the three manly sports is horse racing and, in fact, it doesn't involve men at all but children from five to nine years of age.

To watch the finish we drove several kilometres out into the country and walked some distance on the pungent sage-covered steppe with grasshoppers snapping and popping all around us. The race is a long one, starting 38 km away in the empty land beyond the hills. When we first arrived there was no sign of dust in the distant gully from which the riders would emerge, so we were treated, quite unexpectedly, to the sight of young men in white coveralls dropping from small planes and floating down out of the bright blue sky suspended from multi-coloured parachutes that always opened to a sigh of relief from the assembled watchers. The Mongolians have added a modern category to their three "manly" sports—not at all untypical; they really are daredevils!

The last jumper had scarcely landed when we saw the first telltale clouds of dust and then, all of a sudden, they were upon us and flashing by, hundreds and hundreds of galloping children, helmets forward and capes flying, riding their little Mongolian ponies to the finish line. What an extraordinary sight! The winner was a seven-year-old girl whom we watched next morning on television solemnly receiving the award from Tsedenbal. He stooped down to embrace her, but she did not smile. Any girl who can ride like that doesn't have to be cute for a president!

In the evening we dressed up and went to the official reception at the national palace where we were offered *koumiss* (fermented mare's milk) and other goodies and chatted with friendly Mongolian officials and our diplomatic colleagues. Then the British Ambassador and his wife and the Finnish Ambassador, a *very* nice man who had come from Moscow to present his credentials, joined us in our hotel suite to finish off our bottle of scotch and watch the fireworks bursting forth from the surrounding hills.

I must tell you about one more thing, although this letter is getting longer and longer. Having done my duty by the museum of the Revolution, I managed to get proper directions the following day and found the museum of Fine Arts. After two or three rooms of ancient artifacts and complicated religious hangings, I suddenly and without any preparation at all found myself among a group of sculptures of such surpassing beauty that I could hardly believe my eyes. I kept coming back to them after visiting other rooms as if returning to a sanctuary. There were more than a dozen pieces, and all of them, as it turned out, by the same remarkable artist, but I was particularly drawn to a group of five contemplative Buddhas. I was completely captivated by the perfection of their beautiful bodies, the grace of their positioned hands (the mudras), and the peace and serenity of their expressions. I have since learned that the figures are 72 cm high, that they are made of gilded bronze, and that they were created in 1683 by an extraordinarily wise and gifted monk named Zanabazar, who had been proclaimed the Dalai Lama during a visit to Tibet at the age of fifteen. He spent most of his long life as the Chief Lama of Mongolia and devoted it to transmitting to his people the religious promise of Lamaism by building temples and founding monasteries, developing a new Mongolian script for the transcription of foreign texts, and, above all, by creating works of great art that express "the divinity of the soul through the beauty of the human body." Luckily, on my way back to the hotel I found a just-published book about Zanabazar in the foreign currency shop. It was put together by a Mongolian artist and contains many superb photographs. This is particularly fortunate because all of Zanabazar's surviving works are in Mongolia and I'm not likely to see them again. The five Buddhas that were such a revelation for me are considered to be among his masterworks. To contemplate them is to feel in some indefinable way both tranquil and free. I can't explain why, but when I read in the book about the attributes of these Buddhas I could only wonder at the genius of the sculptor. Akshobhya suppresses wrath; Vairochana suppresses obtuseness and ignorance; Ratnasambava, pride and greed; Amitabha suppresses self-interest and passion; and Amhasida, envy. I could not say the same for the bust of Lenin on the staircase or the outsized and laboriously executed embroidered portrait of Tsedenbal in the hall of honour that I passed by as I left the museum.

I don't suppose I will ever go back to Mongolia. I regret not seeing the Gobi Desert or High Karakorum or the monastery at Erden-Tsu. But, according to our colleagues, travel there is full of the kinds of restrictions we're only too familiar with in the USSR and the Mongolians (as we found out for ourselves) ride cars rather like horses! But I'm very glad we had our two trips and I'll always remember the old men and women in their *dels*, the large families of rosy-cheeked, black-haired children, the racing girl, and the Dhyana Buddhas of Zanabazar.

LETTER NUMBER 56

Zavidova, August 21, 1983

We have come to Zavidova for the last time and I am writing this letter to you sitting in the little summer house by the tennis court. I am surrounded by fragrant, colourful phlox and by small boys on large bicycles who are racing around shouting at one another in Arabic (I think!). The sky is blue and the air is clear but the wind is chilly and the birch leaves have begun to turn yellow. Caroline Lussier, Monique's daughter, who has been studying folk dancing in Poland and has now come on to visit us for two weeks, is braving the breeze and sunning herself on the dock. Geoffrey is in the dacha writing I'm not sure what, as he has been all weekend, breaking off from time to time to play tennis. It's surprising that no one is on the court now. Yesterday the Japanese were out in strength in their neat tennis whites with their fancy racquets but that group didn't stay over and the Latin Americans and the Yugoslavs who are walking up and down the road don't seem to be keen players. Caroline is amusing herself trying to identify the various languages she overhears. Yesterday the Polish Embassy sent a whole busload up to hunt mushrooms so she was in her element! We didn't realize who they were until, having rowed across the Shosha to the beach and picked our way among the "meadow muffins" into the woods, we came upon them wandering about with their wicker baskets. Later we went for a walk through those fields bordering the Volga that some of you know well from other seasons. Now there are lots of sunflowers and some of the corn was over our heads. We stole a dozen ears and felt slightly guilty as we carried them past the miliman at the gate. He looked benevolent or perhaps he was just admiring Caroline, who was also carrying a large sunflower. We boiled the corn very briefly and took it to share with the New Zealand Ambassador, Frank Wilson, and his wife Marina, a couple of other New Zealanders, and an engaging group from the Irish Embassy who had all come together for a delicious cookout. We wrapped ourselves up in blankets as the stars came out, and ate British steaks and New Zealand (what else?) lamb shashlyk, and drank Irish whiskey ... In a little while we will set off by motor launch for a short trip down the river and then we will pack up and return to Moscow. I am sure that when I think in the future about our time in the USSR my most nostalgic thoughts will always make their way to Zavidova and to the countryside of the Upper Volga.

Caroline arrived full of anticipation from Warsaw on Thursday evening. After living for three months on a student's stipend in Lublin, *her* first impressions of the Soviet Union are quite different from those of our guests who come directly from the West. She hasn't yet met our niece Barbara and our nephew David, who will return from their trip to Leningrad and Kiev with their mother, Geoffrey's sister Patsy, on Tuesday morning. It will be interesting for the young people, in particular, to compare their experiences. It has been delightful for us to have all these visitors. Geoffrey has quite relaxed with them although now he has to gear himself up for the arrival tomorrow of the Parliamentary Delegation led by Jeanne Sauvé, the Speaker of the House of Commons. Quite a large group, too; more than fifteen, including spouses. After three days in Moscow they will go to Central Asia and thence to Leningrad where Geoffrey and I will join them for the last two days of their trip. They are guests of the Soviet government and no doubt they will be looked after very well. But we will, of course, have a dinner for them and be involved in organizing other events.

Although I mailed my last letter to you early in August, it has actually been a month since I wrote you because that letter ended with our return from Mongolia on July 15. We came back to Moscow then to find ourselves in the middle of a film festival. François Mathys had enjoyed himself thoroughly as Chargé d'Affaires in Geoffrey's absence, largely by looking after our Canadian delegation. Of course he would have done that anyway. It was comprised mostly of people associated with *The Tin Flute*, which was our official entry in the competition. The film had its world première on the night that Gabrielle Roy died, which was a little sad. It was well received and popular with the Soviet public although our passionate film buff, Nina Ryan, who managed to see at least fifteen films during the Festival, found it a bit too sentimental. On the other hand she really liked *La Quarantaine*, an NFB film about a group of school friends from a poor neighbourhood of Montreal who meet again in their forties. She thought it was much more original. We had the film group in for a very enjoyable lunch (I was particularly taken with the actress Marilyn Lightstone, and with Jacques Godbout, who was one of the judges) but we were unable, unfortunately, to get to any of the Canadian showings. We only managed the official closing ceremonies, which were incredibly boring and where the criteria by which the judges were asked to select their winners were only too blatantly revealed. Marilyn Lightstone did, however, receive a special award from the Soviet Women's Committee, as *their* choice for best actress. Apparently she is excellent in *The Tin Flute* and I look forward to seeing it when I come home.

Before the film festival was over, another delegation arrived from Canada, this one consisting of George and Alison Ignatieff, LBP's old colleague Walter Gordon, Bob and Stephanie Reford from the UN Association, and Rob Byers from York University. They had come for some round-table discussions with the Institute of the USA and Canada and we saw quite a lot of them, of course, although there was no Embassy participation in the talks. Mr. Gordon was in remarkable form after making such a long trip at his age and Geoffrey went with him to call on Mr. Gorbachev who, now that he has been there, seems to take a special interest in Canada. The Ignatieffs had brought along their son, Michael, and his wife and much of the interest of the visit, for all of us actually, centred on Ignatieff family history. Michael is planning to write a book about it because it *is* fascinating and is connected with many significant events in Russian history, far more than I had realized. It was Michael and Alison's first trip, and the only other one that George had made since his abrupt departure at the age of six was as a young diplomat in 1955, when LBP was the first NATO foreign minister to visit the Soviet Union after the Iron Curtain was dropped. They visited the old family residence in Leningrad, which is now a wedding palace, but had to give up on George's grandfather's tomb because it was too far from Kiev to be reached in a single day's drive. They were very well received everywhere.

Early in August we had another official visitor, the MP Marcel Prud'homme, in his capacity as the head of the Canadian delegation to the InterParliamentary Union, but before he came we did manage to get one short holiday, three days in Yalta over the first of August

weekend. It was a mixed experience. The flights in the new 300-pas-
senger Airbus were okay although on our way down, since we were
carrying a load of young Pioneers to Black Sea camps, we were treated to the soundtrack of a whole series of what must have been Tom
and Jerry-type cartoons ... *not* soothing! And the night we arrived
there was a horrendous thunderstorm that made the sea cold and
filled it with jellyfish, provided you could make your way into it
across the golfball-sized pebbles without getting a foot cramp or
falling to your knees. The hotel was huge and expensive and it was
practically impossible to get a decent meal. *However*, the town itself
has considerable Mediterranean charm, hills and cobbles and
cypresses, I got to visit Chekhov's house, which I loved, and up
behind the hotel I quite unexpectedly came upon a beautiful hillside
park, full of wonderful trees and flowers, cedars and oleanders and
roses, well-kept paths, little pools and tumbling streams, and almost
no people. They were all down beside the sea, ample flesh exposed to
the sun, turning themselves by slow degrees on their wooden couch-
es in order to roast every bit of it! So I could sit undisturbed in the
shade, inhaling the fresh smell of cedar, and reading all about Lady
Diana Cooper in Philip Ziegler's biography, a distant world, another
time! I can't even imagine her in a Chekhov tale!

LETTER NUMBER 57

September 21, 1983

This will be my last letter from the Soviet Union. I don't know
when it will reach you. The courier is coming down by train from
Helsinki on Friday and will be leaving again the same way. It is even
possible that we will be in Canada by the time this arrives in your
mailbox! Not too likely though, as we are planning to spend six days
in England on our way home. We still expect to leave Moscow on
September 29 and are booked on the only Western airline flying in
and out, Austrian Airlines. As a fallback position we have also made
a reservation on the train to Helsinki on September 28. In some ways
I would prefer to depart that way, as leaving from a train station with

friends crowded on the platform has a special old-fashioned quality. I have fond memories from the old days when we always arrived and departed from the post by train and boat. However, we'll see.

Although the terrible gloom of the days following the airliner tragedy (KAL 007) is beginning to dissipate, the atmosphere in Moscow during these first weeks of September has been very sombre. The pressure on Geoffrey has been particularly hard and he now has a bad chest cold as well as a sore tooth, which is one of the reasons we may travel via Helsinki. I, luckily, had the company of my sister-in-law Dot, a trip to Novgorod and Leningrad, and a series of beautiful sunlit days to offset the general sense of depression, but he did not have much relief from the tasks imposed upon him by the circumstances or from his own feelings. We have been much saddened, both by the tragedy itself and by the official Soviet response to it. The statements and actions of the government have tended to confirm my worst impressions of the whole system. Here I speak only for myself, but I keep wishing that it could have been otherwise, even though I realize that would have been totally out of character once the Western reaction, which was also predictable, had set the tone. We had some very interesting Canadian Christians here this past week on a special mission that had been organized before the shooting down and I could not help but reflect that "Love thine enemy" has always been one of the least popular and most difficult of Christ's injunctions. Rightful indignation slips so easily into self-righteousness and I'm afraid that sanctimony is no more effective than selective economic sanctions in producing desired behaviour from those against whom they are directed. After three years in this country I am not at all sure that it is possible for outsiders to force the kinds of changes that would modify the political system of the Soviet Union so that it conformed better to the character and the potential of its many peoples. However, I *have* decided in my own mind that one factor more than most is responsible for fostering inhumanity in the system, and that factor is official secrecy. I'm not against secrets as such. Every self-respecting person needs some. But the institutionalization of secrecy, which is so characteristic of a closed society like this one, does nothing but breed fear and mistrust, wild speculation, and complete misunderstanding. This has been particularly brought home to me as a result of the recent events. Only yesterday I was talking to someone who had been convinced that the airliner was not, in fact, carrying ordinary passengers at all. When I told her that, among the debris that has been recovered from the crash, there has been found the body of a child she was absolutely horrified. And immediately set about to speculate as to why the Soviet Air Command hadn't sent at least twenty planes into the air to surround the plane and force it to land. After all, as she *had* been informed, there had been plenty of time. Of course I don't know whether that would have been at all feasible but her comments and the rest of my conversation with her revealed that by totally depersonalizing the airliner the authorities had deprived this kind and generous woman and so many others like her of an appropriate and humane response to a human tragedy. The very existence of the passenger list has been kept a secret. So my tentative conclusion is that one of the things most needed to bring about the kind of relationship between this country and the rest of the world that will enable all of us to breathe a little more easily is *not* more moral condemnation, goodness knows their daily lives are saturated enough with it as it is, but more straightforward humane information, information about human beings. This is an objective that is hardly served by cutting off all cultural and educational and sport contacts. I can understand why we sent the Russian circus home from Canada, and it was probably the wisest thing to do in the circumstances, but it really is a great pity that so many thousands of Canadians couldn't get to see it and that the circus folk could not get to know Canada.

I am sure that all of you who have been to visit during our stay here will understand the tremendously mixed feelings with which I am leaving. I am so glad that so many of you have been able to come at all seasons of the year and have been able to appreciate some of the things that make this country a great one as well as a scary one. On Sunday, the extra day that was given to Dot owing to the rescheduling of her return flight, we went out to Peredelkino. The weather was glorious and the air was suffused with that golden autumn light that particularly suits the Russian landscape. We met Victoria and her mother down by the village pond and went with her to her aunt's dacha, where we had tea and apples amid affection and laughter and surrounded by all of her family, who had gathered for the weekend. Then we went to explore the cemetery overgrown with Michaelmas daisies. There was a small group of people near Pasternak's grave. One of them, an older man with a bald head, was reciting poems from *Dr. Zhivago* with such passion and such beauty that even the cows in the neighbouring field seemed to tremble. And up beside the village church with its twisted and coloured domes three old men were telling stories.

The rest is detail. The packers come on Monday. On Tuesday I turn over my blue Zhiguli to UPDK to sell for me. There are farewell calls, lunches, dinners. I take each day as it comes, trying to cheer up Victoria, make Tamara laugh. I am in a strange state, I don't really know how to describe it. But I do know that I am longing to see you all and that up in the Gatineau on Thanksgiving Day we will know that we are home at last!

AFTERWORD

It is now exactly twenty years since we left the Soviet Union and I am back in Moscow as part of a delegation accompanying Governor General Adrienne Clarkson on her state visit to Russia. How things have changed! Relations between our two countries are now so much better than they were in our time. The purpose of this visit is to celebrate their improved status and to explore our areas of common concern in the North. We are both large countries, neighbours across the Arctic.

So much has happened over the last twenty years. Mikhail Gorbachev brought openness, Boris Yeltsin ushered in democracy, Vladimir Putin is now a democratically elected president, and Russia and the US are allies in the war against terrorism. And all this with relatively little bloodshed or destruction. The economy has sputtered, however, and the social costs of transition have been high. It seems that Russia is in the process of becoming a "normal" state, in which some people have a lot of money and power and many more are very poor. The Russian friends with whom we have maintained contact, mostly middle-class professionals, have absolutely no desire to go back to Soviet times, of course, but they do worry about the elderly and about the very young, who have lost their privileged place in Russian society.

The Embassy looks much the same, although much of nearby Moscow has changed. The vast church, destroyed by Stalin, whose foundations were transformed into the heated pool where Geoffrey used to swim has been rebuilt in all its gaudy glory. A huge statue of Peter the Great rises above the Moscow River, buildings have been restored and refurbished, expensive stores line the main avenues. As for the traffic, what a nightmare!

On a more personal note, Nikolai is still at the Residence and Natasha is still trying to teach Russian to Canadian newcomers. Victoria, who remains a close friend, has moved to the Australian Embassy. Ilya the driver, alas, has died. Most of my correspondents are still alive, though, except my mother, my aunt, Bill Kilbourn, and Pat Rand, and those who are the same age as we are are all doing as well as our aging bodies permit. Our children have all married, one of them twice, and have interesting jobs. We have eleven grandchildren.

On our return, Geoffrey left External Affairs to become the founding director of the Canadian Institute of International Peace and Security. When he retired from that he wrote a book about his father's time as Minister of External Affairs entitled Seize the Day: Lester B. Pearson and Crisis Diplomacy (Carleton University Press). Then he became actively involved in voluntary and academic organizations connected with international affairs, most recently as president of the United Nations Association in Canada. He is an Officer of the Order of Canada. As for me I spent the rest of the 1980s writing Children of Glasnost (which was published by Lester and Orpen Dennys in 1990) as well as presiding over the Canadian Council on Children and Youth. In 1990, I co-founded and then chaired the Canadian Coalition for the Rights of Children until my appointment to the Senate in 1994 as a voice for children.

And here I am back in Moscow in my new role, fascinated as ever by this extraordinary, tormented, complicated, soulful country, and hoping that my letters from one particular period in its long history will enrich your understanding of it, as writing them enriched mine.

Moscow, September 2003

CANADA/RUSSIA SERIES

Vol. 1: John Woodsworth, Russian Roots & Canada Wings. Russian Archival Documents on the Doukhobor Emigration to Canada. With a Foreword by Vladimir Tolstoy (1999).

Vol. 2: J.L. Black, The Peasant Kingdom. Russia in the 19th-Century Russian Imagination. With translations of Alexander B. Lakier's travels through Central Canada, 1857, and other real and fictional accounts by Marina Sabanadze, Yana Kuzmin, George Bolotenko, and Larry Black (2001).

Vol. 3: Vadim Kukushkin, Carter Elwood, Mikhail Klochko: Soviet Scientist, Cold-War Defector, Canadian Storyteller (2002).

Vol. 4: Landon Pearson. Letters from Moscow (2003).

THE CANADA/RUSSIA SERIES BY PENUMBRA PRESS

Canada and Russia have more in common than is usually assumed. They share most of the world's Arctic lands; they have similar geographies, wildlife, and indigenous northern peoples. They are the world's two largest countries, both of them federalist in structure, they are multi-lingual and multi-national in population make-up. They have been members of opposing alliances, yet they have been allies. They once were, and may again be, each other's leading competitor for natural resource markets. It is better known that they have differed enormously in their political and social systems until very recently.

The purpose of the Canada-Russia series of monographs is to reveal that side of the relationship that is least known in Canada, i.e., the Russian perception of Canada from the early 19th Century to the present. It is, in fact, always useful to see ourselves as others see us. In the case of this series, readers can learn what Russians know — or believe — of Canadians, and what Canadians who have lived in Russia know — or believe — of Russia.

The Series began as a by-product of a long-term project initiated by J.L. Black, an history at Carleton University in 1997. With the help of a generous grant from the Donner Canadian Foundation, the Centre for Research on Canadian Russian Relations (CRCR), of which Black is director, organized 'search and copy' expeditions to Russian archival holdings, finding, photocopying and re-locating to the CRCR thousands of pages of documents related to Canada. The CRCR now has nearly 20,000 such pages, all filed and catalogued — and this extraordinary, and unique, collection is still growing. Imperial Russian and Soviet books, reports and travelogues related to Canada also were copied or purchased. Hundred of those are now on the CRCR's shelves.

An important condition of the Donner Foundation's sponsorship was that gathered materials be made available to Canadian researchers. The Series is helping to fulfill that commitment.

The first two volumes of the Canada-Russia Series were direct results of research in Russian archives: the first is made up of translated documents on the Doukhobors who emigrated to Canada from

Russia in 1899. By means of original documentation translated and edited by John Woodsworth of the University of Ottawa, the volume tells the story of the Doukhobor emigration in a way never before seen by Canadians.

The second issue is a monograph on Russian perception of Canada in the 19th century. Relying almost entirely on Russian archival documents, Larry Black draws a picture of Canada as a vibrant, peaceful and democratic young nation state evolving in purposeful contrast to images of a violent and greedy America and an aggressive and arrogant Britain. Canadians will be surprised to read that Russians were, indeed, involved in our Rebellions of 1837/38; that the Trans-Siberian RR was modeled after the CPR; that the famous anarchist Kropotkin toured Canada and worked briefly at Ottawa's experimental farm; and that the Russian navy's capture of Canadian fishing ships on the Bering Sea led directly both to the first international agreement on protecting fur seals — and to a short story by Rudyard Kipling.

Our third and fourth volumes differ greatly from the first two, but serve the same purpose. Short stories written by Mikhail Klochko reveal why that Russian defector fled the USSR, where he was a scientist of considerable standing, for Canada in the 1960s. The book is edited, with a long and insightful introduction, by Carter Elwood, a professor of History at Carleton, and Vadim Kukushkin, a citizen of Russia who is a History Ph.D. candidate at Carleton. There is a certain convergence here.

Our fourth volume is made up of letters sent to friends by Landon Pearson during the three years she spent in Moscow where her husband Geoffrey Pearson was the Canadian Ambassador. These letters are a careful explication of a Canadian's impressions and judgements of Soviet life and society in the early 1980s. In addition to their own great merit as a mirror of contemporary Soviet life and habit, the letters provide interesting contrast to Klochko's earlier musings, and also reveal that much had not changed.

J.L. (Larry) Black, Director CRCR
Professor Emeritus
September 2003